DANGEROUS WRITING

DANGEROUS WRITING

Understanding the Political Economy of Composition

TONY SCOTT

UTAH STATE UNIVERSITY PRESS
Logan, Utah
2009

Utah State University Press
Logan, Utah 84322-7800

Manufactured in the United States of America
Cover design by Barbara Yale-Read

ISBN: 978-0-87421-734-6 (paper)
ISBN: 978-0-87421-735-3 (e-book)

Library of Congress Cataloging-in-Publication Data

Scott, Tony, 1968-
  Dangerous writing : understanding the political economy of composition / Tony Scott.
      p. cm.
  Includes bibliographical references.
  ISBN 978-0-87421-734-6 (pbk. : alk. paper) – ISBN 978-0-87421-735-3 (e-book)
  1. English language–Rhetoric–Study and teaching (Higher)–Political aspects–United States. 2.
English language–Rhetoric–Study and teaching (Higher)–Social aspects–United States. 3. Academic
writing–Study and teaching–Political aspects–United States. 4. Academic writing–Study and teaching-
-Social aspects–United States. 5. College students–United States–Economic conditions. 6. College
students–United States–Social conditions. I. Title.

  PE1405.U6S4 2009
  808'.042071073–dc22

                                    2008047646

There are two kinds of saviors: those who want to soothe the souls of the suffering and those who want to heal the sores on the flesh of the suffering. Sometimes I wonder which is right. Sleep well. The couch may not be as comfortable as your leaves of grass, but there is a roof over it.
NGUGI WA THIONG'O, *Wizard of the Crow*

And in the final analysis, it doesn't bother anyone much that politics be democratic so long as the economy is not.
EDUARDO GALEANO, *The Book of Embraces*

CONTENTS

ACKNOWLEDGMENTS

Many thanks to Laura Bartlett-Snyder, Marc Bousquet and Leo Parascondola, who have helped me to think through the primary issues that I raise in this book since graduate school. I also thank Lil Brannon, who has commented on this work in its various phases and who has also been a steadfast source of support and an invaluable and committed partner in dialogue. Michael Spooner who has been an extremely supportive editor and moved this book smoothly and steadily toward publication. Others who have provided valuable critical feedback on parts, or all, of the manuscript: Jeanne Gunner, Lisa Melencon, John Tassoni, Nancy Welch, and the anonymous peer reviewers who read the manuscript for Utah State University Press. Finally, I would like to thank all of those students and teachers who were willing to participate in the research. For all of its problems and challenges, this is still the best job I know.

Parts of chapter four were published in "How Soon Is Now?: Writing Work, Education, and Fast Capitalism." in *Open Words: Access and English Studies* 2.1 (2008): 4-21.

DANGEROUS WRITING

INTRODUCTION
Embodying the Social in Writing Education

Over the past four years I have gone through numerous jobs and have experienced the good, the bad, and ugly aspects. Learning from what I have come to see has taught me that the workplace is not always as pleasant as what you wish it to be. I have worked at places where I have not been treated as an equal, been sexually harassed, discriminated against, and have had issues with management. Through times of triumph I have learned to pick and choose my battles where, as an employee, I could still have my pride, dignity, and self-esteem. . . .
                    "Mariah," university student and waitress[1]

By the time she had reached her junior year as an undergraduate, Mariah already had an extensive work history at the wide, low-paying, low-security bottom of the fast-capitalist economy. She had worked in a daycare center and at a number of jobs in restaurants and retail. Much of that work had been for national chains. At twenty-two, she had been sexually harassed by a manager on one job, asked to wear more revealing clothes on another, left another job because of a hostile work environment created by racial tensions, and not paid by an employer who suddenly closed his doors and disappeared. Mariah sees higher education, in part, as a chance to eventually move out of these types of jobs—in the meantime, she has tried to live life as a university student and a worker in low-status jobs with as much dignity as possible.

A classmate of Mariah's, Teresa, worked as an assistant manager at a discount shoe outlet. Teresa is in her mid-twenties and has also worked in a variety of jobs, including as a telemarketer and as a clerk for a newspaper. By the time she took the job at the shoe outlet she was married and both she and her husband were in school. She says that she became an "hours whore," taking all the shifts she could get at eight dollars an hour to make ends meet. At least in terms of responsibility, this raised her status on the job considerably. In a store that relied almost entirely on part-time labor—a very common way of avoiding paying benefits—Teresa was

---

1.   Student quotes used with authors' permissions as part of a reviewed and approved research project.

eventually asked to work full-time: "Turnover is a fact of life for any retail store; in this case, it worked in my favor. I quickly earned seniority and full-time status as old employees left, some before I learned their names, and new employees joined the staff." Full-time status meant health insurance coverage, a much-coveted benefit at this level of the economy that many postsecondary students as well as their part-time teachers don't enjoy. Her manager, however, began to take advantage of her, giving her his managerial duties—opening, closing, doing accounting, and even taking money to the bank alone after hours—without commiserate pay. Shoplifting was an ongoing concern at her store, and when she was threatened by a group of organized, brazen shoplifters, she quit. She got an administrative job on campus, and after a few weeks went back to visit the store (and buy cheap shoes): "Only three of my former coworkers still worked at the store and all of them were looking for new jobs in the area. It's not surprising—retail wears you down."

So, apparently, does restaurant work. Marshall, a twenty-four-year-old waiter at a restaurant, initially had high enthusiasm for the amount of quick money he could make waiting tables. His enthusiasm faded over time, however, as he began to lose respect for his managers and question how the work was starting to change him. While working on this job at a well-known restaurant chain, he grew cynical about the difference between the restaurant's carefully maintained public image and what he saw as a fundamentally exploitative work environment, and about a corporate structure that maintained a solid cap on advancement and hired upper-level management only from outside the company. He connected his own discouragement with the self-destructive lifestyles of many of his coworkers. His attitude eventually turned extremely negative:

> On good days, I still hated the job. I could only admit to the day's goodness in light of the hatred I had. I existed in a state of constant melancholy. I held open contempt for everything the restaurant stood for; I willingly expressed it to any who would listen, including management. I was just regarded as the weird guy. No one cared about my contempt, they weren't agreeable or offended.

Marshall came back to school—he had dropped out—in part because he felt that his self-esteem was suffering as a restaurant worker, and he was slipping into a self-destructive lifestyle himself (drug and alcohol abuse and late hours spent out after work are a normal part of the culture at this restaurant). He continues to work, but he believes that school gives him the feeling that he is moving forward, not wholly defined by the work that he continues to do for twenty-five or more hours each week. His work while not a student before returning to school therefore seems to function as a kind of cautionary experience for him, motivating him to stay in school and avoid the lives of many of his coworkers.

Camille, a mother of a one-year-old son, describes the beginning of her day like this:

> Waking in the morning, I get out of the bed to begin my work day. I usually take a shower, dress myself, and dress my son. My son and I then go off to work together—into our living room. Yes, to arrive at my job doesn't take a thirty minute drive or even a ten minute sprint. I can be in my office, ready to start work for the day in just a few steps.

Twenty-three-year-old Camille runs a day care out of her home, with some help from her fiancé. After waking their son and getting him dressed, she springs immediately into action—making breakfasts and performing the dizzying array of tasks it takes to get her house ready for the children. Eventually, eight children—ranging in age from twelve years old to three weeks—are under her care at some point during the day. Her typical day is thus a blur of drop-offs and pickups, meals and regulatory-oriented paper work, dirty diapers and lesson plans. And yes—she also comes to class, occasionally with the one-year-old still in tow.

Over the past three years, I have centered sections of both a first-year course and an upper-division writing course on the theme of work. Students write essays in which they examine their work histories and experiences; they interview other workers as part of broader research projects; and they do secondary research on issues related to work in the current economy. The lives of Mariah, Teresa, Marshall, and Camille are typical among my students. They sat relatively close to one another in a single section of a writing class. Most of my students describe lives lived at the insecure bottom of the service economy, where according to U.S. Department of Labor statistics the overwhelming majority of new jobs are now created (U.S. Department of Labor 2008). They move from job to job, often working for employers who have obviously built high turnover into their business plans. They struggle with lower-level managers of widely varying competence who are also poorly paid and whose status is nearly as marginal as theirs. A few are self-employed—Camille running a day care center, another student doing contract office work from home. Far more work for companies that are household names:

Target, Nordstrom, Chili's, Starbucks, Barnes & Noble, Gap, UPS, Wal-Mart, Office Depot, etc. Carefully maintained, glossy corporate images are often a stark contrast to the gritty, everyday realities of workers at these companies.

In addition to being workers, they are also (mostly) full-time students at a large, urban university. As working, "nontraditional" students they are hardly an isolated demographic in higher education. In fact, according to the National Center for Education Statistics (NCES), a significant majority of all postsecondary students (73%) are now best (if ironically) classified as "nontraditional," and the overwhelming majority of all post-secondary students are in "second-tier" institutions (National Center for Educational Statistics 2006, 25).[2] Regardless of their ages—and postsecondary students are now older than they have ever been (according to the NCES, 39 percent are now older than twenty-five), students are spending much of each week in the alienating world of low-end service economy work. Moreover, many institutions of higher education have begun to adopt service-economy characteristics—in terms of their rhetoric (as students are increasingly referenced as "education consumers" and curriculum is approached as a portable commodity); in their marketing techniques; in the articulation of their goals; and in their positioning and management of teachers (see, for instance, Apple 2000; Blackmore 2000; Bok 2003; Miyoshi 1998; Schugurensky 2006; Slaughter and Leslie 2004; Smith 1999). Among the oft-cited characteristics of the "new" or "fast-capitalist" economy is its increased reliance on "casualized" labor, and its steady reconstitution of higher education as an ongoing training mechanism for continually displaced, often chronically partially-employed workers. Job insecurity is now very consciously linked with enrollment and goals in higher education, as colleges openly market themselves as paths to economic competitiveness, and programs—Masters-level programs in particular—are developed and marketed with displaced white-collar professionals in mind.

Postsecondary students are far more likely to be part-time workers now than they were in 1970: 80 percent work some amount of regular hours as they go to school and 39 percent work an average of thirty-five

2.   John Alberti provides a thoughtful way of distinguishing "elite" and "second-tier" institutions (2001, 564–65). He draws on NCES statistics, but manages to articulate the distinction without denigrating the "second-tier." According to NCES numbers, only 24 percent of colleges are classified as Doctorate, Liberal Arts, and Baccalaureate—it is from this already limited pool that "elite" colleges would be drawn.

or more hours per week (National Center for Educational Statistics 2005). Their teachers are very much a part of the part-time economy too. A survey sponsored by the Coalition on the Academic Workforce (whose membership includes Conference on College Composition and Communication and The Modern Language Association) found that 93 percent of all introductory classes in freestanding writing programs were taught by non-tenure-track faculty.[3] Moreover, 60 percent of *all* undergraduate writing courses were taught by contingent faculty ("Report on" 2001, 338). Given the low pay, lack of security and benefits, and high turnover at this large and expanding lower echelon of postsecondary education, teachers themselves are often far from the ideal of success that is marketed by many institutions of higher learning. Though typically these factors are ignored or left on the margins of discussions of literacy and pedagogy, the harsh logics of the fast-capitalist economy profoundly shape the contexts of postsecondary writing instruction in the United States.

In 1988, Janice Newson and Howard Buchbinder noted the rise of what they called "the service university" in their important *The University Means Business: Universities, Corporations and Academic Work.* They argued that universities would in future years be shaped by conceptions of higher education as a competitive moneymaking enterprise in which operations are rationalized for economic efficiency; vested faculty act as "entrepreneurs"; and knowledge is created, marketed, and sold as a commodity. Newson and Buchbinder read the tea leaves correctly. Ensuing research and scholarship (including the important work of Michael Apple, Sheila Slaughter, Larry Leslie, Gary Rhoades, Randy Martin, and Carlos Alberto Torres) has tracked the substantial changes that have occurred in funding, policy, authority, and mission in American higher education over the past three decades that have served to bring about the service university. This conversation and body of research is now well-developed and very consequential to writing education. We need to understand how changes in the economics of higher education are shaping writing education and how we should respond.

John Alberti has made the case that pedagogical models and theoretical discourse still tend to assume "elite" universities, and the largely privileged students who populate them, as the norm—even if it is a largely unacknowledged norm. A variety of factors, however—including open

---

3.   The majority of those classes, 75 percent, were found to have been taught by part-time instructors and graduate assistants.

enrollment and the terms of the fast-capitalist marketplace—have radically changed both who students are and how they experience higher education. Most postsecondary students are now not from privileged backgrounds, and most institutions are not elite or very exclusive, but are what Alberti calls "second-tier" or "working class." Acknowledging this doesn't diminish the importance of the work of those of us who are at less exclusive institutions, quite the opposite: it necessitates a now long-overdue change in general perspective. If we

> focus on those "second-tier" schools as the norm, we can take their institutional structures and ideological formations not as pale imitations of "real" college but as defining the major trends and developments, for good and ill, of higher education in the United States, developments that, not coincidentally, parallel the rise of both composition studies and the multicultural challenges to questions of canon and cultural authority. (2001, 567)

Alberti focuses on issues of access and economics at second-tier, working-class schools as he connects institutional issues (funding, admissions standards, etc.) with a multiculturalist curricular agenda. Economic class should not only be among the categories of difference that are recognized in multicultural agendas, but the lived experience of class should be "a catalyzing force for scholarly and curricular activism at working-class colleges and universities" (581). Multicultural political agendas should not be idealized in the cloistered classes of a well-positioned and well-financed economic elite; they should encompass issues associated with the economics of higher education as they are played out in the lives of all students—including the nontraditional majority—who are attending institutions under widely varied circumstances. He advocates an approach that combines curricular reform and service learning to build "multicultural coalitions" in the communities within which schools are located.

Rhetoric and composition scholarship has now long recognized that writing in industrial and civic spheres can only be adequately understood when situated in particular places and times. However, as Alberti, Bruce Horner (2000), Richard Miller (1998), James Zebroski (1998), and others have argued, the field has tended not to study and conceptualize student writing in the same way as writing outside of educational settings. "Writing program" discussions often do focus on institutional, material concerns, but from an administrative perspective. The emphasis is therefore on factors like compliance requirements, budgetary issues, part-time and contract teaching labor, assessment, and the place of writing in general education and English curriculums. Systematic connections are rarely made between these factors and the character of literacy and learning as manifested in day-to-day classroom activity. In contrast, scholarly discussions of writing pedagogy—method, purpose, and praxis in writing classrooms—tend to account for factors other than the institutional settings of writing education: textuality, rhetorical theory, ideology, technology, revision, gender, race, and so on. Though everyday institutional practices and the material terms of labor for teachers and students have a profound effect on the character of writing pedagogy, they don't often appear in research- or theory-driven discussions of postsecondary classroom pedagogy. Advocating a more "ecological" approach to research in the field, Margaret A. Syverson notes that researchers of postsecondary writing, for all of their insistence upon the importance of location, "have been somewhat atomistic, focusing on individual writers, individual texts, isolated acts, processes, or artifacts" (1999, 8).[4] Jeff Grabill argues that the fact that research in professional writing often accounts for institutional factors is one of the primary characteristics that distinguishes it from research more directly focused on writing pedagogy in postsecondary classrooms (2001, 16). The perception of "the social" in writing doesn't account for how the immediate social contexts of postsecondary writing are institutionally constituted. We don't, for instance, have a developed body of work that examines how the institutional positions of teachers (part-time or full-time but non-tenure-track) shapes how pedagogical praxis is carried out in classrooms. Most undergraduate writing courses are now taught by non-tenure-track faculty, but composition scholarship continues to be written largely from the perspective of tenure-track teacher-scholars who don't address the consequential differences between how they and contingent teachers are positioned in writing classrooms.

In this book, I join those who suggest that pedagogical goals and practices are an integrated piece of broader, situated institutional concerns. My perspective, however, is primarily political economic. I explore

---

4.   There are some notable exceptions: Margaret Marshall and Bruce Horner, for instance, discuss the relationship between the material terms of teaching labor and pedagogy in postsecondary writing. Nevertheless, the field has a surprising, and perhaps telling, dearth of research that critically examines the effects of managerial practices (programmatic policies and goals, evaluation procedures, required syllabi, etc.) on writing pedagogy and student learning in postsecondary writing programs.

relationships between postsecondary writing, institutions of higher education, and the world of service work in fast-capitalism, with a particular emphasis on class. The terms of work for teachers and students in writing education are not subsumed by the academic field of rhetoric and composition. Teaching, administrative, and student work occurs on contended, highly politicized terrains and is shaped by economic logics and constraints. I describe student writers and their texts as pieces of broader material processes in which consciousnesses and institutions are continually being created: the socio-material terms of labor for teachers and students are at least as relevant to these processes as any research, past or present.

Throughout the book, I argue that the creative powers of teachers, students, and writing in postsecondary institutions are prevented from reaching their full potential by two primary factors.

1. A carefully circumscribed view of "the social" that has prevailed in the so-called "social turn" in rhetoric and composition prevents recognition of the immediate, dynamic relationships between student consciousness, institutional logics, and acts of production. This constraining view masks the internal, historically derived contradictions of a field that is closely tied to an institutional requirement (first-year composition) but has also been significantly shaped by open enrollment and the progressive politics of the 1960s and 1970s. The administrative logics of writing programs—formed in response to institutional and economic pressures—are, in many ways, at cross-purposes with the more radically material and politically aware conceptions of pedagogy and discourse that are suggested by a fully "social" or "post-process" view of writing. Those logics push practices in the field toward more easily commodified and administered pedagogies and away from the immediate, the creative, and the politically meaningful (and perhaps dangerous).

2. A continued reliance on dated conceptions of higher education and generic identity categories prevents us from constructively naming the terms of work and education in fast-capitalism, even as the lines between public educational institutions and private industry have become increasingly blurred. The political economy has changed dramatically over the past three decades—these changes have been characterized in various loaded terms, but

generally they are described as a movement from an "industrial" to a "postindustrial" or "fast-capitalist" economy. Though some scholars have addressed those changes, the field has not developed a discussion of what they have meant to our work. "Class" is too often a generic identity marker that is contained within "tolerance" projects, rather than a part of a politically actionable vocabulary that enables understanding of how we are positioned in terms of power and relations of production. To borrow Deborah Brandt's term, the institutional "sponsors" of postsecondary writing—along with the terms of labor and economic structures that are created and sustained by those sponsors—remain largely invisible. Conceptions of what exactly is happening when our students write therefore often don't make space for a counter-hegemonic consciousness or politics because they don't account for how the political economic shapes labor and writing education at the level of institutional architectures. Still overused and underscrutinized, "academic writing" is a strategically vague, inadequate description of what happens when students write in academia.

I will argue that in order to find sustainable footing on the educational terrains created within the political economy of fast-capitalism, writing pedagogies should adopt a more dynamically social, yet materially grounded, praxis. This requires not only a recognition and critique of the terms of student labor as a facet of the political economy, but also of the increasing synergy between the aims and logics of the fast-capitalist marketplace and administration in higher education. The economic lives and struggles of Mariah, Teresa, Marshall, and Camille aren't suspended when they walk onto campus. Academia doesn't just produce academics, and writing teachers generally don't determine the terms of their own work. New approaches to critical pedagogies should focus on critique of the political economic circumstances of work both outside and inside of higher education, and on transcending the conceptual limitations of a now institutionally appropriated, identity-oriented rhetoric that obscures as much as it reveals about labor, class, and the daily lives of most students in higher education.

In addition to its secondary research, the book will draw upon two primary sources of research. One is a study of the genre function of textbooks. It is based primarily on interviews with twenty-one writing faculty, and positions textbooks in relation to the terms of teaching work in composition. The study provides a useful means of understanding the relationship between teachers' professional standing, the textbook industry, and writing pedagogy. A second study is a class-ethnography that centers primarily on student texts and illuminates much about the working lives of students, how they see their work and education, and the possibilities and shortcomings of various approaches to examining work in writing classes. It uses discourse analysis as a means of understanding how students continually create identities through their writing. What emerges is a complicated portrait of students rhetorically negotiating the figured worlds of work and higher education, working through their own complicated political economic identities and lives.

I have seen the tensions, contradictions, and opportunities for change that I examine in this book firsthand. I was a working-class, first-generation college student who (with the help of Pell grants and student loans) financed his own education working a variety of jobs including landscaping, construction work, waiting tables, working in warehouses, agriculture, and even in a meatpacking plant. I was an adjunct for two years, teaching days at an urban university and then working the second shift loading and unloading trucks at UPS—sometimes alongside some of my own students. I was also a teaching assistant (TA) in a Ph.D. program who worked with other TAs and adjuncts out of a crowded basement office. At this writing, I am an associate professor and the director of a large, and in many ways very challenged, first-year writing program that is staffed almost entirely by part-time and full-time non-tenure-track teachers. My experiences and ongoing struggles to understand my professional work inform, energize, and bias my research and writing.

In the remainder of this introduction, I more fully introduce the term "political economy." The term has a long history and therefore carries quite a bit of baggage, but it is nevertheless well worth the trouble. A political economic perspective offers a means of understanding current writing and teaching praxis in composition that could generate creative, integrative new ways of doing work—writing work, teaching work, and administrative work—in rhetoric and composition. It connects the macro with the micro, grounding conceptions of work in the material conduct of that work. I then relate a political economic perspective to what Bruce Horner has called the "dominant conception of the social" in rhetoric and composition—a theme that will be explored in various ways throughout the book.

I won't argue that a political economic perspective will lead anyone out of the allegorical cave and into the pure light of perfect knowledge. Nor will I even attempt to account for all or most of the many possible political economic factors about which critically reflective teachers and scholars are, and need to be, concerned. This book will, however, offer a kind of conceptual webbing on which we can position the factors that shape writing pedagogy that we feel are most important. In so doing, it is my hope that it will expand the scope of what professionals in the field feel is relevant to day-to-day writing pedagogy, including the organizational cultures created by writing programs; the positions of teachers and students as workers in the current economy; the embodied, consciousness-shaping performances of that work; and the increasingly pervasive influence of the textbook industry. I hope to provide a useful way to see and act upon the challenges, frictions, and immense creative possibilities of a more fully social approach to learning and acting with writing.

BROADENING "THE SOCIAL TURN"

The Political Economy

I start from the assertion that writing, even writing in school settings, is embodied, creative production that is significantly shaped by political economic factors. To clarify, I am using "embodied" in a historical materialist way. In *Capital*, Marx uses the term *verkörperung*, which is translated as "embodiment" and also connotes "physical realization." For Marx, "embodied" labor is both material thing and process. It references bodies laboring, engaging in this or that productive activity at a given time; it also references how that labor is imbricated within relations of production that abstract and commodify it. Marx was careful to show that these two forms of labor are conflated in capitalism: this parallels the conflation of use-value and exchange-value and is thus a primary source of contradictions. In chapter 1 of *Capital*, he uses "embodied" in his descriptions of how labor is abstracted through commodification:

> If then we disregard the use-value of commodities, only one property remains [of products], that of being *products of labour*. But even the product of labour has already been transformed in our hands. If we make abstraction from its use-value, we abstract also from the material constituents and forms which make it a use-value. It is no longer a table, a house, a piece of yarn or any other useful thing. All its sensuous characteristics are extinguished. Nor is it

any longer the product of the labour of the joiner, the mason or the spinner, or of any other particular kind of productive labour. With the disappearance of the useful character of the products of labour, the useful character of the kinds of labour embodied in them also disappears; this in turn entails the disappearance of the different concrete forms of labour. They can no longer be distinguished, but are all together reduced to the same kind of labour, human labour in the abstract. (1996, 128 [emphasis mine])

It is through this process of abstraction that products appear on shelves seemingly completely detached from the labor that went into producing them. In "concrete," material settings, real material bodies labor and produce—and the fruits of that production have use-value. A pair of pants can be worn—and the worker who created the pants might be able to exchange them for something else of relatively equal use-value, a shirt perhaps. However, both the labor and the use-value of products are commodified by capitalism: concrete human labor is made to "disappear" as it is abstracted through exchange. Currency and circulation enables the pants and the labor that went into producing them to become a form of exchangeable capital, and this creates a system in which alienation and large-scale exploitation are possible. Workers are alienated from the products they produce by the terms of their labor, and they aren't in a position to reap the benefits from the exchange of product for currency. Pants may be made in sweatshops for pennies on the dollar in remote parts of the world, but then appear on shelves at the Gap or Target far removed from laborers and the circumstances of production. Political economic analysis can enable an understanding of teaching and writing as concrete *and* commodified labor. It can help us to see important aspects of both the writing as embodied labor (for instance, teachers teaching and writers writing) and the writing abstracted (writing education as it is embodied within disciplinary and institutional frameworks)—ultimately, it can help us to see the ways that teachers and student writers are alienated from what they produce by the terms of their labor.

The term "political economy," however, has a very old history and is richly textured and potentially slippery. As it is now generally understood through the lens of contemporary economic theory, "classic" political economic thinking had its roots in the eighteenth century, perhaps most notably in the work of Adam Smith and David Ricardo. When Smith described his utopian model for industrial capitalism in *Inquiry into the Nature and Causes of the Wealth of Nations*, he described a system in which people do the work to which they are "naturally" best suited. They do it cooperatively and according to a very calculated organization so that the dual goals of individual realization and collective efficiency and prosperity are achieved. Smith's utopian model therefore carried common assumptions of the Enlightenment: he sought to realize what he took to be a *natural* order through a *scientifically* managed system. Liberal, political views of individual freedom and self-realization—natural essences and rights—were joined with positivistic views of scientific efficiency and progression.

When reading Adam Smith now, through a lens tempered by a few centuries of industrial capitalism, one might easily adopt a sobered view. Beside his crisp, clockwork vision of a free people working in an efficient, harmonious system, one might juxtapose deeply troubling, even nightmarish images: child labor and coal-blackened skies; company thugs and tent-city massacres; poisoned rivers and technologically advanced armies that wipe out entire cities with impersonal, industrial efficiency; the synchronized bodies of Fritz Lang's *Metropolis*, wearily pulling levers according to the relentless timing of a giant steel clock. Again and again, in site after site, human bodies and labor have been employed in projects and within systems that can't, by any stretch, be said to have realized human potentials. But in the public discourse we don't typically see those images juxtaposed with Smith's utopian image of a natural, rational, generally beneficial order through capitalism. Among the reasons that his articulation of free market liberalism persisted as an ideal is that Smith so beautifully joined a political ideology with a material economy—creating a tantalizing vision of people working together in organized, efficient systems that best realize productive and creative potentials, rather than exploiting them. Smith's political economic system elegantly brought Enlightenment individualism and industrial capitalism under one umbrella, marrying a philosophy of personhood, freedom, and governance with a material science of economics and production. In the popular imagination, it continues to survive as a platonic essence, sullied only in actual applications for this or that reason. It can work, so the thinking goes, if only we get this or that right—"There is always room at the top." If certain people do not thrive, it's not the systemic structure itself—the poor can be wealthy, too, with better schools, more discipline, more gumption, etc. Higher education figures heavily into this thinking, as it is often constructed as an equalizer, a means of righting social wrongs and enabling one to create one's own destiny. A statue outside of my own office building is of a man chiseling himself out of rock. Marketing in higher education, especially at institutions like mine, consciously draws on the "bootstrap" image of realization through individual accomplishment in a free society.

Marx would develop a different way of doing political economic analysis. Marshalling extensive research on the factory system in England, Marx situated human labor in broader systems of production, exchange, and wealth accumulation. His method was to move from the particular/material to the systemic and the historical. He painstakingly followed raw materials labor and goods through processes of production and circulation, eventually contextualizing specific material artifacts and labor within those processes. In so doing, he created a portrait of how everyday human labor is positioned within (and shaped by) circulation, valuation, and exchange. Through political economic analysis he showed how the terms of labor are historically produced and how they, in turn, become the causes of history. The conception of the free, rational "individual" was integral to Smith's Enlightenment conception of the political economy. In that conception the individual exists independent of the economic and exercises rational choice based on self-interest. Marx countered the figure of the rational individual with the political economic subject, whose labor and identity are significantly shaped by her terms of production. Rational choice, in Marx's formulation, is shaped not only by the limitations of the choices that are genuinely available to people of different economic classes, but by a class consciousness continually recreated in day-to-day life—through work and socialization. Identifying how exploitation, stratification, and injustice are built into the material terms of industrial labor for workers, Marx explained how alienation and conflict are inevitable outcomes of the political economy of capitalism. In so doing, he established a relationship between human labor, identity, and the political economic. Social class is produced by history, power, and the terms of labor—rather than being achieved individually through merit and the development of cultural distinction.

Though it developed diverse early roots in the work of, among others, Adams, Marx, David Ricardo, and William Stanley Jevon—all of whom used the term "political economy"—the contemporary field of economics has dropped the term "political." This reflects a general turn toward the mathematical and axiomatic and away from a broad political, historical, or rhetorical disciplinary orientation.[5] Some have associated this turn with a giving up on the project of a hopeful, generally beneficial theory of the economy. Those who, for instance, call current economics a "dismal science" argue that it has succumbed to a neoliberal form of reflexive realism that valorizes individual agency and rational choice as a means of subordinating or eliminating altogether questions of the greater social good or positive systemic transformation (Morrow 2006, xxi). Though created by a system that is historically contingent and changeable, capitalism's inequities are naturalized, and the focus of economics becomes more exclusively tactical. Nevertheless, the combined term "political economy" continues to have currency in a variety of contemporary fields—including political science, sociology, anthropology, geography, and (to a lesser extent) rhetoric. Within those fields, methodologies and connotations vary, but political economic perspectives continue to be characterized by examination of the relationship between the systemic/ideological and the particular/material. It names systemic relationships that connect specific acts of production with broader political cultures, policies, and systems of valuation. The combined term usually references the material situation, the circulation of resources, and *the socio-material terms of production*: the details of how goods are produced, how they are circulated, and how human labor is positioned and valued. Much of this discussion draws on the conceptual vocabulary of Marx and historical materialism. It views economic relations as historically *produced* by human actions; therefore they are contended and transformable, not natural or preordained. Likewise, it views identity and human agency as a part of the material, rather than existing in some transcendent external essence.

Political scientist Andrew Sobel succinctly describes the two realms of political economies—the macro and the micro: "Macro politicaleconomy investigates associations between political activities and substantive performance of an economy" (2005, 24). Broad economic indicators that are reported in the media and occasionally even

---

5.   From this generalization about the orientation of economics as a distinct field, one quickly moves into highly contentious territory that is outside of the scope of this work and its author's field. For instance, the neoclassical view has been supplanted by far more dynamic models of understanding. One generalization that might be sustained, however, is that contemporary economics is primarily concerned with mathematically measurable factors, rather than with historical context or how production and consumption are politically structured. Even this distinction is contentious, however.

explicitly mentioned in political debates are part of this macro-realm of the political economy: the gross domestic product (GDP), unemployment rate, inflation rate, interest rate, trade deficits, etc. These indicators are referenced as evidence of how the economy is generally doing. Macro-level indicators touch virtually every aspect of governmental policy—from educational and environmental to health care and social security. Sobel points out that we can see these indicators as both initiators and results of governmental policies. In contrast, a "micro political economy approach focuses on the processes that influence, motivate, and constrain the choices of individual political actors. In this approach, political economy describes the processes of choice that lead to government policies and to social, economic and political outcomes" (25). So the micro-level of the political economy is concerned with the choices and actions of particular agents in specific situations. Here the realm is local—what economic and political choices do agents make, and what are the assumptions and desires that shape them?

Importantly, the term "political economy" therefore necessarily assumes a dynamic and integrated relationship between the macro and the micro: micro-level choices about investments or a particular election might very well be influenced by macro-level trends—interest rates, unemployment rates, GDP levels, etc. These particular ("individual") choices simultaneously serve to embody the macro-level indicators—people's investments, savings, and debts are (after all) what create the broader trends. At the end of the day, micro-level actions are therefore inseparable from the macro-level factors: the distinction is a matter of emphasis and perspective rather than material reality. Once quantified and publicized, macro-level indicators influence decision making again in a continual feedback loop. While we might, for the sake of focus, separate certain aspects of the political from the economic (and certain aspects of the macro from the micro), the fact is that they are deeply, inextricably intertwined. Broad trends and political policies—systems that organize and value human labor—have profound effects on individuals; in turn, individual decisions and actions are what embody and enact those broad trends, policies, and systems. "Economy" isn't the sum total of a set of formulas or quantified indicators: those are only attempts to understand and describe a dynamic, codependent, evolving material entity.

Rhetoric and the Political Economy

Smith and Marx were doing rhetoric even as they did economics. In *The Wealth of Nations* Adam Smith helps to create the vocabulary and ways of knowing for classic economics (McCloskey 1994). Likewise, in *Capital* a rhetoric emerges that carries its own vocabulary—and with it, its own actionable ways of knowing. "Exchange value," "surplus value," "circulation"—even the fundamental connotations of "labor," "production," and "history"—change in Marx and the conversation that followed. As Foucault describes the author function, he points out that Marx, like Freud, initiated a new discourse as a necessary accompaniment to a new way of seeing the economy. The vocabulary doesn't just describe, it enables and acts upon: it is a means of understanding but also of articulating and potentially transforming. Revolutionary shifts of paradigm require equally revolutionary rhetorical shifts.

Victor Villanueva has argued that rhetorical study should refocus itself on the political economic, noting that the distinction that has arisen between political economic study and rhetorical study has always been unnecessarily limiting. Villanueva contends that rhetoric and political economy are both rightly seen as analytical praxis—ongoing efforts to understand and act—rather than as static bodies of disciplinary work and knowledge. Because both have to do with analysis *and action-in-the-world*, rhetorical analysis and political economic analysis significantly overlap in their purposes: "Let me put it this way. The role of rhetoric, according to Burke, is the demystification of the ideological. The role of political economy is the demystification of relations tied to the economic. If we're to understand where we are and what is happening to us—and maybe even to affect it—we need the tools provided by both" (2005, 58). Villanueva argues that the study of rhetoric has been somewhat shackled by its situatedness in literary-studies-dominated English departments, which relegate rhetoric and writing to a subordinate, skills-centered role. When writing became an introductory course in English departments dominated by literary studies, it had a corresponding subordinating effect on rhetorical study: "Rather than rise to the level of the architectonic, rhetoric had become confined to learning to write about literature." This subordination and orientation have changed to a certain extent in recent decades; however, contemporary rhetoric and composition as a whole has not assumed a political economic orientation. Villanueva points out that when we do mention the political economic, it is usually secondarily in discussions of theorists like Raymond Williams, Walter Benjamin, or Paulo Freire, rather than as an emphasis in its own right (59). Still being carried out in the diminishing but still-long shadows of literary studies, rhetorical analyses often stop at textual representations as their own ends, rather than broadening the scope to recognize how cultural representations are historical process—subsumed within the circumference of political economic structures and also substantially involved in constituting those structures. As Villanueva writes: "Economies are carried rhetorically. We cannot discuss the ideological and thereby rhetorical reproduction of beliefs about gender, race, class, age, nation, religion, or any other of the axes of difference—without a grasp of how such axes are embroiled in the economic" (64). The implication is that rhetoric is not just the production of knowledge, but embodied material praxis with language. Like economic analysis, rhetorical analysis is tied to ongoing action in the world. Moreover, rhetoric is necessarily concerned with the consciousnesses that are constantly being reformulated through that situated rhetorical praxis.

To return to the statement with which I started this section, "writing, even writing in school settings, is embodied, creative production that is significantly shaped by political economic factors." The analysis I offer seeks to work through aspects of the relationship between writing education as concrete production—teachers and students laboring—and writing education as it is abstracted and commodified in scholarship, textbooks, program administration, and within broader conceptualizations of the university as a part of the fast-capitalist economy. Writing and writing education are not inert, prescripted product, however: they are production. Writing education isn't just shaped by political economic factors, it also produces the political economic. Also, in spite of all of the efforts to control it through such methods as prescriptive academic modes, the encouragement of homogenized "objective" authorial positions, and emphasis on structure and grammar, writing—by its very nature—continually squirms beyond containment. It remains stubbornly and deliciously varied, and sometimes in the hands of those who are skilled and determined, consequential and dangerous. It is this active, hopeful, potentially transformative aspect of writing toward which this study will eventually turn.

The Social Turn in Rhetoric and Composition

According to what economic logics are the labors of teachers and students being situated? How do those logics shape what is produced? How, and for what interests, are alternatives omitted or constrained? I see a new focus on the political economic as a potential means of expanding the truncated view of "the social" that has come to characterize much of "the social turn" in rhetoric and composition studies. A focus on the political economic can enable more strategic integration of pedagogical, administrative, and scholarly praxis. There is now a widespread consciousness of the overuse and exploitation of contingent labor in composition, but little research connects the managerial logics that shape the systems of labor that flourish in writing programs to the assumptions that shape teaching and writing in the classes of those programs. We discuss, with a high level of sophistication and nuance, ideology as it plays out in student texts and in writing classrooms, but we don't integrate factors like the working lives and histories of students or the public, consciously constructed and market-targeted images of sponsoring educational institutions. Rather than rigorously seeking to understand how what we do is shaped by how we do it, the field's normal science continually sutures the split between disciplinary ambitions and projections and the material realities of writing education. It continually finds means of turning away from the contradictions that become apparent when the immediate and the material are juxtaposed with the structural and cultural.[6]

Because of the material realities of postsecondary writing education, significant aspects of "the social" in rhetoric and composition are compartmentalized as a means of perpetuating the normal science of the field. Unfortunately, this compartmentalization serves the cost-cutting agendas of upper-level administrators in higher education well and it has its antecedents in the institutional history of the field. Because of the

---

6.   For instance, rhetoric/composition professionals fight for the legitimacy of rhetoric and composition as an academic field even as, at many sites, writing programs hire large numbers of people who have little or no background in the field to teach it. The field has broadened the scope of writing program administration as a scholarly endeavor and professional identification, but the specialization might not exist if contingent teaching faculty were not used to teach most writing classes. Indeed, the expansion and solidification of program administration as a professional specialization *relies on* the continuation of policies and practices that deprofessionalize the teaching of writing. We build first-year writing programs around "academic writing," but staff many or most classes with teachers who don't actually do any academic writing and don't have full institutional status as academics.

relegation of so much of writing education to "writing programs," professionals in rhetoric and composition (to a greater extent than those in other humanities fields) have been administrators as well as teachers and scholars, and those roles create continuing contradictions. As writing program administration has become an increasingly established professional identity—with many now primarily self-identifying as writing program administrators (WPAs) and some even establishing courses of study that center around administration—an administrative ethos has concurrently arisen. It is important to explore the ways in which this administrative ethos is distinct from a scholarly ethos, and how it positions postsecondary writing in terms of internal institutional dynamics and the broader factors that increasingly shape writing pedagogy, like mandated large-scale assessments. I discuss these distinctions in ethos in chapter 1.

Intractable contradictions between pedagogical practice and administrative and scholarly work are historically produced. Solidifying as a new dominant trend in rhetoric and composition studies in the late 1980s and early 1990s, "the social turn" is best described in terms of its emergence from what might be described as an institutionally appropriated and inoculated form of process pedagogy (Trimbur 2000). Unfortunately, but not surprisingly, the logics by which the social turn has been prevented from reaching its fullest potential—the means by which it has been constrained and gradually reconceptualized to conform to institutional and professional prerogatives—is a continuation of what had happened with process. In her historical essays, Sharon Crowley describes the development of process pedagogy; its proliferation as the dominant approach in college writing occurred within the context of the campus unrest of the late 1960s. As an institutional requirement steeped in hierarchical notions of literacy, the first year composition (FYC) class became a point of contention during that period. According to Crowley, universities responded to student and teacher dissatisfaction in a number of ways, including through abandoning the requirement or lowering the standards for exemption (1998, 205). It was during this period that process pedagogy began to gain ascendancy. Crowley argues that process was adopted in composition, in part, as a response to dissatisfaction among politically progressive and leftist students and faculty with the irrelevance of existing, heavily institutionalized curriculums—an attempt to make writing relevant to volatile, impassioned, rapidly changing times. The various characteristics of writing pedagogy that came to be called "process"—workshopping, lending students more authority and control over their texts, multiple drafts, etc.—were touted as a means of countering a more staid, conservative, institutionally driven form of literacy instruction that did not reflect or respond to broader socio-political changes. So within the professional discourse of the emerging field, the binary was between an establishment literacy and accompanying pedagogical practice (that came to be called "current traditionalism") and a more democratic, politically progressive literacy and pedagogy (that gelled under the umbrella of process).

Turning this binary somewhat on its head, Crowley drains process of some of its counter-hegemonic aura through describing it as a kind of palliative political adjustment. Neither a teacher-sponsored exercise in revolutionary practice nor a teacher-centered extension of a formalist literary tradition, process was a "less radical way to respond to students' insistence on 'relevance' in their courses" (205). Lending students more authority certainly had a democratizing effect and was consistent with a more general project of undermining the authority of institutionally rigid, teacher-centered approaches to pedagogy, but it also had the effect of "displac[ing] some of the responsibility for classroom activity away from [teachers] and onto students" (207). It offered a way for institutions to encompass volatile political discourse without changing foundational structures or risking many careers. Crowley describes how process, over time, even came to be adapted to current-traditional instruction, ironically reinscribing the basic tenets of the pedagogical philosophy it was supposed to replace. Process, especially as it was commodified and standardized through textbooks, was gradually reduced to "pedagogical tactics" that often are employed within pedagogies that carry rigid notions of correctness and are re-centered, if more loosely than before, on academic modes. The adoption of process was, therefore, the new field's first response to a threatening crisis. It pragmatically but brilliantly saved a lumbering system of writing education through providing an informed, palliative way to move through a crisis without substantial structural changes in the writing requirement or the terms of work for the people who teach most writing classes. Eventually, it would become commodified dogma in the realm of FYC textbooks and writing program orientations, far removed from any counter-hegemonic moment.

Crowley puts the history of FYC as an institutional requirement at the center of the problem that developed with process:

> Theorists of process constructed a self-directed student who would take control of his or her own writing process; this projected student subjectivity was to replace the docile, rule-bound, grammar-anxious student subjectivity produced by current-traditional instruction. The institutional paradox, of course, is that students are forced to take the class in which they are to be constructed as self-directed writers. (1998, 217)

The requirement, and the professional and profit-making apparatuses that have grown around it, reasserted the technocratizing logics of institution and administration. Paradoxically, these logics were an ideal fit with current-traditional approaches to language and literacy, and they therefore resurfaced (if altered and politically adapted) within process approaches. Joseph Harris has elegantly described this technocratized version of process as a "new formalism":

> The problem with the older current-traditional approach to teaching writing, as has been argued over and over, was its relentless focus on the surface correctness of student texts, so that writing was reduced to an empty tinkering with verbal forms. But the advocates of process did not redirect attention to what students had to say so much as they simply argued for what seems to me a new sort of formalism—one centered no longer on textual forms but instead on various algorithms, heuristics, and guidelines for composing. This new formalism has proven little different from the old, as those versions of process teaching that don't work toward a very familiar set of therapeutic and expressionist goals instead work toward an equally familiar set of technocratic ones. (1997, 56)

In their study of the emergence of basic writing as an emphasis in rhetoric and composition, Bruce Horner and Min-Zhan Lu note a scientific positivism in the version of process and academic writing that emerged in the 1970s and 1980s. They describe a tendency in this period to see writing in acultural, ahistorical terms that emerged in the work of, for instance, Kenneth Bruffee, Peter Elbow, Thomas Farrell, Janet Emig, and James Moffett. Writing in this work was divorced from the messiness of cultural conflict and divergences and isolated as a manageable and *natural* therapeutic process in which problems with not only writing but thinking could be resolved. Addressing how "community" is constructed as homogenous and free of conflict in the work of Bruffee and Farrell, Lu describes how writing classes assumed a "healing" aura. Writing classrooms were sites in which students' differences, struggles, anger, and frustrations are socialized away in pedagogies that avoid conflict and aim toward resolution: "They sustain the impression that [students'] experiences ought to and will disappear once the students get comfortably settled in the new community and sever or diminish their ties with the old. Any sign of heterogeneity, uncertainty or instability is viewed as problematic; hence conflict and struggle are the enemies of basic writing instruction" (1999, 39). Horner and Lu link this homogenization tendency—which is really a tendency to erase difference and ameliorate class conflict—to both right-wing pressure to create a "depoliticized" curriculum, and to a perceived need to build the field on an "objective," scientific (rather than on more of a historical materialist) foundation. Lu is particularly adept at showing how Vygotsky and Freire were co-opted in ways that "amputated" their Marxist orientations and appropriated them for a largely dehistoricized pedagogical project (1999, 66–69). The field's understanding of the social nature of writing thrived on ideologically cleansed notions of social development that saw conflict and struggle as problems to be transcended, rather than as legitimate responses to injustice and inequality.

The initial promise of process pedagogy may have been as a means of doing writing education in a more immediate, varied, and perhaps even politically consequential and creative way, but it was grounded by composition's ties to the institutional requirement—to textbooks; to standardized programmatic curriculums; to low-status, often inexperienced teachers; and to the managerial ethos produced by the field's increasing identification with program administration. In theory, the social turn might have served as a corrective to the institutional co-option of process. In an influential *College Composition and Communication* review from 1994, John Trimbur even described it explicitly as a means of moving into a "post-process" phase in the field in order to refocus on social justice issues—to make writing more politically relevant. At least as a stated set of assumptions for new approaches to pedagogy and research, the social turn moved the focus of the field away from isolated texts, standard academic textual forms, and solitary authorship and toward a view of writing as situated social action. It emphasized sophisticated cultural adaptability—to situated genres, to specialized discourses, to communicative norms, and so on. Process pedagogies that had succumbed to the steady lure of generic modes (argumentation, expository, etc.) were to give way to those that focused on reaching particular audiences with particular messages in particular ways. Perhaps most importantly, the social turn reflected a more constructivist view of subjectivity. While process still relied on a self-knowing, self-contained notion of individual identity, many articulations of the social turn were informed by an understanding of identity as a more fluid, socially constructed entity that is continually created through discourse. The term "discourse communities" entered the field's lexicon at this point, particularly in work that described how students should be taught to adapt to "academic writing." This conception of writing supplanted a conception that maintained rigid separations between authors, audiences, and contexts. Indeed, "audience" as a distinct area of research emphasis fell by the wayside as meaning-making came to be seen as cooperative, negotiated, and heavily dependent on cultures and artifacts. Certainly, the ways that scholars like David Bartholomae and Patricia Bizzell framed the project of FYC in terms of entering the "community" of academic writing had a profound effect on writing pedagogy in the 1990s and would come to narrow the scope of the social turn. In both Bartholomae's "Inventing the University" (1985) and Bizzell's *Academic Discourse and Critical Consciousness* (1992), two highly influential works of the period, the "social" function of writing was formulated as socialization into academia.[7] Many first-year writ-

---

7.   However, the way that they described both the socialization and the communities are somewhat distinct. Bartholomae argued that students can be taught to gain a degree of authority in academic settings through adapting a discourse that, he admits, is largely alien to them. To borrow the language of Bahktin, students gain authority within the contexts of their schooling through *ventriloquating* the voice of authority—of academics. In a widely cited passage, Bartholomae admits that these attempts to project an authoritative, "academic" voice are typically problematic and uneven. The problem, as Bartholomae puts it, is that students must learn to:

> speak not only in another's voice but through another's code; and they not only have to do this, they have to speak in the voice and through the codes of those of us with power and wisdom; and they not only have to do this, they have to do it before they know what they are doing, before they have a project to participate in, and before, at least in terms of our disciplines, they have anything to say. (156)

Bartholomae leaves the socialization process open-ended. He doesn't claim that most students easily, if ever, achieve what might be called "mastery" of academic discourse. Rather, successfully "inventing the university" will likely lead students to write "muddier and more confusing prose" (162). Moreover, the kind of authority students will typically achieve is described in a very qualified, limited way: "Our students may be able to enter into a conventional discourse and speak, not as themselves, but through the voice of the community" (156). When students "invent the university, it is "not as themselves": it remains alien to them. Bizzell linked writing more closely to socialization and suggests that the learning of academic conventions in writing is also the learning of academic habits of thinking. Students entering basic writing classes not only have deficits in writing, but deficits in thinking: "Students who struggle to write Standard English need knowledge beyond the rules of grammar, spelling and so on. They need to know: the habitual attitudes of

ing textbooks and curriculums continue to be based on the learning of "academic writing" as an entry into "the academic community." The title of the second class in the two-section FYC sequence at my own university is "Writing in the Academic Community."

Important questions have arisen about the project of enculturation into academic communities through writing. How exactly does this socialization into academic discourse happen? What is the difference between academic writing and consciousness and mere mimicry? Is the discourse that occurs across academic writing singular and stable enough to have its own term—and even if it is, can it be learned by those who have not been socially initiated? Finally, what is the long-term worth of spending so much time and effort teaching academic writing to students when most will never actually be academic writers? As early as 1989, Joseph Harris critiqued the tendency to genericize academic writing, pointing out that "the learning of a new discourse seems to rest, at least in part, on a kind of mystical leap of mind" (17).[8] In the ensuing years, the general understanding of discourse communities has likewise been deepened and complicated, particularly in genre studies. Important work by Carolyn Miller, Charles Bazerman, Amy Devitt, David Russell, Anis Bawarshi, and others supplanted "discourse communities" with more dynamic conceptualizations of what happens when people communicate in particular social settings.[9]

There is scant evidence that this more complicated view of genre and situated writing has shaped the conceptualizations of "academic writing" that continue to define basic and first-year writing curriculums. Moreover, and more to my point here, "the social turn" was rarely explicitly articulated in relation to the material terms of teaching and learning in postsecondary writing. Through its narrowed focus on "academic writing" and its comparative lack of interrogation of what higher education is and how it is changing, the social turn has been sandbagged and appropriated by the same institutional and political pressures that

---

Standard English users toward this preferred form; the linguistic features that most strongly mark group identity" (1992, 86).

8. Harris advocated seeing academic "communities" as more conflicted, more diverse, and more materially situated than "the idea of the university" suggests.

9. "Discourse community" conceptualizations of situated language use were critiqued as too static, too rigidly bounded, too suggestive that one could adapt to a discourse through explicit instruction rather than long-term immersion. Discourse communities have been largely replaced in the field's scholarly vocabulary by terms like "systems of genre" (Bazerman 1997) and "the genre function" (Bawarshi 2003).

homogenized process. The field has favored a "social" view of literacy and learning that, paradoxically, may have more to do with avoiding the more important and potentially even revolutionary aspects of the social in writing than embracing them. Though founded on a constructivist sensibility, the social turn has unfortunately often been characterized by a turning away from an imperative to understand and account for how consciousness, institutions, and politics are socially produced and reproduced at the material sites of writing education. Even as they emphasize the importance of specific audiences and locations, "social" approaches to discourse and pedagogy have stubbornly continued to reinscribe the figure of the writer as an autonomous actor in stable, external socio-political spheres. Wrapped in the freshly spun gossamer of culturally sophisticated techne appears the same old self-interested, self-contained individual that was carried from current-traditionalism through process—only now rather than navel-gazing, to which she was given during the more expressivist phase of process, she focuses outward to adapt to given rhetorical situations in ways that meet her own rationally (and privately) conceived ends. The "social" subject of composition is therefore often still a modernist subject, even if now she is dressed up in fast-capitalist garb for adaptation to the information economy. She understands that writing is "social" and cultural but typically only in a very constrained way. Rather than *encompassing* the writer and her spheres of practice, "the social" and the relevant space for action with language are often only recognized *between* them (see figure 1).

Left out of pedagogical practices driven by this view are sticky but essential issues that come with a recognition of how motivations and identity themselves are continually formed and rearticulated *through* discourses—and, perhaps more importantly, how everyday labor both shapes and comprises social contexts, including the educational institutions in which teachers and students work. Through coping adjustments that keep the structure of the current system of requirements and teaching labor largely intact, in a sense these aspects are continually "black-boxed" and moved safely outside of the concerns of writing pedagogy.

Surveying the scholarship of the late 1980s and into the 1990s, one can see considerable anxieties about the potentially revolutionary ramifications of a more fully social view of writing education emerging concurrently with the social turn. Maxine Hairston began to make her famously controversial arguments for the teaching of "craft" rather than "art" in the late 1980s and early 1990s, and the critiques of Freire that

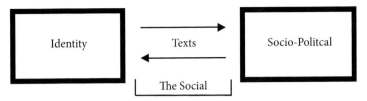

Figure 1. The Containment of the Social

have become de rigueur over the past decade have also tended to posit a carefully circumscribed view of the social against what is conceived as heavy-handed political activism in the "consciousness"-focused aspects of critical pedagogy. Juxtaposed against the now stock character of the soapbox Freirian pushing her own politics under the pretense of doing writing education is the image of the more humble, more responsible teacher helping her students reach their *pragmatic* goals for writing—which they, unlike the soapbox Freirians, recognize and respect (often as a safely privatized black box).[10]

In these articulations of the proper goals of writing pedagogy, the sphere of the social is limited to behavior with language at the moment of articulation, rather than subsuming the messy ongoing dialectics of consciousness and institutions. The outcome of social pedagogy is individual adaptation. So writers are still imagined to enter an institutional sphere that is largely stable and external to them, write within that sphere as they develop their now "socially" adaptive "craft," and then move on through various other (still stable) spheres in their (still private) life trajectories. Writing is still "craft," even if enacted with greater social awareness, and transformative potential is contained by the assumption that one can separate craft from ideological enactment with real social and political ramifications—in short, the radical likes of Vygotsky, Bakhtin, and Bourdieu are reconstituted and redeployed toward the ends of the information-age economy. Craft can somehow be learned and practiced *with awareness of* culture and ideology without concern for the inevitably problematic and anxious dialectical thicket of institutionality, consciousness, and action-in-the-world. The messy factors that make writers always already real, evolving, and consequential

---

10.   The dichotomy tends to obscure that critical pedagogical approaches are extremely varied, and in my experience typically employed by teachers who are particularly sensitive to their students' opinions and desires; students' positions within, and desires for, education are also widely varied and complicated, in spite of their economic class (Seitz 2004)

agents in already real, evolving, and consequential material locations are left outside of the sphere of disciplinary concern.

Reactions to politically focused pedagogies over the past ten years continue to suggest that a focus on ideology in writing classes too often comes at the expense of writing proficiency and they therefore advocate a curious kind of self-conscious instrumentalism. Interestingly, many acknowledge the political aspects of teaching and writing, but in the next breath push them aside in order to focus on "writing." This double-move is couched in uniquely liberal terms of empowerment and presented as a means of respecting students' opinions and *their own* goals for higher education. This is the case, for instance, in arguments for the importance of recognizing students' instrumentalist goals in writing pedagogy through giving them a job-ready form of literacy (see, e.g., Miller 1999; O'Dair 2003; Smith 1998). These arguments at once acknowledge that identity is socially constructed and sometimes even that education is a powerful site of cultural interpolation, but then also reessentialize consciousness in an effort to recognize and respect students' now-privatized desires and experiences. In a recent *College English*, for instance, Sharon O'Dair (2003) admits the power of education to enact "embourgeoisement" and alienate students from home cultures. She therefore concedes that postsecondary education can be a powerful mechanism of socialization. However, she nevertheless advocates an instrumentalist approach that consciously attempts to minimize that socialization in order to locate the proper process of social formation elsewhere (home? friends? workplace? K-12 education? pop media? religion? all of the above?). She argues that it is not our business to fundamentally change how working-class students see the political economic—they have their own reasons for coming to school. They should therefore have an "excellent primary and secondary education, as well as excellent secondary and postsecondary vocational training," because this is what is best suited for a working-class consciousness—which remains intact—if not implicitly naturalized, at least external to higher education. "Excellence" in writing is consciously limited to instrumentalist categories not problematized by the field's many ideological critiques of standard written English.

Others assert a more subtle distinction between language practice and social practice in order to advocate a writing pedagogy that tries to keep its political aspects—which they carefully acknowledge—safely bracketed. In another recent *College English* article, Harris asserts that he is not convinced that there is any necessary link between learning a critical practice and acquiring a critical consciousness—or any other kind of consciousness, for that matter. But this doesn't strike me as a problem. For if our aim as teachers is to help students take part in the cultural and political discussions of the day, then we need less to influence their attitudes (which strikes me as a kind of intellectual canvassing for votes) than to help them learn to deploy more powerful forms of reading and writing. (2003, 578)

The pedagogy in this piece on revision is built on compartmentalization as a means of scouring away much of the untidiness that comes with a fuller conception of the social (and the political) from the craft of textual production. In his construction of the student as a blackened center, a lacuna that critiques, Harris separates the term "critical" from "critical consciousness" in the hope that it can refer "more concretely to writing that responds to and makes use of the work of others" (578). He argues that he doesn't want to "depoliticize the teaching of writing" but he does nevertheless want to foster among students an understanding of what he calls the "distinctive moves and gestures" of academic writing without explicitly discussing them as political. He thereby asserts the stability of both students and the institutional spheres within which they operate (mostly limited to a conception of the academic here) as a way of distancing his model from pedagogies that he believes are "far more social than textual," which he suggests is a shortcoming (580). While the political has now long been acknowledged, including with sophistication and insight by Harris himself in other important work, as being deeply intertwined with language and education, the political is here revisioned in the narrowed way that has to do only with electoral politics ("canvassing for votes") rather than the ongoing, dynamic social formation of values and identities.

As more textual and less social beings, students assume a rather ghostly not-quite-presence in the writing classroom and within institutions. Harris takes issue with Ira Shor because Shor imagines the goals of teaching in terms of "shifts of consciousness rather than changes in practice" (2003, 578). Can we separate critique from the consciousness of the critic? Can we separate practices from consciousness? If we choose to try, what are the goals and ramifications? I don't think we can talk about "distinctive moves and gestures" in academic cultures without also recognizing that routinization, everyday social rituals, discursive commonplaces, and textual genres are precisely what constitute and inculcate ideologies. "Changes in practice" are recursively, inextricably bound with "shifts of consciousness." To suggest that they are not is to suggest that practice and consciousness are not deeply interlinked. The foundational work that gave rise to a contemporary, social conception of language and learning, from Vygotsky and Bahktin to Raymond Williams and Bourdieu, describes language-use as both a molder and an outcome of material, social—and thus ideological—processes. When we articulate, we do; we act upon ourselves and our environments. I argue in this book that the normal science of the field encourages these contortions in order to contain the potential dangers, and the innate resistance to standardization, suggested by the more expansive view articulated at the onset of the social turn by people like Trimbur, James Berlin, Crowley, and Shor. Paradigm-threatening anomalies that continually emerge out of specific material locations and undermine generalized conceptions of writers learning writing—such as those associated with the terms of student and teacher work, and the rapidly changing business of higher education—are continually, and sometimes very cleverly, swept to the margins in the interests of maintaining disciplinary and programmatic regularity. After rhetorically strategic asides about the politics of discourse and the role of language in ideology, scholars assume the mantle of the wizened pragmatic realist and find inventive ways back to the safety of "academic discourse": clear and rational motivations $\rightarrow$ carefully crafted texts $\rightarrow$ stable, generalizable contexts. The inconvenience and messiness of particular people writing with consequences within complicated, evolving milieus is regularized to provide a stable, manageable object of study and education. As Horner argues, the pervasiveness of a narrowed view of the social "testifies to the dominant's seizure of the definition of the social as uniform, all-encompassing and static rather than as a dynamic ongoing process of struggle among heterogeneous and conflicting forces" (2000, 216).

Paradoxically, as I argue in chapter 2, it is the material terms of writing instruction and program administration themselves that help to make the constrained view of the social so intractable in composition pedagogy. Many who teach writing in postsecondary institutions may not have the educational backgrounds necessary for a nuanced understanding of writing and pedagogy as constitutive acts within political economic spheres. Moreover, writing pedagogies that explore questions of individual and social formation as they relate to discourse inevitably bring ideology to the fore and are therefore potentially controversial.

They run counter to the hardly invisible administrative/institutional hand that shapes writing program decisions concerning curricular goals, textbook choices, criteria for evaluation, and so on. Politically safe writing pedagogies lead to more efficiently administered programs and more portable pedagogies that can be commodified in various profitable ways, such as through composition textbooks and the increasing array of software tools that are being created for, and marketed to, writing programs.

We have not adequately historicized the social turn in terms of its synergies with the hegemonic fast-capitalism that emerged during the 1990s and its largely unacknowledged reflection of a neoliberal view of rhetoric, politics, and the public sphere. Through continually inventive ways of keeping the scope narrow, "social" pedagogies carefully preserve important elements of the liberal political imagination. They enable authors with still-private, autonomous motivations to achieve their goals with awareness that they will need to adapt their messages to specific situations in order to be effective. They thereby offer a truncated conception of the creative and productive possibilities of writers within a naturalized status quo. Authors with privatized political consciousnesses are free and individualistic choice-makers working within stable milieus that define the choices and opportunities for expression—the model of authorship is therefore consistent with consumerist conceptions of democracy created by hegemonic capitalism. Individuals compete in the "marketplace of ideas": in this marketplace, the best ideas that are articulated most effectively win out. Basic "social" questions about how desires and motivations are continually formed through discourse and learning, who has the real power to speak and be heard, and the inequalities and injustices that are hardwired into societal structures all remain in the murky background—at once acknowledged and defined outside of the proper sphere of pedagogy.

MAKING WRITING DANGEROUS

In this book, I argue for a more active view of the social as a means of connecting writing more immediately to material concerns. I argue that we should risk letting our practices as teachers, scholars, and writers be dangerous. The students I described at the beginning of this chapter—Mariah, Teresa, Marshall, and Camille—should certainly not be targets of a resocialization project with preordained and overly determined political ends. Nor should they be robbed of the opportunity to more fully evolve in ways that are personally and politically transformative. They should—they have the right to—have the opportunity to find opportunities for creative work through developing an understanding of the dialectical relationships between language, materiality, social relations, and consciousness. As Gee writes, "language has meaning only in and through social practices, practices which often leave us morally complicit with harm and injustice unless we attempt to transform them. . . . any proper theory of language is a theory of practice" (2005, 8). For this book I would alter that to "any proper theory of writing is a theory of practice." Neither the student nor the educational institution are transhistorical givens. Each is continually recreated through daily labor and therefore is subject to positive change and hopeful possibilities. Writing education can be characterized by ongoing struggles to understand and positively transform the particular historical and material circumstances of production inside and outside of academia.

In chapter 1, "Professionals and Bureaucrats," I examine the challenges and contradictions of teaching writing in higher education. Arguably, the general ethos that the field of rhetoric and composition has constructed for itself is averse to institutional hierarchies. The academic field's "we" is clearly sometimes intended to subsume contingent writing teachers, and sometimes clearly not. While the impulse to generalize might derive from an egalitarian impulse, the line between egalitarianism and a manipulative and even cynical appeal to populism can be murky; avoiding recognition of institutional hierarchies is also a means of preserving and exploiting them. Though they differ in other aspects, the field's most widely cited histories associate the rise of composition studies with the rapid growth in required writing sections that came with open enrollment. This growth led to an increasing awareness that, in spite of the long history of the requirement, little was actually known about how to teach writing well. Because these classes were largely covered with contingent teachers, it also led to the creation of a professional layer of WPAs who not only manage FYC in English departments but who primarily self-identify as WPAs. The result of that growth has been the development of a professional/scholarly realm that grew out of the first-year requirement, but which now often seems removed from the daily labor of teaching required introductory writing classes. I argue that in order to articulate the ongoing role of FYC in rhetoric and composition, it is important to explore more thoroughly the sometimes directly contradictory relationship between a *scholarly profession* that seeks full status as a legitimate academic discipline and a *bureaucratic practice* that has a legacy grounded in labor exploitation and oppressive conceptions of literacy and higher education.

Chapter 2, "Writing the Program: The Genre Function of the Writing Textbook," proceeds from the professional/bureaucratic distinction established in chapter 1. The chapter presents some of the research from a study that examines how twenty-one writing faculty in a particular program conceptualize, choose, and use textbooks. "Rhetoric" is a contentious ongoing discussion among scholars; a textbook, in contrast, is primarily a commercial enterprise, and the successful commodity should be designed with the primary consumers in mind—the decision makers. In some cases decision makers are WPAs who make texts mandatory for their programs. In others, as in this program, it is left to the teachers. The overarching point is that those two realms, the scholarly and the commercial, are fundamentally different in important ways—and they carry their own loaded and consequential rhetorics. As this study suggests, textbooks do significantly shape pedagogies in many classes, and they are often chosen for reasons other than the soundness or the currency of the theoretical basis on which they are founded. Rather, a whole host of far more pragmatic concerns drive textbook choices. When they choose textbooks, the teachers interviewed for this study aren't nearly as concerned with theory and research as they are with factors like cost, the usability of the instructors' manual, layout, and whether the book includes clear assignments. So textbooks are more properly understood as a situated work genre that responds to, and in turn shapes, programmatic prerogatives. They are less accurately seen as an extension of the scholarly realm of rhetoric and composition. I argue that they are therefore a part of the administrative apparatus that often very strongly works against the more fully social, potentially transformative view of writing described above. Textbooks help to "write the program" through responding to its need for standardization and efficiency.

In their oft-cited study of the language of "new" or fast-capitalism, Gee, Hull, and Lankshear have argued that "we have yet to fully invent an adequate language of critique for the new capitalism" (1996, 42). Chapter 3, "How 'Social' Is Social Class Identification?" examines distinctions in how class can be examined in writing classes. Critical approaches to writing pedagogies are still typically centered on fostering identification within social categories. In this chapter, however, I examine the various names we give to class experience. Do they, for instance, emphasize the social markers of class, or do they emphasize situatedness in relations of production? Do they they reflect an understanding of the changes that have occurred in the political economy over the past four decades? A significant transformation in the political economy that began to become clearly hegemonic in the 1970s shifted agency from labor to management based largely on the belief that a globally competitive economy required giving management maximum flexibility. Job security as a fundamental right of citizens and an essential component of general well-being fell away from the political economic discourse and out of legislative policy decisions. In its place came the so-called "global" or "fast capital" era of managerial flexibility and worker insecurity—an era in which government hesitated or refused to intervene in employer/worker disputes (and when it did, usually acted on behalf of employers). A host of governmental policies and historical contingencies have fundamentally changed what it means to work in the United States and how people see themselves and their work in relation to the broader political economy. I argue that examinations of class that emphasize markers or habits of consumption are at risk of becoming appropriated by now highly adaptive institutional structures and thus drained of their counter-hegemonic potential. I advocate strategies that foster a rhetoric of identification and social justice in writing pedagogy that accounts for the position of higher education in the new economy.

In chapter 4 I focus on student work. "Students Working" begins with a discussion of the clash between the still solidly upper-middle-class aesthetic of higher education and the day-to-day lives of the nontraditional, working students that actually are the majority of postsecondary students. I describe a political economic model for writing pedagogy that uses the material terms of labor and institutionality as starting points for writing and research. Within this model, students write about work and working lives and critically examine the circumstances of their own educations. They examine the terms and significations of fast-capitalism and casualized labor—for instance, what it means to be an "associate" at a retail store, a "contract worker" at a cable company, or an "adjunct writing instructor" in an English department. Importantly, however, this model doesn't leave its own immediate institution unexamined. Students are encouraged to connect the dots that lead from the material terms that shape their lives as students and workers to broad economic trends and the politics and discourses that sustain them. This chapter also draws on analysis of student texts to explore contradictions between the "figured worlds" of higher education and work.

Finally, in chapter 5, "Writing Dangerously," I argue that this pedagogy only makes sense when enacted against a backdrop of institutional change. We can struggle to resolve the contradictions that exert a perpetual drag on our field through seeking to make administrative, scholarly, and pedagogical work *a singular praxis*, an extension of integrated— if actively contentious and evolving—philosophies of labor, literacy education, organization, and culture. Rhetoric and composition might be able to move into a post–writing program era. Pedagogies that come from the assumption that writing is a powerful social praxis cannot be enacted where labor is not even afforded the dignity of a truly professional status. Positive models exist for writing programs that have made the decision to take the necessary, if difficult and even painful, steps to reduce or eliminate reliance on contingent labor. Hopeful, empowering writing pedagogies will (and can only) be, an extension of hopeful, empowering organizational frameworks.

1
PROFESSIONALS AND BUREAUCRATS

The state didn't send out the secret police to transform higher education into an entrepreneurial sector; we have done that all by ourselves by taking on the ethic of managerialism as the practice of institutional life.

Stuart Hall

I recently became the head of a first-year writing program that is in a situation that I very deliberately call a "crisis." The character of this crisis, however, is all too familiar to many who have done program administration work at large, public, "second-tier" institutions. Prior to my becoming director, there was little general knowledge among tenure-track faculty of what goes on in the first-year writing program—who is teaching what under what conditions. I consider promoting awareness of the terms of labor in the writing program a fundamental part of my job as head of the program, and an essential piece of any strategy of transformation. Starting from the premise that what we do is powerfully shaped by how we do it, I am trying to move the program away from a rather deeply entrenched "new formalism" and toward a more social approach to writing. I am also trying to dramatically curtail the program's use of part-time teachers. These two factors—pedagogical philosophy and terms of work—are connected within a broader economic and institutional dynamic. The shift in teaching philosophy cannot (and should not) be enacted without a concurrent shift in the terms of labor for teachers in the program.

My university is in a high-growth urban region, and its enrollment grows steadily year by year. The university projects continued steady annual growth over at least the next decade. The writing requirement is currently two sections—typically taken in fall and spring of the first year. To accommodate steady annual growth in enrollment, the writing program has expanded by an average of ten sections per year over the past ten years. During the year in which I began directing the program, it staffed and fully enrolled almost three hundred sections.

This rapid annual expansion in sections has been covered entirely by contingent teachers. This year, over 50 percent of our first-year courses were taught by part-time teachers. Less than 1 percent were taught by tenure-track faculty, and only about 8 percent were taught by teaching assistants. The remainder, about 40 percent, were taught by full-time, non-tenure-track lecturers. In the first-year writing program, part-time faculty outnumber our full-time, non-tenure-track faculty by two to one. Consistent with the national average identified by the American Association of University Professors, our part-time faculty also turns over by about a third each year. We are a public university in a so-called "right to work" state: this means that our part-time teachers and lecturers have had the right to engage in collective bargaining taken away from them. Part-time teachers with MAs at my university make about two thousand dollars per class before taxes and receive no health care coverage, no paid vacation, and no assurances of employment beyond the current semester.

Because our steady growth in enrollment is being covered by a concurrent steady expansion in contingent hires, the department faces the same dilemma that English departments across the country often face. A number of responses are possible. Do we, for instance, just stay the course and increase our already-heavy reliance on a contingent instructorate in an atmosphere in which we have to make annual arguments for every new full-time hire? Do we revisit the first-year requirement—perhaps eliminating it or cutting it to one semester? Do we change the numbers of people who are required to take FYC through testing and adjusting exemption requirements? These are complicated questions involving a host of elements, including financial considerations, core requirements, and general curricular philosophies and goals. Disciplinary turf issues also enter the equation. Some colleagues in rhetoric and composition vehemently oppose cutting the requirement, in part because they feel that surrendering the first-year requirement means surrendering important disciplinary "turf" or the field—diminishing the overall position of writing.

Over the years I have been struck by how different FYC becomes depending on what we need of it at a given time—by how the enterprise is compartmentalized based on rhetorical expediency. In what sense is FYC the special "turf" of rhetoric and composition? How do those of us who self-identify as professional compositionists occupy it? Do we own it at all times or just when the turf is at stake? It is common in instances like discussions of the first-year requirement to retreat behind old, familiar battle lines, referencing present and past denigrations of our field by literary faculty, and fortifying our collective professional identity through protecting FYC as the "turf" of writing.

Situations like this necessitate a more fully three-dimensional discussion of the FYC requirement, and undergraduate writing more generally. They need to be informed by a nuanced understanding of the deep connections between the political economic terms of labor in composition; the pedagogies that are encouraged by, and practiced according to, those terms; and the assumptions and institutional practices that shape them. They also need to be informed by a more complicated and up-to-date understanding of the history of the academic field of rhetoric and composition—particularly the professional dynamics that have emerged over the past three decades and the economic logics that now shape our work.

Being a professional in rhetoric and composition has required a willingness to cope with the unique contradictions that come with being in a scholarly field that is intimately connected to the introductory-level institutional requirement of FYC. My sense is that most Ph.D.s in rhetoric and composition are not prepared by our professional training or our scholarly discourse to fully grasp and effectively account for the organizational and professional contradictions we encounter when we enter into our professional lives. For the most part, we learn that we are doing scholarly work within an academic discipline *and* we do administrative work: we don't struggle to examine the two as a part of a more general political economic framework. Rather, most of us are compelled to adopt a peculiar, transposable ethos that moves—sometimes opportunistically, sometimes desperately—from the scholarly/professional to the bureaucratic/managerial to the pedagogical, depending on the work we are doing at a given time. These roles are juxtaposed, often daily, but they are rarely brought into dialectic in scholarly forums. We assume a natural and rightful identification with FYC teachers, even as we expect full status as professional scholars and managers of FYC labor, without rigorously exploring how material conditions create irreconcilable contradictions between these roles. Our lives as administrators, scholars, and teachers therefore tend to play out in distinct realms, with their own distinct discourses and concerns. Discussions of pedagogy and literacy theory rarely deal with the material conditions of teaching and writing in the university. Discussions of academic labor and writing program management rarely touch on the specific effects of faculty hierarchies and pervasive managerialism on day-to-day pedagogy—or literacy in the university more broadly.

In this chapter I will describe the nature of this compartmentalization and its consequences for both the scholarly field of rhetoric and composition and for postsecondary writing education as a situated material practice (the two are not synonymous). I will start with a discussion of the issue of ownership of the first-year requirement—a primarily historical and institutional question. I then move to a discussion of the necessity of distinguishing professional from bureaucratic subjectivity, arguing that professional training in rhetoric and composition tends to avoid the distinction—with negative consequences.

US AND THEM

A number of very widely read histories—including those by Sharon Crowley, James Berlin, and Susan Miller—have dealt with the complicated history of the first-year writing requirement. While there are certainly important differences in their approaches, Crowley, Miller, and Berlin approach the issue of institutional position primarily in terms of the historical relationship between composition and the more powerful literary studies. Crowley points out that both fields have developed problematic relationships with FYC. Since its inception, the FYC requirement has been used for social and intellectual gatekeeping and enculturation. Moreover, because composition has been situated within English departments dominated by literary faculty, it has been assumed that writing instruction is intellectually unchallenging—and thus marginal to the primary, more important work of literature. Crowley points to the elements of classism, racism, and ideological interpellation that have long been intrinsic to the writing requirement. As she describes it, FYC is grounded in nineteenth-century hopes for literacy, assumptions about who

> was, and who could become, "an educated person" and about the most efficient ways of fitting people to compete aggressively, if obediently, in a capitalist society. Freshman English has always been a gesture toward general fears of illiteracy among the bourgeois, fears generated by America's very real class hierarchy. (1998, 235)

Crowley believes that the first-year writing requirement is too firmly grounded in this "oppressive institutional history" to be salvaged.

Also making primarily historical arguments, Susan Miller and Jim Berlin have examined the practice in terms of its ongoing and semiotic relationship with literary studies. They argue that composition has survived and flourished, in part, because it has functioned as "the other"—the necessarily inferior half of the literary/composition binary. To sustain its own status, literary studies needs composition as a foil against which it can assert its identity and superiority. Sacred texts gain their status and sanctity only when juxtaposed with the mundane and the everyday. As texts have been differentiated by level, so too have students by the level of development they are believed to have achieved. Miller makes the case that composition classes were initially offered as a way to differentiate economically privileged white males from the immigrants, women, and first-generation college students who were starting to find their way into American universities in increasing numbers with the development of a fully industrial economy. An early incarnation of composition was developed at Harvard. Charles William Eliot, who became president of Harvard in 1869, sought to admit students from "all conditions of life," but those students would not be accepted as is; rather, they would be uplifted—made legitimate—by their literacy education, through a combination of composition and literature (1991, 52). Composition's function within this curriculum was as a type of filter: it certified that deserving students, with a little help, were worthy of joining their social betters and moving fully into higher education. It was therefore identified with basic learning, "thought of as *freshman* 'work,' not as the study of writing throughout college" (53). More advanced work that can be embarked upon once students pass through the literacy gate became the realm of literary studies. Berlin makes a similar argument that identifies a consequential binary between composition and literary studies. Within English departments, composition classes enabled those texts deemed "literary" to become more highly valued in comparison to the functional, everyday, nonartistic writing that constitutes the realm of rhetoric and composition. Modernist claims concerning the distinction and transcendence of certain texts have been all but destroyed in literary theory; nevertheless, they can still resonate in departmental justifications for the subordination of writing to literature. The imagined trajectory of "basic students learn basic writing before they move on to the consequential work of literary study" has been functionally beneficial for those who work in literary studies.

This territorial distinction has played itself out in the ways that English curriculums are structured as well as in hiring and promotion practices. While literature classes continue to be staffed primarily by tenure-track faculty, FYC and undergraduate writing—at least at large, public universities—continue to be taught primarily by people whose position at the university is tenuous: contracted, non-tenure-track faculty; graduate students; and part-time lecturers. This work has certainly been important to the general understanding of the professional ethos and institutional position of rhetoric and composition. However, while I am certainly persuaded by arguments that literary studies needs composition, I am also convinced that composition now needs literary studies, and that the contentious relationship between the two fields has enabled compositionists to mask certain aspects of our own problematic and sometimes opportunistic relationship with FYC. Professional enculturation into the field involves learning how compositionists have often had to work against literary studies to establish the field—oftentimes this "comp/lit" battle is playing itself out in low or high frequency in the very programs where we are doing our graduate study. This split has served a number of necessary functions in the construction of the professional identity of those of us who work in rhetoric and composition. Within the disciplinary metanarrative of rhetoric and composition, literary studies has been the elitist "other" against which "we" have struggled on a variety of fronts—"they" are the British and "we" are the Irish. Literary studies certainly bears much of the weight of the formalist conceptions of literacy against which expressivist and process pedagogy asserted itself—incompletely, as I argue in the next chapter. Moreover, because literary studies was well established before the open enrollment era, and contemporary composition came about much more recently in response to open enrollment, rhetoric and composition has been able to cast itself as the politically progressive, democratic element of English departments that might otherwise be more exclusionary and elitist. Finally, because the exploitation of writing teachers and the basement-status of writing education predates the rise of contemporary composition as a scholarly field, many in composition studies have continued to include contingent instructors who teach FYC in the field's "us." This "us" is broad enough to include those primarily contingent teachers who teach the vast majority of writing classes and the tenure-track Ph.D.s who have truly professional status, do research, and manage writing programs. But the way that we tend to distinguish ourselves from literary studies has enabled rhetoric and composition to largely avoid recognition and examination of our own opportunistic and contradictory relationship with FYC.

PROFESSIONALS AND BUREAUCRATS

The scholarly field's strong identification with FYC is certainly logical. The rise of contemporary rhetoric and composition as a scholarly field has been as much an effect of the first-year requirement as its cause. In a sense, all fields produce what they study: literary studies, for instance, continually reproduces (and changes) the contents of the category of study called "literature"—and while the subject might appear stable, even minimal scrutiny shows that it isn't. Contemporary rhetoric and composition studies is unique, in part, because a considerable part of its subject was produced by a bureaucratic imperative. The subject/object relationship between our field and what it studies is especially murky among academic fields in the humanities: what we *study* as scholars is more intimately, recursively involved with what we *do* as teachers and administrators.

The rise of composition studies has been concurrent with the rise in numbers of people who attend postsecondary education and enroll in basic and first-year writing classes. While FYC certainly existed for a century prior to 1970, it was the late 1960s and early 1970s that saw the development of what can be called "contemporary rhetoric and composition studies." During this period, the contemporary field began to form as a distinct academic "discipline" with all of the institutional apparatus that the term implies. It developed with the assertion of its territorial claim over required writing classes—basic and first-year writing—as a substantial portion of its object of study. Bruce Horner and Min-Zhan Lu (1999), John Trimbur (in "Cultural Studies . . ." 14), James Slevin (1991), and Ira Shor (1980) have described the importance of basic writing classes to the field's emerging disciplinary identification during this time. Surveying these various descriptions, Horner notes a consistent linking of basic writing with the politically progressive project of democratization. Trimbur, Slevin, and Shor

> all identify the lessons and insights of teaching from this period in political terms: a "movement" for "cultural democracy" that explicitly called into question the social and political role of educational institutions and the politics of representing students, or prospective students, and their writing in particular ways, e.g. as "literate" or "illiterate," "college material" or "remedial," "skilled" or "unskilled." (Horner and Lu 3).

The ethos of the field has deep roots in the project of democratization and open access to education. This democratization subsumed both texts and writers. Rhetoric and composition not only stood on the importance of texts not distinguished as "literary" by whatever the current dominant terms of distinction are in literary studies, but also on the dignity and legitimacy of those student writers historically excluded from higher education and the corridors of power.

Ironically, the field's more noble purposes have created what are perhaps our deepest and most problematic contradictions. The emergence of the field and the growth of the territory it claimed led to the creation of a professional layer of WPAs who not only manage FYC in English departments but who primarily self-identify as WPAs. A vibrant, important body of scholarship has grown with the expansion of access to higher education over the past four decades—as have tenured positions, graduate programs, journals, scholarly books, mounds of FYC textbooks, and endowed chairs in rhetoric and composition. In order to articulate the relationship between FYC and rhetoric and composition, it is important to explore more thoroughly the field as an ongoing, strained relationship between a *scholarly profession* that seeks full status as a "legitimate" academic discipline and a *bureaucratic practice* that has a legacy grounded in labor exploitation and oppressive conceptions of literacy and the political function of higher education. Professionals in the field are certainly generally aware of this relationship. However, it is far more rare to conceptualize present rhetoric and composition in terms of the deep contradictions created by its history; this is the conceptualization that is required and enabled by a political economic examination. The work of the field has been produced by a material history, and its work is being done according to historically produced hierarchical relationships and within economic constraints that considerably shape its character and aims. In spite of the institutional legitimization of a fully professional echelon of scholar/teacher/administrators, the work of teaching composition has remained largely both bureaucratized and deprofessionalized. We have argued for the dignity of students from all walks of life, even as we have managed, researched, and theorized a project that continues to be built on labor conditions that aren't conducive to living with dignity (a living wage, health insurance, and secure employment).

While the general ethos that the field has constructed for itself is averse to institutional hierarchies, many of our practices continually maintain exploitative hierarchies. It is useful, if uncomfortable, to view the work of our field in terms of a hierarchical split between "professionals" and "bureaucrats." This hierarchy needs to be continually named and examined. During normal times, the entire project of FYC operates cheaply and, for the most part, quietly on a largely separate track from the rest of an English department—typically with a professional compositionist at its helm. In my department, entire years go by without a single section being taught by a tenure-track faculty member other than the director of the program. Yet when the project becomes threatened in some way—as when it is suggested that the first-year requirement be eliminated—the flinch-response is to circle the wagons and defend "our" territory. I don't think that FYC is rightly the territory of the *scholarly* field of rhetoric and composition at most universities—rather, FYC is a separate colony of English studies over which rhetoric and composition now asserts a propriety interest as it cultivates and manages it for its own benefits as well as for the benefits of departments. Professional scholars are developing the management of FYC into a science (see, e.g., Miller 1999); some professionals develop textbooks for it and we write articles and books that theorize it, but day-to-day teaching remains in the hands of people who might have minimum or even no formal education in the field and a tenuous professional and institutional status. The professional work of scholars of rhetoric and composition is not only substantially produced by the bureaucratic requirement, it is produced by the positions and opportunities created for us by the ongoing use of contingent labor to teach writing. "We" (professional scholars) might claim it as a part of what we might call our "disciplinary imaginary," the terrain that we consider a part of our professional focus, but we have a much less legitimate claim over it if we view it as labor—as embodied day-to-day practice. Thousands of sections of FYC taught in the United States every year are the labor of people who don't have professional status in the field, and may not even primarily self-identify in the scholarly discipline. This scholarly/teaching work distinction mirrors the more general debate over who actually owns the labor of workers and the products of that labor in any given workplace. How do our institutions position writing teachers in relation to their work and the products of their work?

Though people have discussed the ethical problems with the use of contingent faculty in writing for years, there has been little exploration of how institutional status and professional identity shape writing pedagogy and research—how the entire system functions, or dysfunctions, as a whole. How do the parts fit together? It is important to examine what it means to be a "professional" who works within a field that is the effect of a bureaucracy—maintaining a relationship with FYC, but (at least at M.A.- and Ph.D.-granting institutions) rarely actually teaching it. It is also important to examine what it means to be a contingent teacher of FYC who works within an institution in which she doesn't have full or even partial professional status.

Max Weber articulated his highly influential "theory of bureaucracy" in *The Theory of Social and Economic Organization* (1964), and Weber's work is still the starting point for discussions of bureaucracy and professionalism in organizational theory. Describing bureaucracy in very neutral terms as a social-ordering mechanism, Weber advocated it as a means of rationalizing social relationships within organizations in a way that mirrored the rationalization of material environments with technologies. Bureaucracies can therefore usefully be seen as a social technology: they are formed to improve organizational efficiency and consistency through regularizing human activities and behaviors. As Weber developed "bureaucracy," he anticipated structuralist and postmodern illuminations of the relationship between social context and subjectivity. He described a bureaucracy as a *Lebensführung*, or "order of life," within which a particular ethos develops. A worker's organizational identity— the character and goals of her work, the foundations on which she bases decisions—are largely determined by her bureaucratic culture. Within effective bureaucracies, workers become useful, consistent instruments of the organization.

In addition to coming to terms with the nature of the *bureau*, contemporary organizational theory has struggled to locate distinctions between professional and bureaucratic roles and functions (Du Gay 2000; Scott 2001). The distinction that is typically inferred between the two terms centers around the degree of autonomy, level of expertise, and the extent to which one's work is managed by explicit, technical rules. Of course, the line between "professional" and "bureaucrat" should not be seen as overly hygienic: in real situations, professional and bureaucratic roles and identifications can be mixed and complicated. Generally, though, work in the professional realm is not subsumed by the goals and structures of particular bureaucracies. The ethos of professionals is more geographically and organizationally portable. Professionals may work within or manage bureaucracies, but they are considered experts in their fields, have a high degree of autonomy in their work, have high social prestige, don't have to conform to many explicit rules that determine their daily work, and often belong to national organizations that certify qualifications and determine membership. In contrast, the work and professional identities of bureaucratic employees are far more subsumed by particular organizations. Bureaucratic workers are generally less expert than professionals (or at least their expertise is less portable, more closely tethered to the operations of a particular site); they carry less social prestige; and their daily work is more highly managed according to terms that they may not have a hand in establishing. Generally, professionals are valued for the expertise they can bring to organizations to help determine and meet goals; bureaucratic employees are valued for the degree to which they can efficiently fill the established roles that will help organizations reach their goals.

It isn't difficult to see bureaucracy at work in the administration of the typical large FYC program, nor is it too difficult to recognize the innate hierarchy in the professional/bureaucrat distinction in academia. A distinction has historically been maintained between the professional work of scholarship, which is typically constructed as intellectual and the product of highly sophisticated training, and teaching work—which is constructed as a technical skill that is *naturally* acquired by scholars with little or no specific training (Marshall 2003; Schell 1998; Strickland 2001). Teaching is consistently coded, and therefore undervalued, as feminine in the profession through its association with day-to-day, materially situated practice and its subordination to the "male" world of scholarship, and women disproportionately occupy non-tenure-track positions in English departments (Enos 1996; Fontaine and Hunter 1992; Holbrook 1991; Miller 1991; Schell 1998).

While composition exists as a "professional" endeavor as defined by all the traditional measures—i.e., through sustained, varied, sophisticated scholarship; the existence of distinct professional organizations; and the establishment of programs, tenure-line positions, and endowed chairs that are explicitly designated in the field—FYC at most large institutions remains a fundamentally bureaucratic project. Professionals theorize FYC, manage it as WPAs, and a few even teach it regularly. Meanwhile, the work of the average FYC teacher is dictated primarily by local administrative prerogatives and has little direct relationship to national scholarly conversations in rhetoric and composition. The local administrative objective is typically to maintain a quality university-wide writing requirement as cheaply and quietly as possible. At medium-to-large universities, over nine out of ten FYC classes are taught by contingent labor. Within that realm, all the characteristics we associate with professional status—autonomy, prestige, expertise in the relevant field, participation in professional organizations, and so on—are either scarce or nonexistent ("Report on" 2001). The realm of professional rhetoric and composition is certainly concentric with the realm of bureaucratized FYC, but the former by no means subsumes the latter.

A FYC program can, however, be a ready-made organizational instrument of rhetoric and composition theory for the professionals who wield it—FYC is a bureaucratic tool that can be effectively used to instrumentalize a particular view of literacy and learning. If you are a professional in rhetoric and composition who believes that writing portfolios, argumentation, critical pedagogy, or service learning are the way to go in FYC, then you can build a program around it. You can advocate or require specific texts and syllabi; you can develop training sessions, workshops, and required graduate courses around your particular view; and you can evaluate teachers based on their effective pursuance of goals that you develop and articulate. Because at most institutions the vast majority of FYC faculty have a more bureaucratic than professional status, their institutional function is to do the curriculum, not develop it.[1] This is not to say that the work of all contingent writing teachers is heavily prescribed, nor is it to say that many contingent faculty aren't innovative in informed and important ways. Nevertheless, distinctions in the institutional status of teachers have a profound effect—in particular classrooms and in aggregate—on how we see and do writing education.

From a satellite view, the broad surface of the ongoing struggle between literature and composition might persuasively be articulated as "them vs. us." However, within the "compartment" of program administration, the "us" of composition is strained to, and perhaps beyond,

---

1. Certainly, the degree to which the teaching work is actually determined by administrative decisions varies from site to site. At my university contingent faculty are given much agency concerning the pedagogical choices they make. In contrast, a nearby institution prescribes nearly every aspect of its writing classes: insisting that all instructors use a common syllabus, a common text, common assignments, and a common rubric for evaluation. Moreover, a particular type of agency can be exercised by those who work within the confines of organizations, and this controlled but not wholly determined form of agency has been articulated in a number of influential studies. Berger and Luckmann (1967) described the relationship between individuals and organizations as dialectical rather than determined and therefore accommodating of a degree of deviation and novelty; others, like De Certeau and Bourdieu, have further elaborated theories of agency within highly rule-governed societal contexts.

the breaking point. Professionals and bureaucrats experience FYC in remarkably different ways; they have very different interests, roles, and dispositions; and the work that they do—including how they approach writing education in the classroom—is an extension of positionalities within relations of production.

LEARNING COMPOSITION

Though rarely explicitly acknowledged, socialization into the profession of rhetoric and composition often involves learning to live with the tension created by the field's relatively recent struggle toward *professional* status and a continued, complicated relationship with the long-established *bureaucratic* project of FYC. If it isn't an exercise in denial of the political economic, it is certainly at least an exercise in the bracketing of the political economic. The professional ethos that many of us who hold Ph.D.s in rhetoric and composition learn to assume in our graduate educations compels us to ignore the conditions that define the undergraduate writing instruction we do as TAs and adjuncts throughout our graduate study. Rather than exploring the contradictions that come with already being university writing teachers but not yet professionals, most of us learn to compartmentalize, survive, and move on. In the program I attended, those whom the university deemed most promising (based primarily on GRE scores) received research fellowships and were exempted from teaching work altogether, reifying the broader institutional distinction between teaching work and intellectual development and inquiry. This sent an early message that promising scholars should not be burdened with the work of teaching writing, and that teaching could simply be learned "on the fly" when graduates landed jobs. Those graduate students who weren't on fellowships taught two/two loads and (depending on the availability of classes) also taught for reduced, adjunct rates in the summer. The adjuncts and TAs who staffed the university's writing classes shared cramped office space, telephones, and sometimes even the carrels at which we were required to hold weekly office hours. Some graduate assistants were chosen to serve as "assistants to the writing program director": among the perquisites for these positions were a course release and use of a desk in a smaller office on the third floor, which was shared with the two other assistants to the director.

The layout of the building made apparent the conceptual borders that distinguish professional from bureaucrat, faculty from staff, writing instruction from fully legitimate higher learning. The everyday happenings in the building further reinforced these distinctions, and for those who were in the doctoral program, necessitated the adoption of plural identities. The same people who were "graduate students" or "doctoral candidates" upstairs in classrooms or in faculty offices were also "scholars" and therefore "professionals-in-training." Within that compartment, developing professionals discussed the most relevant and advanced research in the field, envisioned and pursued research projects, prepared papers for conferences and publication, went to national conferences and joined professional organizations. We also attended departmental social functions for tenure-track faculty, and some even enjoyed personal relationships with faculty that were not fully circumscribed by school-related work and responsibilities. Downstairs was quite a different world. There, everyday material reality was not defined primarily by our status as future professionals, but rather by our status as already-realized teacher-workers fulfilling designated roles in a particular bureaucracy. We worked alongside our contingent "colleagues" teaching the hundreds of sections of FYC and entry-level technical writing courses offered by the department each year in a way that was consistent with the general philosophy of our writing program. There we also met with students—some of whom seemed as embarrassed as we by our institutional status and material circumstances—ate our lunches at a makeshift break area, and competed for time on the handful of networked computers we were intended to share.

It would be difficult to overstate the difference between the "rhetoric and composition" that we discussed and theorized upstairs in classrooms and faculty offices and the, in terms of our scholarship, largely invisible FYC teaching labor that we performed out of the basement carrels. "Upstairs" we talked about Aristotle and Burke; postmodernity and technology; gender and race; current traditionalism, expressivism, and process; deficit, cognitivist, and social constructivist models; portfolios and assessment, etc. We learned the prevailing orthodoxy, which defines itself against the unsophisticated authoritarianism of current traditionalism and the quaintly modernist naiveté of expressivism. We learned that context is always important, that discourse must always be understood and negotiated in terms of power, and that privilege and hierarchies must be continually recognized and questioned. And yet, strangely, the relationship between "composition" as a professional, scholarly endeavor and the fully bureaucratic, institutional context of our everyday paid work in FYC remained vague. The socio-material realities of the teaching labor we already performed rarely entered our scholarly discussions in meaningful ways. The economic terms of the work (broad administrative funding decisions as well as our own lack of benefits and low paychecks); the ways in which we were evaluated and monitored as teacher-workers; the feudal power disparities created by a dynamic within which our managers were also our teachers, dissertation directors, and mentors; the various material strains exerted on our teaching work as a result of our tenuous institutional status and our precarious economic circumstances (circumstances that for many led to semisecret additional jobs outside of the university)—these were not an integral part of the way we were encouraged to understand truly "professional" work in the field. Within a highly regarded curriculum that covered everything from advanced theories of discourse to empirical research methodologies, we became expert at contextualizing writing education everywhere but in our own building and working lives.

What is the broad impact of this mode of socialization on postsecondary literacy instruction and the concerns of research in the field? Among the characteristics of the professional culture of rhetoric and composition is the omission of the embodied, bureaucratically situated labor of contingent teachers as a factor of significance in the professional, intellectual realm of the field. Rather, in graduate schools, most of us learn to adopt the compartmentalized subjectivities that allow us to avoid recognizing the inherent contradictions of our work throughout our professional lives. Absent a defined status as university workers already doing legitimate, important work for our departments and universities, we learn to separate most of our bureaucratic *teaching* work from our efforts to advance toward a *professional* career. The socialization of the professional compositionist often involves assuming the efficacy of FYC and assuming that we are to be its managers and theorists. Even as we are taught to admire a historical devotion to "the noble work of teaching," we also learn that research, publication, and the establishment of a scholarly presence are minimum requisites for professional status. Teachers of FYC are everywhere and nowhere. They are not the primary audience of scholarship in composition; the primary audience is other professionals. Absent the professional legitimacy and status that would come with the fuller recognition of the teaching work they are already doing for the university, graduate students defer professional legitimacy until they have acquired a Ph.D. and a tenure-track job. In the process they learn that they are different from the part-timers and contract staff with whom they typically share offices—"staff" are labor, "TAs" are management/professional trainees. Peripheral, but progressing toward *the real* according to the terms of the discourse of scholarship and workplaces, graduate students learn to identify with their managers/mentors and work toward joining their ranks. Meanwhile, rhetoric and composition as a field of research and intellectual inquiry remains strangely "out there," detached from the material realities of what they are already doing in their everyday lives as writing "staff." At least in terms of FYC, teaching is more interesting and even relevant as the subject of professional conversations than as praxis. Pedagogy certainly remains the focus of composition scholarship, but the conversation is framed in a way that removes the teaching of writing from its material, bureaucratic context.

By the time many of us do achieve a professional status in the field, the routine contradictions of the profession have often been so deeply internalized that they can seem natural and inevitable. This is not to say that they are invisible, however. It is not that most of us don't understand that the use of contingent labor to staff so many undergraduate writing classes is a serious problem. It is nearly impossible to be naive about the terms of teaching labor in composition, and so it is difficult to be subject to "false consciousness" in the dogmatic Marxist sense. Rather, we tend to both admit the issue and dismiss it—a process that is enacted largely beneath the level of the primary scholarly discourse of the field. In so doing, we engage in a brand of what Slavoj Zizek describes as "cynical reasoning" (1989, 29). We recognize the distinctions between the layers of labor in our profession, but we are conditioned to couple that recognition with a dismissal of its significance to the general profession and perhaps a lack of faith in our ability to address it. Professionals don't allow the dirty work of day-to-day bureaucratic administration to spill over into the more advanced, legitimate work of scholarship. The seeming lack of interest of many who mentor graduate students into the field further conditions future professionals not to deem the problem worthy of interest or energy. Indeed, this cynicism can sometimes even pass for sophistication and be interpreted as a sign of maturation. Applying complex analytical paradigms to critiques of cultural hegemony and social injustice are appropriate for scholarship and classroom discussion—for broad-ranging theoretical discussions of race and gender, for instance—but applying the same analysis to the bureaucracies many of us create and maintain within which graduate students' teaching work is conducted puts one at risk of being dismissed as naive or out of touch. Professionalization through graduate studies therefore often carries an implicit denial of the material. Our professional lives as scholars and future-classroom-teachers move on a different track from our working lives as already-classroom-teachers. Within this logic, until graduate students realize that professionals manage (rather than being subject to) the flawed, innately contradictory, bureaucratic enterprise of FYC, they are not yet ready to assume the sober work of leadership in our departments and professional organizations—work that involves budgeting, hiring and firing, making policies, and troubling compromises. Some even see this role in a kind of benevolent way—the WPA "looks out for" adjuncts in the department, protecting them as best she can. The "canny bureaucrat" who makes deals with administrators in the best interests of contingents fills such a role (Harris 2000; Miller 1999; Porter et al. 2000). Whether covertly benevolent, nakedly managerial, or both, graduate students learn to enter the terrain of FYC as administrators and the terrain of broader academic careers as scholars in the traditional mode.

PROCESS, PRODUCTION, AND MYSTIFICATION IN COMPOSITION

Pedagogical technique also now helps mark the distinction between composition professionals and FYC. While contentious and ongoing theoretical discussions inform pedagogy within the professional realm, FYC has not been directly responsive to the sophisticated critique and pedagogical theory that has come to define the theoretical mainstream over the past decade. Few textbooks designed for use in FYC courses reflect the "post-process" informed critiques that have defined much of the recent scholarly discourse.[2] Few invite students to examine the power dynamics, cultural milieu, and material conditions from which they write—fuller examination of context might evoke uncomfortable or even dangerous questions about the very historical and organizational logics that create writing programs and profitable lines of writing textbooks. Portable and easily digested by the nonspecialist, most composition texts therefore seem frozen in the particular version of process that gained ascendancy in the late 1980s and early 1990s. In other words, they tellingly fail to embrace the more radical implications of a fully social view of writing.

---

2.   I examine textbooks, and what they can tell us about postsecondary writing education, with much more depth in the next chapter.

Recognizing and perpetuating the distinction between the professional and bureaucratic realms in the field, publishers have clearly identified contingents as an important marketing niche and now often even bypass "professionals"—who often don't use textbooks in their writing classes—and appeal directly to both the disaffection of FYC workers and the rhetoric of empowerment that ironically frames their pedagogical project. For instance, Houghton Mifflin maintains a Web site designed to market writing textbooks directly to non-tenure-track faculty, and they unabashedly appeal to the disgruntlement and lack of institutional standing of this niche. "Wishing you had a voice?" the promotional materials for the Houghton Mifflin Web site ask—then visit "adjuncts. com." The opening statement at the Web site seeks to express empathy for a target audience that feels undervalued: "At Houghton Mifflin, we understand the valuable role that adjuncts play in higher education, and we hope the information on this web site helps you negotiate those challenges." At the Web site visiting contingent teachers will find interactive features, various kinds of support materials, and (of course) composition texts from Houghton Mifflin (Houghton Mifflin 2004). Houghton Mifflin enacts a marketing strategy that identifies alienation and voicelessness as defining characteristics of this market niche and subtly constructs itself as an understanding entity, in contrast with the exploitative bureaucracies within which many adjuncts work but don't feel valued. The Web site offers interactive forums, textbook reviews, pedagogical advice, and even links to *The Adjunct Advocate: The Magazine for Adjunct College Professors.*

Of course, the goal of any publisher is to sell books. And in the content of textbooks the focus moves from the potentially voiceless teaching subject to the student who, herself, stands in need of the critical thinking skills and nurturing pedagogical stance that defines empowering process pedagogy. The marketing and the introductory descriptions of composition textbooks draw expertly on the rhetoric of student empowerment that has become entrenched as the normal science of FYC. With the strange, powerful magic offered by these textbooks, the adjunct who can only wish she had a voice is transformed into someone who is able to show students how to find theirs. Consider the following passage from a popular FYC text published by Bedford/St. Martin's. Through the text—produced, marketed, and sold by a major publisher—the professional/theorist speaks directly to the FYC teacher/worker:

Traditional textbooks too often place students and teachers in opposition: The teacher acts as the provider of knowledge, while students are positioned as passive absorbers of this wisdom. *Work in Progress* would, I hoped, foster the development of a genuinely collaborative community, grounded in mutual respect and a shared commitment to learning. Learning and teaching are, after all, both works in progress. (Ede 2001, vii)

Can the "genuinely collaborative community" envisioned by Ede here be fostered by a textbook? Answering this question may require another: is "the teacher" in this classroom a part of a "genuinely collaborative" professional culture, or is she expected to come out of a more rigidly hierarchical culture in which she is largely invisible and has little or no professional standing, and then manage to create such a culture within the walls of her classroom? This passage appeals to a broad "we" that can be taken for the national, generic ethos of FYC. Indeed, it reproduces the field's disciplinary imaginary—one that places an all-inclusive com-position against the elitist tradition of literary studies, as it denies the material, institutional realities of teaching and learning in postsecond-ary writing. "We" are invited to approach this textbook as teachers who are fully aligned with process/empowering pedagogy and the values it carries. "We" don't subscribe to banking models within which teachers are authoritarian dispensers of knowledge and students are "passive absorbers" of that knowledge. "We" embrace a democratic model that fosters "a genuinely collaborative community, grounded in mutual respect and a shared commitment to learning." We value collaboration. We emphasize process rather than product. We respect our students and the knowledge and experiences they bring into the classroom. We are definitely, absolutely, 100 percent not current-traditionalists.

My question is where are "they"? Increasingly, those who are teach-ing FYC were themselves FYC students in process classrooms. The pedagogical values and assumptions concerning literacy and learning that process carries are the clear dominant in FYC. It is true that what gets called "process" is, in practice, often what Joseph Harris has called a "new formalism": it is "process" employed toward technocratic ends (1997, 56). Nevertheless, at least to the degree that orthodoxies can be maintained among a variously trained, ever-evolving, casualized instructorate, process is the orthodoxy. Ironically, this construction of empowering pedagogy helps to enable the misrecognition of the clearly disempowering socio-material conditions that define work in FYC. When we place the teacher of FYC in a position of authority, casting her in a struggle against authoritarian pedagogies, we (mis)place her in the professional realm of pedagogical theory and research, masking the powerful political economic forces that determine the shape and conditions of her work and her students' work. Few of us can fully believe in this mirage, but it is a part of the necessary game we play in scholarly and administrative discourse: it keeps discussions of academic literacy and the bureaucratic aspects of writing programs moving along on their present, distinct tracks.

Primarily through the employment of contingent labor, English departments deliver large numbers of sections of writing instruction to the university on the cheap. This is perhaps the most obvious relationship through which surplus is extracted within university labor dynamics. It is also perhaps the most mystified and invisible facet of postsecondary education within the general culture outside of academia. In its continually reproduced FYC metanarrative, rhetoric and composition reifies the FYC instructor as a legitimately professional intellectual who engages in an ongoing fight against authoritarian pedagogies and for the empowerment and edification of students. The rhetoric within which FYC is often couched thereby mystifies the material terms of teaching labor. In contrast, broad outcomes statements, new curricular initiatives, large-scale writing program assessments, textbooks, and the philosophies that drive them frame the material terms of everyday production in FYC. Within these selective frames, the labor of teaching is folded neatly into the fully professional work of administrator/researchers, where it becomes visible only in terms of sections filled, outcomes achieved, and curriculums successfully implemented. Instrumentalist management techniques—standardized syllabi, uniform grading rubrics, mandatory texts, mandatory evaluations—can ensure that FYC teachers are present and productive but not granted too much agency even in the classroom. Within our professional rhetoric, we rarely see the contingent writing teacher as a socially, indeed bureaucratically, situated material body—one who might teach many, many writing students but may very well be indifferent to, and bewildered by, the scholarly discourse of rhetoric and composition.

Take, for instance, outcomes statements like one published in *College English* by a group that formed on the Writing Program Administration Listserv (Harrington et al. 2001). The statement lists desired outcomes for the tens of thousands of students throughout the country who take FYC each year. The outcomes generally strike a balance between contemporary research concerning language and learning and the bureaucratic realities of English departments and the universities within which they are situated. What is troubling is the position from which the statement is written, which assumes the naturalness of the authority that WPAs wield over the armies of mostly non-tenure-track instructors who will be charged with meeting these administrative prerogatives. There is no indication that any part-time teachers or TAs were even consciously included in the drafting of the statement. This is a conversation among professionals about the proper aims of the bureaucracies and bureaucrats they manage. I don't deny the usefulness of such statements to WPAs; however, I think they are artifacts of our field that should be critically examined for what they say about our work. Among the questions that should be raised by such a statement: What assumptions about FYC, pedagogy, disciplinary hierarchies, and academic labor dynamics inform it? Why is the theory that informs this statement a contentious, participatory realm for WPAs but a matter of calcified, determining policy for those beneath them? How are people and their work positioned differently in debates about theory and outcomes statements?

TURNING TOWARD THE SOCIAL AS AN ASPECT OF THE MATERIAL

The field is beginning to grapple with the problems presented by the use of contingent FYC labor in its major scholarly forums. That conversation, however, remains primarily administrative or purely labor-oriented. It doesn't address how administration and labor are intertwined with classroom learning and writing, disciplinarity, and the production of professional discourse. Some, for instance, argue that we should accept that FYC classes will be taught by a subordinate tier of faculty whose primary identification is with teaching rather than with scholarship. This teaching tier is distinct from the more professional tier of the field (those who hold Ph.D.s), which Richard Miller describes as concerned with "overseeing the labor of others, interacting diplomatically with department chairs and college deans, working within a budget, writing grant proposals, and performing other such managerial tasks" (1999, 98–99). Miller joins those who generally, if reluctantly, accept the use of a separate tier of faculty to teach writing as an inevitable fact of life and seek pragmatic, locally situated means of improving their working conditions. Typically speaking from the perspective of WPAs, they outline ways that WPAs can work for practical gains within bureaucracies: for instance, through becoming what Miller calls "intellectual bureaucrats" (see also Harris 2000; Murphy 2000; Porter et al. 2000). This position recognizes the bureaucratic aspects of academic work and explores ways to work "within the system" to make the use of contingent faculty more equitable, dignified, and effective. It is important to note, however, that while this strategy might undermine the binary between theory and empirical research, it maintains the binary between professionals and teacher-workers, as it conjures the image of scholar-administrators using research and administrative acumen to enact local change—for, rather than with, non-tenure-track FYC teachers.

A number of problems have resulted from the willingness of many to embrace a managerial relationship with FYC. It emphasizes individual, rather than collective, action, usually ignoring the successes brought about by unionization and essentially giving up on the project of making FYC a more fully professional and intellectual project. Additionally, it can become yet another way of silencing the contingent—as the paternalistic WPA assumes the authority to represent the interests of FYC teachers. Finally, it tends to promote a particular brand of pragmatism that accepts that the ascendancy of neoliberal managerial practices and the casualization of teaching labor are inevitable facts of life. If the field is set to accept the dual assumptions that FYC is rightly taught by a subtier of faculty and that the natural position of the professional compositionist is as manager, we must also accept the unsavory fact that our field has come to depend on the existence of exploited labor for our disciplinary identity, function, and survival. The management function has taken a place among the subjects of our professional work alongside literacy and language. The historic lack of significant, collective action by professional WPA organizations to address labor inequities could already lead one to such a conclusion.

An even deeper problem with embracing a managerial ethos, however, is that it reinforces the historic and ongoing undervaluation—and the feminized coding—of teaching, especially the teaching of writing, within the academy. Rather than finding creative ways to advocate for those who work "beneath" us—a plan that, not so coincidentally, solidifies the position of the WPA—we should work toward a situation in which those who teach writing are legitimate professionals with advanced education in rhetoric and composition. Given the realities of funding, this could very well mean cutting back or eliminating the first-year requirement and allowing writing courses to stand on their own within broader English curriculums. These are the options that I am pushing in my own program.[3] Among the aspects of rhetoric and composition that make it unique in the humanities is that the work of its teachers involves the application of advanced research on literacy and learning, rather than the explication of that research. Margaret Marshall argues that to be more properly valued within our departments, we need to work to increase the visibility of teaching in the evaluation process. When we accept the institutional subordination of teaching work as an immutable fact of life, we don't recognize the manner in which composition scholarship has intellectualized writing pedagogy. She advocates measures designed to make innovation and excellence in teaching more visible—eventually more fully professional—in English and writing departments.

Regardless of the path, we need change not only to address immediate problems that typically fall under "administrative" or "labor" categories; we need to connect administration and labor to the sociomaterial conditions of teaching and the production of research and theory more broadly. If FYC is the "turf" of rhetoric and composition, we should cultivate it as active insiders, erasing the borders that currently characterize the relationship between the professional field and the bureaucratic enterprise. Our scholarship, administration actions, and pedagogy should become an integrated scholarly praxis that is fully historically situated.

This praxis would not only help the field to more progressively address its own labor issues, it would be generative of progressive pedagogies that examine issues of socioeconomic justice. The two are inextricably linked. Systems of pedagogical work—whether "professional" or "bureaucratic"—create the ideological frameworks within which student writing is performed. We have a large body of research and theory that argues that writing is never just writing: it is the formation

---

3.   Of course, there is nothing new in this position. The Wyoming Resolution proposed and endorsed (but not implemented) by CCCC's in 1986 proposed grievance and censure procedures for the exploitation of part-time faculty. The conversation surrounding the resolution connected the terms of labor for teachers with the quality and character of writing education more generally (see Gunner). If more in the field had taken Sharon Crowley's advice and taken measures to eliminate the first-year writing requirement, would postsecondary writing education be in a worse position now? Without relying on the debilitating crutch provided by part-time labor, it is certainly possible that many institutions would have found ways to do writing education more responsibly and more effectively; it is also plausible that the field more generally might have found a more legitimate place in undergraduate curriculums.

of consciousness and the enactment of politics (for instance, Berlin and Vivion 1992; Downing 1994; Fox 1990; Horner and Lu 1999; Shor 1996; Trimbur 1994). In addition to examining pedagogical theory, however, we need to recognize and be more accountable to the relationship between our own labor practices and professional ethos and the character of the literacies that we sponsor and promote in our classrooms. This accountability could help the field to escape the embarrassing and cynical contradictions of promoting empowering models of literacy in classes taught by casualized teaching labor at the very bottom of academic institutions. The production of writing in composition classes cannot be properly or adequately examined in isolation from the conditions and relations of labor in English departments.

2

WRITING THE PROGRAM
The Genre Function of the Writing Textbook

As a political philosophy, neoliberalism construes a rationale for a handful of private interests to control as much of social life as possible to maximize their financial investments. Unrestricted by legislation or government regulation, market relations as they define the economy are viewed as a paradigm for democracy itself. Central to neoliberal philosophy is the claim that the development of all aspects of society should be left to the wisdom of the market.

—Henry A. Giroux and Susan Searls Giroux

This year, like every year, textbook publishers sponsored a book fair and free lunch in my department. Eerily polite and deferential book reps from the major publishers displayed large stacks of texts. While some literary anthologies were among the offerings, the vast majority were textbooks for writing classes, and the annual event is intended primarily for first-year writing staff. Indeed, the reps pay the writing program a fee in order to participate; with the stacks of textbooks, the business cards, and the smiles come free sandwiches and sodas. This event has become an entrenched part of the general scene in my department, coming with the same mundane regularity as the Christmas party and factional squabbling. It is also remarkably different from the other regular happenings in the department because it directly integrates private industry and marketing into the fabric of the departmental culture and work. Publishers make their presence felt in a host of other ways, such as by sending out free textbooks and e-mails that advertise particular books and soliciting paid reviews. A few publishers are now sponsoring research in the field, and publishers are ubiquitous at the annual College Composition and Communication Conference (CCCC) and the National Council of Teachers of English (NCTE) conference. In fact, major events at each conference are sponsored by the publishers and have become deeply ingrained in conference cultures. At the CCCC, meetings with free food and alcohol at publishers' parties are a regular part of the established routines of conference goers. At the NCTE conference, a line at least one hundred yards long typically begins to form outside of the book expo long before it opens on the first day. When the doors are opened, a crush of conference-goers rushes inside to collect promotional giveaways from the publishers. People walk away with bags filled with everything from pens and pencils to tote bags and book covers—all with publishers' logos prominently displayed. These upfront expenditures on building relationships and establishing name recognition are testament to the fact that textbooks are big business. The number of titles available for composition alone is overwhelming. From the major publishers—Bedford/St. Martin's, Pearson, Longman, Allyn and Bacon, and Houghton Mifflin—one can choose from over 500 titles of rhetorics, readers, and handbooks.

The relationship between the textbook industry and college writing says much about the political economy of work in composition. I recently got an e-mail from a publishing rep asking me to participate in what the message called a "Rhetoric Symposium" being held in a southwestern state. The publisher offered to pay for all travel expenses and provide a $250 "honorarium for completing a preparatory assignment and participating in the symposium." Reflecting the murky position of college writing instruction as a quasi-professional, quasi-scholarly endeavor, the description of the purpose of the symposium is a strained conflation of professional development, consultation, and market development:

> The symposium features discussion among fifteen instructors who teach this course at colleges and universities around the country, *and will include in-depth discussions about technology tools.* For two days, we will focus on the challenges faced by you and your students, ways in which other instructors are confronting these challenges, and how we as a dedicated publisher of course materials can support your efforts.
>
> The roundtable forum and small group size allows for lively and engaging discussions. Faculty members bring different experiences to the table, which stimulates rich discussion both during the symposium program and in after-hours conversation. Participants at other symposia have left the meetings with a variety of new ideas to implement in their courses and share with their departments. Discussions span how to best organize course material, how to integrate technology, and how to better motivate students.
>
> This input will help us develop better instructional materials for instructors and your students—participants will impact the publishing decisions we

make. Participants are asked to help facilitate discussion on a particular topic at the symposium. This format allows members of the publishing team to focus on discussion, and it puts control in the hands of instructors! And, we promise that at no time during the weekend will we try to sell anything—this is a developmental endeavor.

As a writing program director with a Ph.D. in rhetoric and composition, I don't think I am the primary target audience of this form letter. As with the www.adjuncts.com Web site discussed in the previous chapter, the rhetoric seems particularly crafted for contingent faculty. This symposium, it is asserted, will put "control in the hands of instructors!" This seems to indicate that the primary target audience is those who don't feel that they have much control, and perhaps don't feel that they have a voice in any professional forum outside of their own classrooms.

There are overt economic factors at play here as well that help to further contextualize the symposium, its purposes, and the complex of motivations and terms of work to which it responds. Textbook marketing techniques, and practices with textbooks, are among the factors that can mark the distinction between a professional and a more bureaucratic orientation in postsecondary writing. Scholars who have professional status tend to learn about and discuss classroom issues in scholarly forums, and those forums lend us a voice, help us to grow as professionals, and provide opportunities for professional advancement. Scholars read and sometimes write journal articles and attend and present at conferences. This activity is institutionally supported, recognized, and rewarded as part of our professional work. Most of us get some measure of funding for travel to conferences; we add publications and conference presentations to our curriculum vitae, and such activities are typically incorporated as important factors in professional review processes. This publisher-sponsored symposium is a part of a process that bypasses that institutionally supported, scholarly realm of rhetoric and composition, describing a forum in which largely contingent teachers of composition talk directly with "the publishing team." Who exactly composes the publishing team (and what its aims and general orientation are) remains vague, but one imagines that this is a group working for the publisher seeking to gain information and feedback from the teachers for new products. Participants are expected to come to the gathering with materials and to facilitate discussions as well as participate. In short, a large part of this exchange can be described as consultation, and consultancy in other industries at similar events is compensated at significantly higher rates: in many industries over $100 an hour, and in fields like medicine and technology over $200 an hour. In this two-day consultation session, however, teachers are asked to work for something for which they are quite likely already accustomed to working: proxy capital. Their own professional development, rather than dollars, is their primary compensation. Fair compensation for travel and professional consultation seems beside the point—this is not a for-profit company looking for information and market development opportunities, but "a dedicated publisher of course materials" that only wants to "support" teachers. Teachers at all levels are conditioned to see their work in terms of social altruism and individual development rather than as adequately compensated, highly skilled professional labor. Many K-12 teachers draw on their own incomes to provide everything from books, paper, and chalk to food for breakfast and snacks for their students. They also often finance their own professional development through paying their own way to conferences and getting advanced degrees. Although higher degrees do typically bring a bump in pay, they are primarily compensated for their extra efforts with love and professional satisfaction. In the humanities in higher education, before we reach an institutionally recognized professional position, we likewise often trade in status and future recognition rather than in real wages. For instance, when graduate students are asked to perform some free labor—help administer a conference, lead a workshop, pick up a job candidate—they are often told that this will be "another line on your vita," or "a chance to better get to know so-and-so."

Eileen Schell writes about "psychic income," another form of proxy capital (1998). She relates a story from Alice Gillam in which an adjunct faculty member complained about her pay and was told by an administrator that she was not working for pay, but for the psychic income of teaching at a university (40). Psychic income is the alleged privilege and status of teaching at a postsecondary institution and the satisfaction that comes with being able to do it well. It isn't real income (wages), nor is it even the type of proxy income that is institutionally supported and eventually realized as professional advancement. Psychic income is a more transparent form of exploitation and it is baldly indicative of low-status work. It is closely associated with "women's work"—work that may be occasionally recognized by a legitimated authority figure for its importance, but not valued in broader political economic terms and which doesn't lead to transferable capital or legitimate professional status.[1] It comes when labor is couched in the language of sacrifice and dedication—rather than credentials, knowledge, and expertise. Psychic income is therefore, as Katherine Wills argues, both a means of justifying low pay among some administrators, and a means of rationalizing the low status that comes with the work among contingent faculty themselves:

> For adjuncts driven by the need of psychic income, fair compensation can take second place to self-perceptions of an altruistic ethos. Women, especially, seem to be willing to work to satisfy abstract concepts of duty or service because part-time teaching falls within a discourse of philanthropy and the respectable, nurturing mother-teacher. (2004, 202)

As Wills points out, psychic income is short-lived: not only do real economic pressures impinge on the lives of contingent teachers, but the more contact they have with the fiercely maintained hierarchies of higher education, the more they realize that their status is never genuine. Wills cites the high burnout rate among contingent faculty as evidence of this cycle of hope and disillusionment. She makes the case that those who seek to enact solutions to the problem of exploited teaching labor in composition through organizing contingent faculty need to account for the powerful but false lure of psychic income (201).

Textbooks are not only an integral part of the cultures of writing programs, they are among the factors that relate work in composition to service work in the fast-capitalist economy more generally. Teachers who work in primary and secondary education are happy to get free pens, posters, and book bags to bring back to classrooms, even when they advertise products. Contingent writing teachers in postsecondary education are targeted by Web sites that show empathy for their institutional positions and events like this "symposium" that *seem* to lend professional status through valuing their opinions and experience. Commodities with well-defined markets, textbooks appeal to a broad "we" that can be taken for the national, generic ethos of FYC—and as textbooks appeal to this ethos, they help to reproduce it.

In this chapter, I will examine textbooks as a part of the past and present political economics of composition. Given their omnipresence, it is surprising that the function and character of textbooks and the

---

1.   See also Enos (1996), Fontaine and Hunter (1992), Holbrook (1991), Strickland (2001), and Wills (2004) for discussions of gender and discounted labor in academia.

textbook industry isn't emphasized more in research.[2] When we do discuss textbooks, it is tempting to frame the material present of our work as an outcome of a *scholarly* past—an effort to reify our own disciplinary legitimacy and professional status. In scholarly metanarratives, our roots are primarily in rhetoric, education, literacy studies, and linguistics. The contemporary field rejected formalism and current-traditionalism (sort of); we moved through expressivism and cognitivism, developing and (in some cases) eventually problematizing "process." Textbooks might easily be thought of as being subsumed within this scholarly trajectory: when scholars tended to be formalist, textbooks were largely formalist; when process gained ascendancy, textbooks became more process-oriented. However, while textbooks do resonate with the most generic aspects of general scholarly trends, they have not kept in step with where the scholarly field has moved. David Bleich notes that textbooks function to homogenize and promote an inert, disempowering "normal science" (1999, 16). Kurt Spellmeyer similarly argues that textbooks are involved in "the social production of banality" and are "almost inevitably . . . out of date by the time they leave the bindery" (1999, 47). Xin Liu Gale and Frederic G. Gale note that

> As composition and rhetoric becomes increasingly a more complex discipline that hosts a diversity of theories, pedagogies, and research methods, one would assume that textbooks, as part of the "disciplinary matrix," would reflect such complexities. However, a majority of college composition/rhetoric textbooks published in the past three decades have failed to fully represent the rapidly changing and richly diverse disciplinary knowledge or to translate successfully the various theories and pedagogies into effective practical approaches for the teaching of writing in colleges and universities. (1999, 4)

Gale and Gale ask "How are we to account for this gap?" I believe that this important question should be examined in terms of the long-established and still-ongoing relationship between textbooks and the use of contingent labor to teach writing classes. Indeed, since the beginning, textbooks have been an important part of the story of the subordinate status of teaching labor in college composition. Textbooks have not

---

2.   A notable exception is the collection *ReVisioning Composition Textbooks*, edited by Xin Liu Gale and Frederic G. Gale. Gale and Gale (1999) note a considerable disjuncture between the degree of presence that textbooks have in the field, and the degree to which they are examined in scholarly work. They found that only one CCCC panel was devoted to textbooks in the 1990s.

only been used as a means of training students, they have also been a relatively cheap and efficient means of controlling the pedagogies that are enacted in writing classes by those who don't have professional status. The question that we have not pursued very thoroughly as a field is what is controlling textbooks and what function are they serving in the contemporary scene of writing education? In order to begin to address these questions, I will survey some of the primary critical treatments of textbooks in the field. I will then relate the results of a study that I have conducted that examines how twenty-one contingent teachers choose and use textbooks in their writing classes. This study provides a revealing, if admittedly limited, glimpse into the complicated political economic dynamics of a first-year writing program.

REQUIRED TEXTS

College composition has from the beginning been intimately connected with textbooks. As stated in the previous chapter, disciplinary histories locate a deeply established subordination of writing work to literary studies within the broader field of English studies, and that has profoundly shaped what we are now. By the turn of the twentieth century, the general content, status, and terms of labor in composition had already been established. Major writing programs were managed by an administrator, and first-year writing was already overwhelmingly taught by part-time instructors and graduate students. "Professors" primarily studied and taught literature, and composition had a firmly secondary status (Brereton 1995, 21). Significantly, a solid semiotic relationship had also been established between textbooks and writing programs. The three primary genres of textbooks—rhetorics, readers, and handbooks—were very much in use in various writing programs by 1900, and of course each carried its own philosophy of language and learning. Rhetorics, for instance, had become an integral part of the program at Harvard, where there was a clear relationship between textbook and curriculum. The course had no outside readings and centered heavily on invention and daily themes. Adams Sherman Hill's *Principles of Rhetoric* (1878) was its only text, and Hill was also the head of the writing program. John C. Brereton calls Sherman Hill's program at Harvard the "first modern composition program" (1995, 8). In contrast with Harvard, emerging programs at many other institutions, such as those at Amherst and Berkeley, did emphasize extensive reading along with writing instruction (11–12). John Franklin Genung, who taught composition at Amherst, had his own best-selling textbook called *The Practical Elements of Rhetoric, with Illustrative Examples* (1885). That pedagogy was focused on modeling rather than invention—but as at Harvard, the textbook facilitated the programmatic vision, synchronizing administrative prerogatives with pedagogical practices for an institutionally subordinate staff of instructors. The textbook was based on a set of theoretical assumptions, but it was used as a mechanism of bureaucracy to turn that theory into day-to-day pedagogical blueprints for those who had little or no professional status or expertise.[3]

From the beginning, an important part of the function of the genre of writing textbooks has clearly been to help to deliver both the content and the pedagogical theory of undergraduate writing. It is important to note that these varieties of textbooks flourished in writing, but not in the other areas of English studies. Literary and critical anthologies certainly existed, and they still exist and help to create and legitimize always-contentious canonical terrains, but they don't function in literary studies in the same way that they do in writing education. Literary anthologies typically only reproduce the primary texts themselves—that is where the areas of scholarly contention are located. In contrast, writing texts are far more prescriptive vehicles of pedagogical theory and practice, containing everything from invention exercises, model essays, and writing assignments to explicit articulations of drafting, revision strategies, readings, evaluative matrices, and source material for research. Textbooks therefore have significantly more influence on what happens in classrooms. As Bleich notes, textbooks (in contrast with other types of books) are "declarative and directive"—they are not the *subject of* interpretation or argument: they *tell how*, and they do so from a position of authority (1999, 16). Textbooks, as a directive genre, don't expose (or invite critique of) the origins or contingencies of their own assumptions and claims. Many even articulate the type of teacher-student relationship that should be fostered in classrooms—often in the context of discussions of process. Bleich argues that the authors of textbooks actually assume their own teacherly presence in the classes: they are coequal with, or even positioned as the founding basis of, the authority wielded by teachers in the classes in which they are used (1999, 17–19).

---

3. A more thorough history of the writing textbook and its relationship to curriculums is not only outside the scope of this book, but one can find excellent treatments of the early history in Brereton (1995) and Kitzhaber (1990). I found Russell (1991) also a very helpful starting point for understanding the history of the textbook in relation to the introductory writing requirement.

Pointing to the distinctions between the ways that textbook author-ship has been perceived, evaluated, and compensated by academic institutions, Susan Miller has argued that more explanation was needed of "the actual function of the textbook and the ways this function con-strains the nature of its authorship" (155). In *Textual Carnivals: The Politics of Composition*, Miller asserted that three things are unlikely about textbooks: "That a textbook will contain any really idiosyncratic view of the students who use it, that it will singularly define purposes of writing in the course it serves, or that it will bring its author 'authorial' acclaim" (1991, 157). In a very clever argument that largely still holds fifteen years later, Miller argued that textbooks point to a paradox: they are deemed essential for the overall function of writing in English departments even as they are considered not really academically meritorious or deserving of the term "scholarly authorship." In terms of professional valuation for tenure and promotion, they are the "bad cop" that goes into the interrogation room and does the dirty work while the "good cop" looks the other way. They also perform essential disciplinary functions for some of the reasons that Richard Ohmann pointed out in *English in America*. Textbooks are among the elements that create a stable subject for composition studies: fixing students, discourse, and the purposes of pedagogy as manageable, generalizable units. As Ohmann put it, text-books position the student as "defined only by studenthood, not by any other attributes. He [*sic*] is classless, sexless though generically male, timeless. The authors [of textbooks] assume that writing is a socially neutral skill, to be applied in and after college for the general welfare" (Ohmann, quoted in Miller 1991, 156). Drawing on Ohmann, Miller points out that textbooks proceed from a view of student writing that is both monolithic and innocuous. Differences between students and edu-cational contexts are minimized, as is the social impact of students' writ-ing: "These books treat the student and student writing as abstractions that will eventually have a social place, but that do not have one now" (157). They create acceptable subjectivities for the procession through higher education and into society. So even as writing may be couched in ways that make it seem empowering, the function of textbooks has been to support the project of FYC as it relates to institutional processes of conditioning, homogenization, and control—textbooks usefully dis-tance writing and writers from the directly consequential. They help cre-ate a generic, politically innocuous middle that students from a variety of backgrounds are invited to occupy so that they might more smoothly move through higher education—a process parallel to gentrification in times when higher education was less accessible, and now might be said to be "middle-classification" in an era in which undergraduate degrees are far more common. "Academic writing" is certainly a centerpiece of this stabilizing process. The linguistic and cultural impurities of class, race, and ethnicity are eliminated not though open contention (we all value diversity!), but by the promotion of an unproblematized standard that omits them at the more fundamental and covert level of structure; marginal or radical ideas and nonstandard dialects are tamed by evaluative rubrics, restrictive assignments, and standardized academic modes that temper diversity and discourage risk-taking. Spellmeyer argues that the act of questioning itself, an act that is central to education, is carefully circumscribed and rendered largely innocuous by textbooks. Even as they purport to support "research writing" and "academic argumentation," textbooks actually "suppress questioning by removing knowledge from the precarious worlds out of which it has emerged—the lab, the library, the household, the battlefield, the stage—and transporting it, now dead and sealed in wax, to a very different kind of place" (1999, 45). This is a place that is institutionally designed to be inconsequential: "The teacher is there to certify the student's mastery of a standardized corpus of facts and an array of normative practices—practices, not incidentally, that require no real engagement on the student's part, or on the teacher's, for that matter." The textbook helps make it possible for the institution to ensure that education "unfolds with regularity and decorum" (45–46).

Meanwhile, as Miller has pointed out, even as textbooks have come to serve this important socializing, homogenizing function in academia, they are also strangely not fully *of* academia. In terms of the ways that authorship is produced by academic institutions, textbooks are neither "authored" in the same sense that academic monographs are authored, nor do the textbooks themselves often rise to the status afforded objects of study: "Instead, we distance textbooks from normal discussions of research activity and withhold our own official and tangible rewards for them" (1991, 157). This positions the textbook author in a paradoxical position in academia that parallels the more general subordinate, contradictory institutional position of composition. English departments are typically unwilling to get rid of first-year writing, in part because there is still a pervasive belief that it is needed as an enculturation mechanism—the cheaply produced Full Time Equivalents certainly don't detract from its continued popularity either. However, FYC is still not usually considered quite *of* the work of most English departments: it is typically administered separately from the rest of the department in a writing program; it is overwhelmingly taught by non-tenure-track teachers who are socially and institutionally isolated from the tenured faculty; and it is not seen as an authentic part of the *intellectual* work of English studies. Those whose expertise is in rhetoric and composition are often hired to make first-year writing disappear in English departments, rather than to work to integrate it more completely into their intellectual centers.

Textbooks also help to position WPAs, writing teachers, and students in relation to each other. It was once not uncommon for WPAs to write their own textbooks and then make them mandatory in programs. They thereby located much of the professional work—work that requires making fundamental decisions about goals and method in writing pedagogy—with the administrator. Positioned as bureaucrats, teachers *do* a pedagogical approach rather than *developing* one. Many programs continue to have mandatory texts (with accompanying syllabi and support materials), a practice that accomplishes essentially the same function.

THE STUDY: THE GENRE FUNCTION OF TEXTBOOKS

This study is actually the product of an earlier study that did not work. For my earlier project, I collected fifty-seven of the best-selling FYC textbooks from three major textbook publishers. My initial goal was to determine the general philosophies of literacy and learning carried in these texts. I developed a preliminary working list of possible categories—current traditionalist, expressivist, process, multiple-literacies, postprocess, and so on. I then began reading through the texts, trying to locate what I saw within theoretical categories. What I found in the vast majority of texts made me realize that this method would not work. The overwhelming majority of textbooks were a theoretical hodgepodge, carrying assumptions about literacy and learning that were sometimes even internally contradictory. Almost all carried the characteristics of a "process" pedagogy, at least in the most superficial, linear sense of the term (i.e., they moved students through progressions from invention to final products over a series of prescriptive assignments). A "process" orientation is among the standard features listed in textbook marketing—what was once pedagogical innovation has become a market standard. Among the features of fast-capitalist business practices—especially in industries like software, entertainment, and publishing—is the development of more market-tested content. The designs and functions of products more expertly anticipate the values of the niches to which they will be marketed. For textbooks to be economically viable, a "process" orientation is as essential as model assignments. However, under the broad banner of process, many also often incorporated elements of other philosophies, formalism for instance, that work against the fundamental assumptions of process. Textbooks that seemed to promote cultural diversity in their readings included assignments and evaluative rubrics that were clearly driven by current-traditionalist views of literacy in their writing sections. A textbook that purported to be based on inquiry-driven research writing provided preset topics and the full texts of sources for specific research papers so teachers would be able to catch plagiarists more easily.

In the process of the research I did learn much about how textbooks are generally structured, how they are marketed, and the values to which they seem to be appealing. At that point, I might have modified a list of categories based on the initial review that could have been more appropriate and fruitful in terms of analysis. However, the failed initial effort at categorization led to more interesting questions that could best be answered by different, more nuanced and situated research methods. I therefore devised a new study that expanded the scope of inquiry from the texts to the social uses of the texts. I used interviews and support materials to address the following two primary questions:

Why do instructors choose particular textbooks?

What are the functions of textbooks in their writing pedagogies?

Genre analysis seemed a good theoretical framework for the development of a deeper understanding of textbooks. Genre analysis ties texts to their contexts, enabling an understanding of not just the typical forms of texts but their social functions. Carolyn Miller's "Genre as Social Action" (1984) and the English translation of Bakhtin helped mark the beginning of the contemporary discussion of genre in rhetoric and composition in the early- to mid-1980s. Previous work with genre had focused almost exclusively on textual conventions—for instance, the standard sections of a research essay or the rhyming schemes of particular poetic forms. This new work expanded the focus of genre analysis from general textual features to the way that communications are typically carried out within their particular ecologies. Genre analysis is no longer a means of classifying texts according to specific features—it is a means of understanding how textual forms shape communications and social relations in specific settings. As Carolyn Miller argued, genre is a means of taking action in specific social contexts. As such, genres shape and are shaped by the cultures in which they are situated (151–65).

This conception of genre spawned a still-expanding body of research that examines the complex relationships between texts and their contexts. Genre is researched as an aspect of social relationships among authors and audiences, institutional hierarchies, actions in work environments, situated professional discourses, and individual and collective agency (see, e.g., Bawarshi 2003; Bazerman 1997; Beebee 1994; Berkenkotter and Huckin 1993; Devitt 2004; Diaz et al. 1999; Freedman and Medway 1994; Russell 1991). Texts respond to social situations and initiate future responses. Genres are therefore often not only *regulative* of texts, they help to create the frameworks of human activities and social orders. Referencing Foucault's "the author function," Anis Bawarshi describes this socializing aspect of certain texts as "the genre function." Texts structure activities and behaviors in ways that define the status quo. Genres are therefore among the artifacts of everyday social life that condition identities and structure social relations.

Genres are also historical and resonate with the histories of their contexts. Charles Bazerman points out how "the emergence of genre goes hand in hand with the emergence of generic situations, with the rhetorical action itself helping to define the situation" (1997, 6–7). Products of exigence, they form as innovative, active responses to situations in particular places and times, and they evolve with the evolution of those situations. Wonderful examples of this process of emergence and evolution can be found in Joanne Yates's work with organizational communication. Yates describes how communication systems were developed by businesses with the rise of industrialization. As the operations of businesses became larger and more geographically dispersed, managers found that existing ad hoc approaches to management were inadequate for controlling complex organizations. They were too varied, too reliant on the expertise of particular individuals, and too subject to misinterpretation. Moreover, there were no regular mechanisms for enacting managerial imperatives quickly and efficiently across the various levels and locations of large organizations. Practices that came to be called *systemic management* were developed in response to these challenges. Communications infrastructures created within managed systems became highly effective tools for the rationalization of operations.

Important organizational genres emerged within these communications infrastructures. These are the texts that are so ubiquitous in organizational settings today that we take their forms for granted—standardized memos, handbooks, training manuals, procedural outlines, checklists, and progress reports.

This study examines how the genre of the writing textbook has similarly evolved to respond to the terms of labor in composition. My choice of methods has benefits and drawbacks. I conducted interviews with twenty-one participants, all of whom teach at the same institution. I also collected various types of documents from these participants (interviews and documents are described below). This research is therefore very limited in scope. A survey conducted among faculty from a large sampling of institutions could have enabled me to make more confident claims of typification. This research was conducted at a university of a particular type, and might not be relevant for other types of institutions—for instance, at small liberal arts institutions that don't experience high turnover, or at institutions that have a very different curricular focus and approach to professional development. However, the sacrifice in scope came with a degree of increase in depth. Conducting lengthy interviews with faculty chosen for their distinctions in rank and experience, doing follow-ups with selected participants, and drawing on secondary materials enabled me to identify salient issues and examine them more fully. Moreover, that all of the participants worked in the same institution enabled me to examine how textbooks function within a particular workplace culture.

Participant Profile

The primary factors in my choice of participants were number of years experience teaching postsecondary writing and institutional rank. Consistent with the national profile of postsecondary writing teachers, the staff at the site of this study was primarily female and overwhelmingly white, and the participants in the study reflected the staff's general ratio. Only one of the twenty-one participants in this study was nonwhite, and only three were male. Participation was voluntary. A total of twenty-four teachers were contacted and three declined to participate—all three cited the busyness of their schedules.

Experience

The range of experience of participants was from one to thirteen years (see table 1). Some already had worked in other careers in a wide range of other professions—from journalism to real estate—before teaching. Some also had experience teaching in primary and secondary grades. As is consistent with national figures, teachers at this institution tend not to have long careers at the contingent level.

Years Experience	1–3	4–8	9–13
Number of Participants	10	6	5

Table 1: Years of Experience of Participants

Rank

Four of the participants were teaching assistants (TAs). Seven were part-time lecturers (PTLs) who are paid per-class and contracted by semester as needed. Ten were full-time non-tenure-track lecturers (FTNTTL) who are salaried and on multiple-year renewable contracts (see table 2). PTLs have no benefits; FTNTTLs do have benefits, including state-sponsored health insurance.

Rank	TAs	PTLs	FTNTTLs
Number of Participants	4	7	10

Table 2: Rank of Participants

With a few exceptions, FTNTTLs tended to be those with the most experience. All PTLs had less than eight years of experience and all TAs had less than three years of experience.

Interviews

I conducted twenty-one initial interviews and six follow-up interviews with selected participants. This yielded 203 pages of transcription. The initial interviews were semistructured (see Appendix A). A standard list of questions was used for each round; however, in each interview I also adjusted depending on what teachers said (Patton 1990; Rubin and Rubin 1995). The interview questions were designed to elicit information concerning the research questions, but I also pursued new themes through open-ended and follow-up questions. Moreover, sometimes it was necessary to deviate from a particular set of questions to make participants more comfortable and interviews more conversational. The follow-up interviews were conducted to verify analysis and discuss—and in some instances significantly complicate and bring about a more nuanced understanding of—the responses of selected participants. For instance, cost was a surprisingly important theme that emerged in the interviews. As the results section below will indicate, it is not only a significant factor in why teachers choose certain textbooks, it also affects pedagogical decisions. Once I identified cost as an important theme, discussing it with selected participants helped me to gain a deeper understanding of *why* it is such a widespread concern. In follow-ups, participants discussed at more length how they believe textbook cost is connected to student evaluations, and also how they relate cost to their own experiences as students. In order to enable me to make more consistent comparisons, I asked the teachers to focus mainly on the second course in the two-course FYC sequence—a course that focuses on argumentation and academic writing. All of the interviews were digitally recorded, transcribed, and coded according to the procedures described in "Transcription and Analysis" below.

Documents

I initially asked participants only to submit syllabi. However, participants volunteered other documents that they felt would be relevant to our discussions of how textbooks functioned in their writing classes. In a number of instances I asked participants to submit additional materials because they were explicitly mentioned (or relevant to discussions) in interviews. I used these documents to verify or complicate statements. For example, when a participant told me that she used the exact assignment sequence offered by her textbook, I was not only able to see this in her syllabus, I was also able to see that she followed the chapters of the textbook in their original sequence as well. Another participant indicated that she didn't feel compelled to cover the textbook in her class, but a later check of her syllabus indicated that almost the entire textbook was, in fact, slated to be covered. When I subsequently asked her about this, she said that she listed so much of the textbook as required reading on the initial syllabus as a goal and then made adjustments as the semester progressed. She believed that this helped her credibility with her students because they saw that she "at least intended" to cover most of the textbook and therefore had not asked them to buy a text that that they did not need. As you will see below, this concern with cost and students' perceptions of whether the textbook purchase was worthwhile was a salient theme in the interviews.

Transcription and Analysis

All recordings were transcribed verbatim. Consistent with an approach to data collection and analysis that has been termed "inquiry-guided" (Mishler 1990), "reflexive" (Atkinson 1990; Emerson, Fretz, and Shaw 1995), and "dialectical" (Emerson, Fretz, and Shaw 1995), data analysis was a recursive process. I recognized that the biases and preconceptions that I brought into the project affected its design and my analysis. This reflexive approach was designed to foster more awareness of these pre-conceptions and enable my conception of the direction of the project, research questions, and methods to evolve. I wanted to recognize and value the participants' voices and knowledge, and to let the data suggest its own analytical possibilities as much as possible. The process was designed to enable me to question some of my initial assumptions, pursue alternative research questions, and develop new interpretive strategies. I asked open-ended questions in the interviews; when a working list of categories and subcategories was developed from an initial analysis, I discussed them with participants. This helped me to understand their relative importance and gain new insights on exactly how or why they were important.

After initial analysis of the documents in light of what I had discovered with selected participants, I refined the working list of categories and developed a list of corresponding codes. When the coding scheme worked satisfactorily, I coded the interview transcripts. I then further refined the coding scheme with a second reader through selective coding. I developed a final list of codes with definitions as a result of this process (see Appendix B). When data was organized according to the codes, it was linked and analyzed with other documents collected for the study (syllabi, curriculum support materials, assessment rubrics, etc.).

PRIMARY CATEGORIES

The research not only revealed a number of surprising, important aspects of textbook use among its participants, it also provided a glimpse into the thinking, professional dispositions, and pedagogical practices of non-tenure-track writing faculty at the institution. I will share the results generated by three general analytical categories: identification, reasons for choosing texts, and authority. In the discussion section that follows, I will elaborate on why I think these particular categories are important and what the research might suggest about the function of textbooks and postsecondary writing at similar sites: medium-to-large public universities that rely heavily on non-tenure-track teachers with little formal training in rhetoric and composition to teach FYC.

Identification

Participants' professional identifications and theoretical orientations were important aspects of this study for a number of reasons. The specific path of inquiry I adopted sought to correlate certain behaviors with texts with people's occupational identities, their years of experience, and their status at the university. On a somewhat deeper level, I wanted to understand more about the degree to which textbooks supplied (rather than conformed to) theoretical orientations, and how they functioned in terms of the teacher's authority.

For instance, I anticipated that textbook choices might intersect with identification in these two different scenarios:

Scenario One: *A teacher has a developed and informed theoretical identification. A tenure-track teacher with considerable graduate study in rhetoric and composition, she has had ample opportunity to think through her pedagogical goals, the assumptions (theories) about literacy and learning that guide her pedagogy, and the ways that her specific methods (assignments, workshops, etc.) relate to those assumptions. This critical faculty has been developed through many of the processes that mark advanced study and enculturation into a scholarly discipline: extensive coursework, relationships with mentors, her own research, attendance at professional conferences in the field, etc. She most likely approaches textbooks as . . .*

Scenario Two: *A teacher has just been hired to teach an introductory writing course as a part-time instructor. She had taught writing at a different institution as a teaching assistant five years earlier. She had one class that focused on teaching writing at that other institution. She has not developed a professional identity as a scholar, and she is not conversant in the scholarly discourse of any discipline—including rhetoric and composition. Moreover, the goals for first-year writing at the institution at which she will be teaching are quite different from where she was in the past. She most likely approaches textbooks as . . .*

In the first scenario, one would expect the teacher to approach her textbook choice with an A > B relationship with theory = A and textbook = B. She has an established professional identity and expertise, and a defined and informed (if evolving) theoretical orientation: she will likely seek a textbook that is at least reasonably consistent with that expertise and orientation. In the second scenario, the teacher doesn't have an established professional or disciplinary identity or expertise, and she has never had the opportunity to develop an informed theoretical orientation in writing pedagogy. Therefore, one might expect her to approach the textbook choice with more like an A < B relationship. In the absence of an established and confidently wielded set of assumptions about literacy and learning, the textbook will likely be relied upon as much to *supply* as to meet a theory of pedagogy. The textbook choice would therefore rely more on factors other than the theory that seems to be driving the book.

None of the participants had an advanced degree in rhetoric and composition, and few had formal background in the field. Two were enrolled in Ph.D. programs at other institutions, but both were pursuing degrees in literary concentrations. Most had taken a course on teaching college writing of the type that is usually required for TAs at various institutions. However, few had taken courses in rhetoric and composition other than a required course for incoming TAs. In short, participants didn't self-identify within the scholarly discipline of rhetoric and composition: none had extensive graduate education in the field, and none did regular research or published in the field. When asked how they self-identify as professionals, the most common answer was as "teacher," "lecturer," or "college instructor." Their occupational identities were primarily tied to teaching, rather than to scholarship or to expertise in an academic discipline.

Significantly, the three participants who did not self-identify in this way were the two who were already in Ph.D. programs, and a third who had been accepted into a Ph.D. program and would begin the following year. The participant who was farthest along in her program—she had completed her coursework and had worked on her dissertation for several years—answered "When I talk to people I usually talk about my dissertation and my field [a literary specialization]." The other Ph.D. candidate, and the graduate student who would begin study in the fall, both self-identified as graduate students rather than as teachers. The numbers here are, of course, much too small to make any generalizations. However, the differences in the answers does point to the possibility that advanced graduate study tends to move people's identities away from the immediacy of teaching work at a specific locale and more toward "graduate student" and then "scholarly" identities that are associated with Ph.D. work in academic disciplines. In the lexicon established in the previous chapter, people move from a more "bureaucratic" identity to a more "professional" identity.

When participants were asked to explain their own general assumptions about literacy and learning in terms of particular pedagogical movements, philosophies, scholarship, or scholars, the responses were generally vague and in a few cases even somewhat defensive. The only scholars mentioned were those who are perhaps most strongly associated with the proliferation of process in the 1970s and 1980s and have subsequently been canonized in process-oriented textbooks: (early) Elbow, Murray, and Moffett. One experienced FTNTTL who had pursued readings in the field on his own was a notable exception, and also mentioned Bizzell, Bruffee, and Burke. The only pedagogical philosophy explicitly mentioned by participants was "process." In nearly every interview, the discussions of professional identification and educational background quickly moved past "scholarly" discussion and toward discussions of particular practices and particular teachers and colleagues. Assertions of expertise were therefore "local": associated with teaching practice and policies—the concrete material conditions—at this particular site.

Consider, for instance, the following responses to the prompt: "Describe your general teaching and learning philosophy." This was followed-up with "What research or theory has shaped it? Can you identify yourself with any particular theories, scholars, or theoretical trends?" A PTL who had taught for six years responded to this question about theoretical orientation with a discussion of her goals as they relate to her practice:

1. I want them to have skills . .
2. to not just sort of leave my class and the university
3. with this isolated body of knowledge . .
4. that is not really going to serve them when they get out . .
5. so we do a lot of work with learning grammar skills
6. learning how to write in a coherent way
7. with a focus on what job are you going to go into . .

8. so that is my main goal

9. that they leave with the skills that they are going to need to
    survive

10. no matter what job they are going into.[4]

Among participating teachers more generally, professional identification was much more based on teaching practices than on scholarly
conceptions or associations, and therefore more practice-centered
than "scholarly." They were generally more comfortable when talking
about *what they do* when teaching than explaining *why they do* what
they do. And when they explained why, the "why" was connected to a
"real world" knowledge, which is where some participants seemed to
be founding their expertise. The positioning of "real world" expertise
in opposition to scholarly expertise, along with the quick turn away
from more abstract scholarly discourse and toward the particulars of
practice, carried an at least implicit rejection of what one might call
"academic frivolity." Certainly in this response, there is heavy emphasis on "skills" you "need to survive" (5, 9) rather on other possible
elements of writing pedagogy that she calls "isolated . . . knowledge"
that are not relevant outside of the university (3, 4). A "real world"
ethos for a teacher who isn't fluent in a scholarly discourse locates
a philosophy of literacy that is based on applicable workplace skills.
Its projected opposite is a scholarly, theoretical orientation that is
diminished by its detachment from the immediate, everyday realities
of economic survival.

When asked about philosophy of teaching and learning, some explicitly described the difficulty that they had explaining their philosophies.
The less-experienced teachers generally said that they were still in the
process of learning. More experienced teachers indicated that they know
what they are doing, but they are not very good at explaining it in what
one participant called "academic lingo." In this program, FTNTTLs are
asked to write a teaching philosophy as part of their evaluation process.
Several PTLs also mentioned having drafted statements as a part of the
required materials to be submitted for consideration for a full-time contract, but they are not requested to do so otherwise. Five participants

---

4.   In the transcription, utterances are broken into units. The only symbol that I use
      is (. .) which connotes a significant pause. After the introduction of a segment of
      transcription, I reference particular lines using line numbers.

mentioned the drafting of this statement when asked about their teaching philosophies. Again, none of the participants had much graduate training in rhetoric and composition and none self-identified within the field. It is possible that the drafting of that philosophy statement is for many teachers the only extended time they devote to reflecting upon and articulating their general theoretical orientations (and the assumptions that drive what they are doing) toward the teaching of writing. When the subject of these teaching statements came up, I asked follow-up questions because I felt that this line of discussion could help to illuminate important aspects of professional identification. The transcripts made it clear that teaching philosophies aren't developed by these participants in extensive dialectic with the scholarship and vocabulary of rhetoric and composition. Drafting these statements therefore seems very awkward, if not troubling, for many of these teachers and points to a clash between two mind-sets that are figured quite differently—the mind-set of a professional academic with a Ph.D. who is conditioned to value a praxis that is shaped through professional dialectic, and the mind-set of a contingent teacher who values applied experience more highly and doesn't see scholarship as very significant to the teaching of writing. One teacher, for instance, indicated that she had

1. spent close to a month
2. the first time I tried to write a teaching and learning philosophy
3. and now I need to redo it . .
4. so it is one of the hardest things
5. to put down on paper
6. or even put into words

Missing is a conceptual vocabulary that enables articulation and perhaps clarity concerning one's aims and orientations. This difficulty with articulating a teaching philosophy at least parallels the hodgepodge of philosophies that can be found in so many textbooks. When asked in a follow-up if the general philosophy of the textbook she uses is consistent with her own, she responded,

1. I pick it mostly for content
2. over what philosophy is coming through

When asked to explain the difference between "content" and "philosophy," she mentioned the features of textbooks—assignments, readings, and exercises—"what the text does for a class" rather than the assumptions that inform the text. Again, the somewhat emphatically stated preference of "content" over "philosophy" carries the implicit suggestion that underlying assumptions and research concerning literacy and learning are not an important consideration when it comes to pedagogy. Theory is contained within academic discourse rather than employed as pedagogical praxis.

Bruce Horner has examined the long association of basic writing with the teaching of "skills." He calls this "practical bent" "problematic," citing Raymond Williams critique of "the practical." Williams locates an element of impatience and willful blindness in the reliance on the practical: "'Let's be realistic' probably more often means 'let us accept the limits of this situation' (*limits* meaning *hard facts*, often of power or money in their existing and established forms)" (Williams, quoted in Horner and Lu 1999, 20). Horner links this to a similar association of impatience with "lore" made by Stephen North. North describes the "habit forming" tendency among those who subscribe to a "bedrock pragmatism" to "become habitually impatient with complicated causal analyses, which in turn makes [practitioners] relatively cavalier about such analyses even for the purposes of inquiry" (North 1987, 40). Textbooks might be said to function as a means of providing a kind of external authorization for practices and assumptions that don't rise above the level of lore. Their directive, authoritative nature might justify a lack of investment in inquiry and the thoughtful, informed interrogation of one's pedagogy.

A little more surprising was how much even experienced teachers relied on textbooks to supply direction for courses over time—well beyond those initial, uncertain years. Going into the study, I expected to find that teachers would rely heavily on a textbook or textbooks early in their careers, but then gradually adopt a more individualized approach as they became more experienced. Among those who had been teaching longer, I expected to see more experimentation and a diminished role for the textbook. However, teachers with three years of experience or less were actually more apt to change textbooks than those who had been teaching longer, and there was little significant difference in how heavily teachers relied on texts to structure their courses over time. Of the eleven instructors who had four or more years of experience, eight reported that they had used their current textbooks for at least four years. They find a textbook that they like and then stick to it, year after year. I came to think of this as "imprinting." Finding something that they feel works well is important. They not only don't want to change, the terms of labor for contingent teachers (high numbers of sections that tend to be full, the maintenance of part-time jobs in addition to teaching) create a disincentive to make significant changes. Participants did indicate that they make tactical changes to their courses over time. However, those changes might be said to "continue downstream" from the text, rather than being made because of more strategic evolutions in perceptions of teaching, language, or learning: evolutions of the type that are fostered by professional development activities like reading scholarship, attending presentations, or participating in discussions at conferences or workshops. Instructors alter the way that they use the textbooks, but the essential structure and philosophies of the textbook continue to substantially drive what they do in the classroom.

One instructor, for example, indicated that she had used the same textbook for the entire eleven years that she had been teaching. She entered the program when it was switching its general orientation away from writing about literature and toward argumentation. At that time she chose this particular argument-focused textbook. It matched well with the curriculum—it had been among the list of texts recommended by the writing program director at that time—and the author had came to the department a number of times over the years that the instructor had used the textbook to talk about how to use it and get feedback for future editions. The textbook author

1. spoke to us and gave us seminars

2. and I started using it because she had a manual with it . .

3. and see what I did

4. and a lot of us did

5. was follow the manual

6. she [the textbook author] had it in an 8½ by 11 [format]

7. so you could just tear out the worksheets

8. and copy them and use them . .

9. so initially. .

10. because we were so new to it all

11. I just saluted and followed her examples every semester

12. and it helped a great deal . .

13. it took several semesters

14. and maybe two or three years

15. until I was comfortable with it . .

16. and um . .

17. I had made up some things on my own to use

18. rather than to follow

19. but it was based on that

The pattern described here was common across participants. Nearly all of those who had taught for four or more years reported that once they found a textbook that they liked, they didn't move away from it; and the individual innovations that they developed over time are built on the same structure and guiding assumptions offered in the textbook (15–19). The textbook supplied the initial framework for the pedagogy, and the essential framework has remained unaltered. Among the participants, finding a textbook that one likes is tantamount to finding a teaching philosophy that one favors; and once a particular path is taken, it isn't likely to be substantially changed.

Below, I provide an extended portion from an interview with another teacher who had been teaching for seven years and who also chose a text during his first year and then never changed. It shows the long-term impact imprinting with a textbook can have on a teacher's pedagogical orientation and practice. This instructor uses the same textbook as his colleague cited above, and also mentioned the author's visits to the department as important to his choice. When asked about the theory that drives the book, he responded with "process," which he described as a deliberate, linear progression through assignments. He then moved on to a more in-depth description of the initial process of textbook choice.

Instructor:

1. The theory that I think drives the book . .

2. well first of all

3. writing as a process

4. they definitely have that

5. and really

6. they take that and apply it to the various steps of the assignments . .

7. and [the textbook author] gives a very detailed instructor's manual

8. which was another reason I didn't mention why we chose this text

9. because we had never taught the course before

10. and had no clue what we were doing

11. and the fact that it came with

12. that very, very detailed instructor's manual helped a lot . .

13. of course, a lot of it we figured out later wasn't so great

14. but at the time it was a lifesaver to see how to structure the course

TS:

1. I can understand how an instructor's manual is helpful

2. when you first begin to teach a class . .

3. can you talk about what happens after that . .

4. when you have had some experience with a class?

Instructor:

1. Yeah . .

2. I don't know how specific you want me to get

3. but I will give you an example

4. [The textbook author] in the instructor's manual

5. breaks down a course into its two components

6. you have the first position paper

7. and then you have a second position paper . .

8. I did that for two semesters I think

9. and it was just completely redundant

10. I got comments from students . .

11. like repetitive assignments . .

12. things like that . .

13. I couldn't argue

14. I agreed with them

15. so I changed that

16. I guess there was over-teaching material . .

17. the students would pick up what they were doing in one class

18. or sometimes two classes

19. but [the textbook author] would overdo it

20. and there was just too much time spent on certain things

TS:

1. So the text is a class by class blueprint?

Instructor:

1. Yeah

2. yes it is

3. oh yes, day by day

4. she breaks it down

5. there are sample syllabi in there

6. and she breaks down each day . .

7. this is for a Monday, Wednesday, Friday schedule

8. or a two-day schedule

9. but she has everything in there . .

10. the framework

11. if you look at the syllabus

12. is still there

13. and it is different too

14. pedagogically speaking

He went on to explain that the book has two assignment sequences that are exactly the same. The book sets up a research paper and then moves students through it, providing the necessary sources for the research in the back of the book. He indicated that he thought this was useful because it "controls plagiarism." It then moves students through a second project that is very similar. Because of the repetition, the instructor changed the second assignment. He uses another reading from the book as a model. However, the students now have to, on their own, find an argument that they disagree with and respond in a letter form with cited support for their arguments. This requires them to use sources outside of the book, but the book still serves as primary support:

1. All of this argument theory [explicated in the textbook]

2. you can find it in the essay [the one he assigns]

3. there is a Rogerian argument

4. it wouldn't have existed at the time

5. but still there are Rogerian aspects in there . .

6. it makes it much more fun

7. it is still a two-component thing

8. only I think it is much more productive

This instructor has initially adopted the exact model offered by the book. He has then gradually deviated. That deviation has been a response to dissatisfaction with some redundancy in the textbook's sequence (26–33). It has therefore been based on practical experiences with the way the book deploys its pedagogy. The adjustments are tactical efforts to find better, more creative, and interesting ways to implement the philosophy and goals that are already driving the text (49–56). As the instructor points out, his syllabus does still show a heavy reliance on the text. The same basic chapter by chapter sequence is still there throughout the term (45–46). There is just some deviation in how the second major writing assignment is approached.

It is also significant that the instructor referred to the author of the textbook either by last name or with a pronoun—rather than giving the title of the textbook or simply calling it "the text." This was common among participants. In spite of the fact that instructors in this program have some latitude concerning the text that they can choose to use, fifteen of the twenty-one participants use the same text. I explore some of the stated reasons why this is the case below, but here I want to point out that these interviews complicate what Susan Miller argued about the lack of authorial status for textbook authors. Certainly, as Foucault famously describes it in "The Author Function," authorship isn't an objective description of the material act of writing texts: it is, rather, a socially conferred status that rests on a host of implicit value judgments. Authorship is conferred differently in different discourses and social contexts and it functions differently in those strata. In the professional, scholarly strata of academia, my strong feeling is that textbooks still don't offer the same authorial status as the authoring of a scholarly monograph. However, in the realm of FYC, textbook authorship is far more highly regarded—possibly even more than the authorship of scholarship. The author of this popular textbook was cited by name throughout these interviews and clearly has "authorial" status among these instructors—most of whom weren't able to name many, if any, active scholars in rhetoric and composition. Indeed, in practice, the authority of textbook authors can be quite profound, as the directive nature of the genre enables them to substantially "author" the classes in which they are used. That said, the author's status isn't scholarly in the sense that she is expected to make persuasive arguments based on primary and secondary sources. What then, is expected of her? What are instructors looking for when they choose texts?

Reasons for Choosing Texts

During the interviews, I asked teachers to talk through their decision making processes when choosing texts for a particular course. As they mentioned specific factors, they were often asked to elaborate. The object of this line of questions was to get as complete a portrait as possible of the spectrum of factors that writing instructors consider when they choose their textbooks. During analysis, these factors were categorized, and then counted for frequency of mention across all of the interviews. Eight categories of criteria were mentioned by at least five participants: cost, support/validation, quality/usefulness of assignments and sequence, quality/usefulness of readings, accessibility, compactness, textual features, and quality/usefulness of instructor's manual. The frequency is summarized in the chart below (table 3).

Category of Criteria	Frequency of Mention (out of 21 participants)
Cost	20
Support/Validation	12
Assignments and Sequence (quality/usefulness)	11
Readings (quality/usefulness)	11
Accessibility	11
Compactness	8
Surface Textual Features	8
Instructor's Manual (quality/usefulness)	6

Table 3: Most Frequently Mentioned Criteria for Choosing Textbooks

In the following, I elaborate on the first five (all of which were mentioned by eleven or more participants). Discussions of these categories will touch on other themes identified in the analysis.

Cost

Overwhelmingly, cost was the most frequently mentioned criteria for choosing texts. Instructors saw keeping book costs low for students as a significant priority that trumped many other concerns. During interviews, many volunteered the precise costs of their textbooks—one instructor even said that a primary reason that she chose a particular textbook was because it could be found used online at various sites for five dollars.

Obviously, the desire to buy an affordably priced textbook is driven by a concern for the finances of students. This is a concern that many of us share. A factor that was rather surprising for its frequency of mention, however, was a personal identification with the financial burdens of students. For some, this identification was directly related to the instructor's memories of their own undergraduate experiences. The interviews were conducted at an institution that serves large numbers of nontraditional students. Moreover, many of the instructors themselves were either graduates of this university or similar institutions that John Alberti (2001) calls "second-tier, working class universities."[5]

---

5.   I cite Alberti here because he is careful not to diminish the value of the quality of

They therefore empathized with the financial struggles of many of their students. For instance, one instructor who self-identified as a first-generation college student volunteered

1. My very first semester of college
2. my textbooks cost six hundred dollars
3. and my family and I were not prepared for it
4. we didn't know
5. so that surprise cost shaped me as a student
6. and sort of shaped the way that I looked at textbooks as a teacher

A TA similarly said

1. All throughout undergrad . .
2. I put myself through undergrad
3. and I was always looking for the cheapest price
4. so I always
5. before I choose a textbook . .
6. I look on the Internet
7. to see how much you can get for it when you sell it back

These instructors consider cost very important and they relate that concern to a personal identification with their financial struggles. At least for some, the concern with cost is clearly related to the fact that they are currently enrolled as graduate students in institutions, or they were recently undergraduates themselves. This describes eight of the participants: four were TAs enrolled in the university's graduate program, two others were also enrolled in M.A. programs and teaching as adjuncts, and two were enrolled in Ph.D. programs and teaching as adjuncts. Some of these instructors volunteered that their own ongoing book costs help them to be more conscious of how much their students are spending.

There is an undercurrent to this empathy that relates to the institutional identification issues discussed above—institutional status

---

education or the students at these institutions.

somewhat parallels an identification within an economic class. The tone in which many participants discussed cost suggested that they didn't feel that cost was a common concern among tenure-track faculty at the university. The "real world" versus "academic" distinction in ethos described above was associated with the ability to empathize with the financial situations of students. Professional worth among "teachers" is not only linked to a devotion to the everyday work of teaching—constructed as distinct from scholarly activity—but also to an ability to empathize with the "real world" challenges faced by students.

An important, somewhat surprising, theme that repeatedly emerged in discussions of cost was the widespread compulsion to cover as much of the material in the textbooks as possible. A part of this compulsion stemmed from a very straightforward cost/benefit logic. The feeling was that if students were being required to buy a textbook, the textbook needed to be used as much as possible. This seemed a powerful motivator for many instructors to include as much of the textbooks as possible in their syllabi—from day-to-day units to assignments and readings. Driving this compulsion was a concern about what students were going to think about the instructor's overall judgment and concern for their welfare, and then subsequently write in their course evaluations. Concerns linked to student evaluations were tied to the need to justify the purchase of the textbook through extensive coverage. Consider the response of a FTNTTL when she was asked why she had recently decided to change textbooks.

1. I got a less expensive book
2. because I remember what it was like being a student
3. and when I found out how much it cost
4. whew . .
5. the first semester I didn't even think about it
6. and I just thought
7. I have all of these wonderful ideas
8. and then I got this book
9. and I didn't even think about the cost . .
10. and then during the first week of class
11. you hear students mumbling and talking

12. and it was fifty something dollars

13. and I had no idea

14. but it was my fault

15. my lack of knowledge

16. then I . .

17. felt that I needed to squeeze every bit out of that textbook

Interestingly, this instructor reports initially having "wonderful ideas" about what she was going to do in the classroom prior to choosing the book (7–8). However, the cost of the book caused her to switch to heavier usage of the book, and away from her own ideas (16–17). Her "lack of knowledge" (15) was experiential—she didn't know that students would grumble about textbook costs, and that was important enough to her to change the way that she approached the structure of the course in order to justify the cost. Another instructor more blatantly made it clear that she believed that the purchase should drive virtually every aspect of the class in order to be justified:

1. If you are going to ask a student to buy a textbook

2. in a lower-level writing class

3. you should use that textbook . .

4. it should be a part of your everyday discussions

5. it should be a part of your weekly readings

6. they should go to those books for assignments . .

7. there is nothing worse

8. that will kill morale in your class

9. than for your teacher to ask you to buy a two-hundred dollar book

10. that you never use . .

11. so weekly

12. daily

13. they have to have their books out on their desks

14. they are doing exercises

15. they are reading probably 75 percent of the text

Again, negative student responses to textbook costs (8–10) leads to more cohesion—in this case far more cohesion—with the specific approach followed in the text. Whether the textbook actually merited this level of focus in terms of how it supports teaching and learning seems marginal: "morale" (8) is substantially built on whether the students feel that a textbook is being used enough to merit its purchase. Similar statements were made with remarkable frequency in the interviews. One instructor described a panicked episode in which she went to the bookstore and found that the textbook she had required came bundled with additional reading materials that she had not ordered. The panic didn't come from a higher cost; the cost was no different with the bundled materials than it had been without. They were nominally "free"—add-ons provided by the publishers.[6] However, this instructor felt compelled to add some of the bundled readings onto her syllabus as the course progressed because she was afraid that students would feel that they had paid unnecessarily for them.

Certainly the high level of concern for student evaluations is related to the contingent job status of these teachers, and therefore shapes pedagogical decisions. PTLs are evaluated exclusively based upon student evaluations. Simply put, low evaluations could mean fewer or no classes for the next term. FTNTTLs do undergo more extensive review in this program, but student evaluations are also heavily weighted in those reviews. Arguably, high student evaluations are the best means of maintaining secure employment.

Support/Validation

The second most frequently mentioned factor shaping instructors' textbook choices was support/validation. "Support" references instructors' tendency to choose textbooks that others in the program have also chosen because they can then build classes that more closely resemble their colleagues' courses. "Validation," which is certainly related, references their desire to build classes that are founded on some external authority and are adequately consistent with programmatic goals. While this program allows instructors to choose their textbooks, the choices

---

6.   Readings and additional materials are bundled with books as a bonus to compel instructors to choose particular texts, and also to field-test new materials for possible inclusion in new editions.

are shaped by a number of factors mentioned by instructors:

- In a class that is mandatory for all incoming TAs, students are asked to evaluate a number of recommended textbooks, and those textbooks are then often chosen by those students for the classes they teach.

- Representatives from two very large textbook publishers are particularly active in this department, and most of the participants have chosen textbooks offered by one of these two publishers.

- There is a clear synergy between the general philosophy and goals promoted within this program—in the TA class, programmatic workshops, and so on—and a few specific textbooks that approach argumentation as a formalistic academic mode.

Even given these factors, it was nevertheless surprising that fifteen of the twenty-one participants chose to use the same textbook from the multitudes of argument textbooks that are currently available. The interviews indicate that an important reason for this choice was that instructors wanted to work among others who are using the same textbook because it creates a common reference point for informal, "watercooler" discussions of day-to-day pedagogy. Participants mentioned the value of being able to discuss particular challenges with other instructors. Some even mentioned the value of having a common set of assignments and grading rubrics.

In addition to the common ground created by the use of a common textbook, however, validation was a persistent theme in these discussions. As one teacher phrased it, choosing a textbook that others in the program had chosen assures her that she is not "coming from left field" with her assignments and general approach. In contrast, a TA in her first year as a teacher said that she had worried when making her choice because the book she had chosen to use "is not on the recommended list; and I think as a teaching assistant you are a little nervous to branch out."[7] However, she decided to use the book anyway because another TA had also decided to use it, and "having another teaching assistant choosing it too sort of validated my using it."

Another way of seeing the validating function of the textbook is that

---

7.   The program does have a recommended text list. However, it also enables teachers to choose their own texts, so the recommended list doesn't seem to be exclusive.

it helps instructors to feel more certain that they are conforming to the general philosophy and goals promoted in this particular program—even if they don't necessarily agree with the philosophy. Using the textbook that so many others are using assures them that they are not going to be too far outside of the program's philosophy, as it is both explicitly and implicitly articulated. One PTL said that

1. The main thing is . .
2. and I don't even know if this is true
3. but I was told that we were required to teach the Toulmin model of argument
4. so I don't really like that model of argument
5. but it is outlined in [textbook author] clearly . .
6. so I use it [that text]

Several others said that they were unsure of what textbook to choose, but this particular textbook seemed to be "everywhere" in the program—on common bookshelves, on recommended lists provided by the program director, and of course the author herself visiting the program to promote the book. This gave them a sense of comfort that using this text would help to ensure that they were, as a PTL phrased it, "on the right track."

In *The Social Construction of Reality* Peter Berger and Thomas Luckmann described the relationship between organizations and the creation of localized knowledges that come to be seen as "objective":

> In the course of the division of labor a body of knowledge is developed that refers to the particular activities involved. In its linguistic basis, this knowledge is already indispensable to the institutional "programming" of these economic activities. . . . This knowledge serves as a channeling, controlling force in itself, an indispensable ingredient of the institutionalization of this area of conduct. . . . A whole segment of the social world is objectified by this knowledge. (1967, 66)

Berger and Luckmann distinguish this type of knowledge from that which might be developed within a disciplinary apparatus, and thus subject to rigorous critique and capable of "subsequently becom[ing] systematically organized as a body of knowledge." Rather, the social construction of this knowledge is much more localized. To a certain extent, the choice of a common textbook creates cultural commonality and the seemingly "objective" knowledge that predominates within a specific locale. This is an important distinction that extends from differences in status and professional training. There is an appeal to a consensus with the choice of a common textbook, but that consensus is exclusively local. While someone who has been professionalized within the field might reference a scholarly consensus or her own informed sense of judgment, at this more bureaucratic level teachers were concerned with programmatic norms and requirements. This highlights how the political economy of FYC makes pedagogy and students' writing much more subject to coercion.

Assignments and Sequence

Eleven instructors volunteered sequence as a significant factor in their favoring a specific text. Consideration of sequence was typically tied to discussions of "the writing process." I put writing process in quotations because this term was used in a very general sense. A "writing process" approach was contrasted with an approach in which students don't do any drafting or revision, and merely turn in a final product—or with an approach that has assignments that don't follow any progressive sequence. Moreover, a number of teachers when discussing their general philosophy spoke of "the" writing process as though it were a singular progression that everyone follows. Many textbooks are structured in a manner that seems to encourage this thinking with linear "process" progressions: invention exercises, then exercises for structuring an essay, then outlines and checklists for revision. As one teacher put it, she liked the way that her text presents "the writing process" because

1. they have a progression in which they take a huge paper . .
2. like a position paper
3. and break it down into little parts
4. like initial proposal and exploratory paper and all of that

Indeed, in addition to being a pedagogical technique and philosophy, process seems to adopt the status of content itself. Students not only go through "the writing process," they learn "the writing process" on more of a metalevel:

1. I liked how this textbook laid out

2. how it presented the information . .

3. it gave kind of an introductory

4. in each chapter

5. definition of what that particular type of paper was investigating or explaining

6. and then it gave some examples

7. and then it talked about the process

8. and I wanted some guidance at that point

9. and time about how to better teach process . .

10. so that was helpful to me

11. and then I wanted that to be a part of the process that I wanted students to see

12. [in altered voice] oh look

13. here is a process

14. and the textbook says here is a process

15. so they trust that

Both teacher and student are learning "the process" from the textbook here. The teacher found "guidance" in the textbook (8), and then students also learn that there is "a process" (14). Again, the pedagogical philosophy of "process" is heavily linked to a linear progression, a blueprint that is provided by a textbook—process commodified for general consumption. One PTL indicated that among the things she most liked about her textbook was that if a student was stuck at any point in "the" process the student could go to the text and it would place them "right [in] the place where you are in the process." Some of the other conceptual aspects that one might associate with "process"—for instance, understanding of how "form follows function," understanding their own histories and habits with language, and leaving space for the particular drafting habits of individual writers—should therefore not be assumed to be a part of this general understanding of "process"[8] (1997).

---

8.   For excellent discussions of how process became homogenized in writing instruction, see Sharon Crowley (1998).

The textbook that is particularly popular in this program, for instance, provides step-by-step blueprints for essays that are in very formalistic academic modes.

More generally, adopting the "process" sequencing of a textbook seemed to take care of a lot of the decision making and work of building a class from the ground up. As a TA put it,

1. I liked
2. from a teacher's standpoint . .
3. how it emphasizes a progression in the writing
4. to where there are assignments that are linked to . .
5. directly to research
6. research is covered in chapter 2
7. and then they have an annotated bibliography that is due . .
8. that kind of leads them into an exploratory paper
9. which leads them into their research position paper . .
10. so I really liked that that book sets up a lot of the assignments

Importantly, the assignments that are a part of most textbooks are among the features that most instructors feel compelled to use when they have chosen a textbook. Even many instructors who didn't volunteer that assignments were a significant part of their initial decision making process said in other portions of the interviews that they either used the assignments in their textbooks or only deviated from them somewhat, such as with a favored assignment that they had decided to add in on their own.

Analysis of syllabi and various support materials indicated a high degree of conformance to assignments outlined in textbooks in the same general assignment sequences advocated in their texts. In some cases, assignments were slightly modified; in others, assignments were used verbatim—some tear the assignments straight out of the instructor's manual and just copy them. Others described the textbook explicitly as a "blueprint" or "plan" with day-to-day assignments that form a logical assignment sequence. Assignments synchronize with chapters in textbooks, so the adoption of assignment sequences nearly always corresponds with a progression through a textbook in a class. Some participants did not provide day-to-day assignments as a part of their materials, and their descriptions of the degree to which their classes generally followed the sequences outlined in their texts was indeterminate. In fourteen cases I was able to make a confident determination of whether their courses followed the linear progressions of their textbooks. Of those, eleven structured their courses around the texts, chapter by chapter, in the same sequence as the texts.

Readings and Accessibility

While over half of the teachers volunteered readings as an important factor in their choice of texts, what makes certain readings good or bad—and how those readings fit into more general pedagogies—varied considerably and was therefore difficult to generalize. Several mentioned the importance of having readings that spark controversy and lead to good discussions and debate. While some indicated that they chose texts in which the readings weren't too hard or long, another mentioned that she wanted readings that challenge her students. Still another wanted readings that represent diverse voices and points of view. The most consistently stated rationale for the use of readings was as rhetorical models. In addition to providing fodder for discussion, readings were intended to serve as the subjects of rhetorical analysis. One teacher even indicated a frustration with students' tendencies to read for meaning, rather than as a means of understanding the rhetorical choices of authors. She assigned them a reading about apes which they found uninteresting, but she said that the point wasn't to learn about an issue concerning apes:

1. You are not reading about apes . .

2. you are reading about writing a persuasive paper . .

3. you know

4. you have to look at it for what the writer's choices were . .

5. you even had things in the margins

6. I mean I tried everything to get them to see that it is a piece of writing

7. that they should look at the organization

8. structure

9. all of those different elements

10. but when it came down to it . .

11. when it was on a subject that they didn't like

12. they put up that wall to where they couldn't see the writer's choices

13. they didn't use it as a model

So the reading isn't serving primarily as a means of learning about a subject, or as a basis for reflection. It is provided by the textbook as a rhetorical model, a form to be emulated. Most of those who mentioned readings likewise indicated that that they liked how their texts matched specific readings with specific assignments, so students have an example. Again, the textbooks provide a blueprint for entire assignments, and the readings are a part of the overall system. This use of texts as models risks deemphasizing their contexts and consequentiality. Texts aren't efforts to make meaning with specific audiences for specific purposes: they are, rather, forms to be emulated. This, along with form-driven assignments pursued in calculated sequences, can be seen as examples of Harris's "new formalism" dressed up in the garb of process. There is an emphasis on form over function that conforms to standardizing logics in FYC.

Authority

Above I discussed the degree to which many instructors rely upon textbooks to provide validation for their pedagogies. The use of textbooks that others are using provides a sense of certainty—it ensures that they aren't "coming from left field" with their approaches. Authority is somewhat related to validity, but it references how teachers feel they are being perceived by students. When teachers buy into, or at least profess, the approach that is being taken by a textbook, the textbook can then serve as a basis of authority for their approach. The appeal to an external authority is related to the institutional status of the teacher. Indeed, this may be a very important function of the textbook genre: that a particular assignment, technique, or evaluative rubric is included in a textbook lends it credibility among students. So the projection of authority relies in part on the degree to which a teacher's overall pedagogy and classroom presence is in synch with the textbook. It derives from a degree of seamlessness. A TA describes the confidence she feels going into classes as being associated with the familiarity she has developed with the textbook. When doing prep work she anticipates the problems that students are going to have with certain terminology—and then makes sure that she is both herself familiar with the term, and that she is using the same terms in class that the book uses:

1. I would say that it [the textbook] makes me feel more confident
2. going into each day-to-day situation
3. because in the syllabus you will notice that I have a kind of general . .
4. [alters voice] OK this is what we are going to talk about today
5. but really . .
6. in prep work it can refer back to that chapter that they are reading
7. and kind of get an idea of where they are standing with the subject
8. OK
9. they are probably not going to understand this term
10. or this term
11. and then I can refresh myself on some of the terminology . .
12. I made a mistake in my other class
13. of using different terminology
14. than what was in the textbook
15. and it provided a lot of confusion
16. so I really like to make sure
17. that I am describing things the way that the textbook is

Here the textbook is driving the pedagogy even at the level of verbally uttered vocabulary. The degree of seamlessness, along with the teacher's reading ahead in the textbook, supply a level of authority. Surprisingly, the degree to which instructors draw on the textbook to project authority and competence doesn't seem to diminish over time. A PTL with six years experience, for example, said

1. I think it definitely gives me more authority . .
2. if I can come into a class with a mini-lecture of ideas

3. that I want them to grasp

4. that is echoed in the textbook that they are reading

5. then

6. that definitely lends authority to what I am saying.

7. when we have talked about it in this way

8. in the mini-lecture

9. and we have learned about it in this way

10. in the book

11. and then we are going to work with it in this way

12. in an activity

13. that whole sequence lends authority to the teacher

A FTNTTL with ten years of teaching experience still feels the need to draw ethos and authority from the textbook:

1. I really feel that the backup that a textbook provides in a class

2. is necessary

3. it backs me up

4. in other words I didn't make all of this up

5. I didn't make all of these rules up

Interestingly, authority and the success of the "process" that is advocated by the book are somewhat synonymous. Another FTNTTL with nine years of experience said

1. I see this class as being in and of itself an argument to students

2. that here is a good process for you . .

3. and so I am up there demonstrating and modeling

4. through the different exercises that we do

5. and then the textbook is also telling them the same thing

6. part of it is

7. I think

8. establishing my ethos as a professor

9. you know

10. I am telling you this

11. but other people think this too

Among the questions evoked by these statements is whether the (at least perceived) need to draw on the textbook for external validation to project authority results from the teachers' institutional status. How do tenure-track Ph.D.s establish authority in the classroom? Do they need to be as concerned about their authority? Do they generally rely on text-books for this kind of external validation?

TEXTBOOKS AND THE POLITICAL ECONOMY OF COMPOSITION

Textbook publishing is a commercial enterprise, and if the enterprise is to be successful, the commodities it sells should be designed with the primary consumers in mind. With the textbook industry, the primary market is decision makers (WPAs and writing teachers). Textbooks are produced to generate profits, and because publishers understand their markets, textbooks respond to the material realities and needs of teaching labor in composition. This is in contrast to scholarship on the teaching of writing—which is primarily written with other scholarly professionals as the audience, and which rarely directly engages with the material realities of who is teaching under what conditions in com-position. It is common to hear "marketplace" used as a euphemism for "democracy"—and one might even hear "marketplace of ideas" used as a euphemism for scholarly exchange and civic argument. According to this logic, the best ideas win out. Discursive spheres should not be conflated, however; what wins out in one sphere might be quickly dis-missed in another. Persuasiveness in scholarly discourse is not derived in the same way, nor does it have the same impact, as persuasiveness in the more overtly market-driven realm of undergraduate writing classes. Scholars do often produce textbooks (though they are hardly the exclu-sive authors of textbooks), but textbooks are only scholarly to the extent that the ethos that comes with scholarship can be used as a means to sell them. They are reviewed and edited primarily for their marketability to writing teachers and program administrators, rather than for their con-tribution to the advancement of the field.

These two discursive realms, the scholarly and the commer-cial, are different in important ways. One can with validity muddy the distinction, pointing to the ongoing, complicated relationship between industry and higher education—a relationship that has gotten muddier in recent years. Nevertheless, scholarly discussions have scholarly antecedents and take place in scholarly forums. Positions are taken, critiqued by informed participants, and become in varying degrees persuasive or influential or not. Much of the distinct apparatus of scholarly discourse—situating one's work in relation to prior work that one is either building upon or taking exception to, the painstaking qualification of claims, the careful employment of specialized vocabularies—is designed to establish ethos, build consensus, and fortify one's work against counterattacks in an ongoing, adversarial scholarly exchange.[9] Scholarly discourse is overtly dialogic in the Bakhtinian sense: it references the previous relevant utterances and actively anticipates future (perhaps aggressively dissenting) responses from informed professionals. The commercial realm works according to different logics. Success is not based on persuasiveness according to scholarly critique, but on sales—"the marketplace of ideas." And, as this research suggests, textbooks might not be adopted according to the soundness, the persuasiveness, or the currency of the theoretical basis on which they are founded. Rather, a host of far more local and practice-driven concerns drive textbook choices in many instances—cost, level of clarity for nonspecialists, consistency with departmental goals, adaptability of assignments and exercises, and so on. Textbooks don't go to any lengths to justify themselves according to prior scholarship that is specifically referenced, nor do they employ highly specialized vocabularies. They are not generally written in a manner that invites or anticipates alternative views of the assumptions of literacy and learning that drive them. Rather, the always contentious assumptions that inform textbooks appear as prima facie facts and are left largely off the table in their content and marketing apparatus. They are more directive than dialogic: they provide blueprints and support materials for writing courses that are deployments of theories rather

---

9.   In *Science in Action,* Bruno Latour (1987) provides a very useful description of how scholarly texts anticipate the dynamics of contentious discursive spheres. Latour uses military terminology when describing scholarly discourse. To bolster her case, an author employs "allies" in the form of citations, often in high numbers, to provide support. As she constructs her argument, she identifies "enemies" and the weaknesses they may use to undermine or destroy her case. Along the way, she uses "tactics" and "strategies" that are standard rhetorical moves in scholarly discourse (30–62).

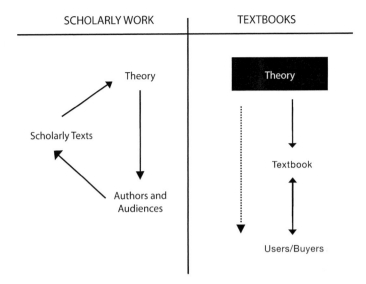

Figure 2. Textbooks and the Genre Function

than being the product of extensive reflection and decision making about theories. They thus construct their readership in a very different way. Textbook publishers certainly solicit feedback from users, but the concern is primarily marketing—not the development of a sustained and evolving body of research.

Ironically, even argument textbooks with titles like *Everything Is an Argument* don't argue for their own efficacy based on sound research or scholarly theory. Everything is an argument—except, of course, why argument should be taught in this way. With textbooks, theory is black boxed. Pedagogy moves downward from theory, employed by those whose primary occupational concern is practice. The agency exercised by practitioners in this model is closer to the circumscribed agency exercised by consumers in neoliberal models of democracy. This is the important connection between professional identification, the terms of work in composition, and a highly profitable industry that is pervasive in the scene of college writing.

To be clear, I am not claiming that those who haven't had advanced training in the field are not often excellent critical thinkers or are pawns of marketing ploys. I am saying that the terms of labor in the field do produce differences in concerns, dispositions, and occupational identification. Without the sort of disciplinary moorings, vocabularies of critique, and responsibilities and opportunities to help *produce* knowledge that come with professional status—and without support for scholarly activity and professional development—identifications and pedagogical orientations will tend to become more solidly moored to the work of teaching at particular sites. Certainly most of the teachers interviewed for this study didn't identify within specific academic fields, and much preferred to talk about specific pedagogical practices rather than the assumptions about literacy and learning that informed those practices. Identification is centered on teaching writing according to the explicit and implicit norms established in this program, rather than on the ability to recursively theorize and thus critique particular pedagogies, textbooks, and programmatic goals. Moreover, concerns about student evaluations and conformity to programmatic norms had a direct impact on textbook and pedagogical choices. The primary considerations were overwhelmingly local. These concerns are doubtlessly amplified by the lack of solid professional standing of teachers whose jobs are riding on consistently good evaluations and the good opinion of the WPA.

There is no forum for questioning the premises of a textbook, only choices from a range of options that are determined by the industry— according to theoretical assumptions that remain largely unarticulated to the consumers. While they have deep roots in the rhetorical tradition dating back to Aristotle, textbooks are also an ever-evolving genre continually adapted to a marketplace—composition teaching, its tasks, and the terms of its enactment as labor. While they adapt to this milieu, they also help to shape it. As they shape it, they tend to generalize and homogenize. They must carry a portable, easily digested pedagogy philosophy. In my survey of texts, I found that very few textbooks designed for use in FYC courses reflect any awareness of the "post-process" informed critiques that have defined much of the recent scholarly discourse. Most continue to draw on a version of the constrained process theory that gained ascendancy in the late 1980s and early 1990s. Most also carry highly formalistic elements alongside the "process" elements. Highly popular argumentation rhetorics, for instance, focus students' attentions on such activities as learning the many varieties of enthymemes, standard logical fallacies, and the nuances of Rogerian argument. They offer assignments, rigidly sequenced step-by-step research processes, and sometimes even the source material for research. Process and argumentative models become objects of curriculum rather than practices and tools employed as a part of consequential, social processes. The immediate, material circumstances of writing remain invisible.

Textbooks also help WPAs to find analogues for their programs in the textbook industry more generally. They therefore both legitimize and shape programmatic philosophies and goals. For instance, having argumentation as a primary focus in your program can be validated by the large number of argumentation texts. Some companies now even offer anthologies of readings to be used in graduate classes for TAs; even in graduate study, teachers are funneled toward particular textbooks, away from competing theories and alternative ways of doing writing education. The education of TAs becomes conflated with market development.

Describing the purpose of his documentary history of composition studies, John C. Brereton wrote:

> This book chronicles the move from composition to every stage of a student's college career to composition confined to the first year, and from a saturation in a rhetorical tradition of some two thousand years to its replacement with a new, streamlined curriculum which . . . emphasized error correction and the five modes of discourse. These were simplifications perfectly suited for the mass production education carried out in so many universities after 1900. How did the rich and complex world of rhetoric get replaced so quickly with composition? (1995, 17)

His answer is that the teaching of writing became relegated largely to the first year and given a lowly post–high school status rather than legitimate postsecondary academic status. I think that is only part of the answer. The other parts have to do with the terms of labor in writing education and, now, the increasing pervasiveness of neoliberal administrative policies in higher education. Writing textbooks are an opportunistic response to our field's inability to change the terms of work in composition and thus reflect the tenuous relevance of scholarship in rhetoric and composition to the pedagogies that are enacted in many postsecondary writing classes. They point to the need for generative rather than directive models of professional praxis that integrate scholarly, administrative, and pedagogical work. They point to the need to recognize and change how we do what we do if we really want to positively shape how writing is actually taught.

3

HOW "SOCIAL" IS SOCIAL CLASS IDENTIFICATION?

What type of consumer is your hybrid offering designed to attract?
Adult learners tend to be more open to an online experience because it
allows them to balance their professional and personal lives with their
educational pursuits. Traditional students—those aged 18 to 24—tend
to want face-to-face, classroom-based learning. Corporations may prefer
a little of both, to allow employees to work and study at the same time.
Segmenting the market by consumer types and needs—adult, tradi-
tional, current, new, credit, non-credit—and designing programs that
fit these segments and needs are important early steps.
                                                      —Kristin Greene

The above quote is from an article published in a recent *Inside Higher Ed.* (Greene 2006) It begins with the question "How can colleges best mix on-campus and online delivery of instruction?"—an initial move down a conceptual road that frames higher education firmly within a business management rhetoric. The phrasing is not "education," but "the delivery of instruction." The distinction is important. Postsecondary "education" typically suggests dynamic interaction, active give-and-take, open inquiry, contentious questions concerning content and pedagogical method, and informed professionals making decisions at the level of the classroom. These aspects of education are difficult to sell, difficult to make portable, and famously impossible to quantify with validity. In contrast, "instructional delivery" suggests a much more stable, transposable entity—something that can be packaged and delivered for a fee: a commodity. Surrounding the commodity is a constellation of contracted relationships—of prescribed roles, identities, values, and niche packaging—that are characteristic of a market. The political economic rhetoric of the article is built on clear objectives and rationalized operations, on organizational efficiency and measurable outcomes. This rhetoric defines education according to the terms of capitalist economics: it is driven by the imperatives of exchange and competition. Success and failure can be quantified according to terms that are established at the onset, as "students" are "targeted consumers" of a product carefully crafted to attract their dollars. They will pay for a product that is necessarily predictable enough to make the exchange "fair" according to market logics of exchange.

Most institutions of higher education continue to project a gentrified aesthetic. Campuses are designed to create the impression of a separate space, at least somewhat removed from the "real world" of direct engagement in economic and civic life. This conceptualization is built into the marketing campaigns of institutions throughout the country. Architecture that is ready-made for pictorial montages; magazine rankings; branding slogans like "Dare to Be Great" and "Thinking Ahead"; and sleek Web sites—in some cases actually featuring models posing as students—are combined in marketing schemes calculated to attract students and dollars.[1] In practice, the boundaries between the "real world" (of adulthood, work, and global capitalism) and the somewhat otherworldly, scholarly aesthetic that still characterizes popular conceptions of college life are muddied to say the least. As David Geoffrey Smith has argued, in contemporary higher education there is an ongoing and increasingly severe clash between "corporate economic fundamentalism [and] the dreams of liberal democratic culture" (1999, 100–1). The working lives of students and many of their writing teachers are significantly shaped by the terms of work in fast-capitalism—on a daily basis. Though typically these terms are ignored or left on the margins of discussions of literacy and pedagogy, economic logics significantly create the contexts of postsecondary writing and learning in the United States. As the discourse and productive logics of the marketplace are aligned with those of higher education, educational and economic production, marketing, and consumption are more uniformly and strategically configured. The kinds of conceptual spaces necessary for the adoption of the critical perspective that many of us consider essential to the mission of higher education are more difficult to foster in environments that are substantially geared toward marketable education that purports to produce marketable students. Moreover, students' and teachers' lives inside and outside of school are shaped by a matrix of political economic factors—from the marketing and administration of their universities to the policies and discourses of their work away from school. The creation of a

---

1.   "Dare to Be Great" is the slogan used by the University of Louisville. The University of Phoenix uses "Thinking Ahead."

space from which students might gain more critical and more strategic understandings of writing and themselves is discouraged by the everyday material processes of work and production in many of today's postsecondary institutions.

The situation is generally discouraging, but far from impossible. A political economic understanding of those everyday processes of writing and writing education can help teachers and scholars to avoid (1) conceptions of postsecondary institutions as culturally elitist, which misidentifies true power structures and (2) homogenized, culturally centered, nonmaterial conceptions of class that prevent more accurate naming of the terms of work and education in fast-capitalism. These terms require creative new pedagogical responses that bring the general and the immediate into dialectic, highlighting contradictions and creating the space for alternative self-authoring.

WRITING CLASS

A number of very contemporary factors make it as important as ever that class be made more conspicuous in the public political discourse, including the growing gap between rich and poor in the United States; the systemic political disenfranchisement of the less- and under-privileged; an increasingly transnational economy that puts labor at a disadvantage globally; and the neoliberal philosophy that has pervaded all spheres of society, including government and education. The argument I will make in this chapter, though, is that critical pedagogical approaches to writing pedagogy that center on explorations of class have generally not proceeded from a political economic perspective, but rather have articulated class as a social identity, an aspect of culture examined in isolation from the political economics of production. This derives, in part, from a reluctance to deploy any potentially disruptive political economic analysis and vocabulary—a reluctance that comes out of the success of the right in stigmatizing leftist speech. It is also a continuing legacy of the position of rhetoric and composition within literary-studies-dominated English departments, where distanced textual analysis tends to be favored over the active view of rhetoric described in the first chapter. The ramification has been a failure to recognize and act upon important shifts in relations of production and the character and function of education, and this failure diminishes the full creative and transformative power of writing education.

An encouraging backlash against postmodernist theory has emerged across humanities disciplines precisely because of the way that it has positioned the function of education and discourse. The arguments are wide ranging, but generally they critique the tendency of postmodernist theory to emphasize textuality and representation at the expense of materiality and history, undermining the possibility of a galvanizing and hopeful politics. Sociologist Raymond Morrow, for instance, argues that

> in its most popular form, as a kind of simplistic reaction against political economy (and critical theory) as totalizing "metanarratives," postmodernist theories proclaimed a radical pluralism and voluntarism oriented toward ahistorical understandings of the here and now. Theoretically, social analysis was reduced to cultural theory and was understood primarily in purely discursive terms that neglected the extratextual dimensions and material aspects of institutions and social reality. (2006, xxii)

A postmodernist perspective has led to text- and identity-focused writing pedagogies that apply class as a generalized category of understanding to discursive representations (such as in literature or pop culture).[2] Class in representations—for instance, in pop culture—is often the subject of critique, but class as a historically produced, political economic position is not. Because it is seen more as a stable category of identity—with which one either empathizes or identifies—than as lived, always evolving, and dialectically shaped, class is treated as roughly equivalent to other social markers that have had their potential as counter-hegemonic political identifications contained through corporate appropriation: gay, African American, etc. Moreover, the position of the critic herself in postmodern analysis is bound to an ethos of skepticism and ambivalence. Class analysis as an aspect of rhetorical study has thus been marred in the quagmire of distanced analysis, losing its power as *praxis* in the fuller sense of the term. Rather than being a part of an actionable political vocabulary that names and addresses the structural causes of injustice and inequity, the rhetoric of class is divorced from political engagement and appropriated within a "tolerance" discourse that is largely silent about political economic justice and process. Alienation among students is an existential dilemma, a generalized cultural "ennui," rather than an outcome of material relations of production on jobs and at school. This is true even of

---

2.   For an excellent critique of postmodern critical theory along political economic lines, see Bauman (1997).

critical pedagogical approaches. As Morrow describes it: "Against the excesses of postmodernism, it can be argued that critical theory without political economy retreats into a free-floating cultural space that loses contact with the historical specificity necessary for its insights as a form of social analysis and critique" (2006, xxii). Ironically, class inequities thus come to seem an organic inevitability rather than a product of specific, changeable material and historical processes. Indeed, this may have evolved as the precise political economic purpose of contemporary text-focused critique. Terry Eagleton argues in *The Illusions of Postmodernism* that critics began in the 1980s to "speak culturally about the material" rather than materially about culture, paradoxically— from a Marxist point of view—displacing bodies from the material into the discursive (48).[3] Mark Wood writes that

> during the 1980s and 1990s, self-identified progressive academics became increasingly disconnected from struggles for social justice, human rights, and ecological sustainability. This was also a period in which many academics, informed by poststructuralist discourses, contended that racial, ethnic, gender, and sexual discrimination and oppression (a category whose ubiquity was matched only by its operational ambiguity) are as significant as capitalist exploitation and state repression. Many theorized social relations as being constituted primarily if not exclusively by discourse, culture, and subjectivity. . . . While much was written about jouissance and the subversive play of libidinous bodies, much less was said about the individuals whose labor made possible this writing. Cyborgs, transexuality, and difference received far more attention than did janitors, the working day, and justice. (2005, 218–19)

Similar cases have been made by Henry Giroux, Zygmunt Bauman, Carl Boggs, David Harvey, and Peter McLaren. McLaren associates postmodern literary critiques with cynicism, passivism, and retreat from intellectual engagement and responsibility. As McClaren describes it, the "hidden curriculum" of fast-capitalist education "is largely the same as it was during earlier phases of industrial capitalism: to deform knowledge into a discreet and decontextualized set of technical skills packaged to serve big-business interests, cheap labor, and ideological conformity" (2000, 33). According to McLaren, "We occupy a time that is witnessing the progressive merging of pedagogy to the productive processes within advanced capitalism. Education has been reduced to

---

3.   Quoted in Wood (2005, 218).

a subsector of the economy, designed to create cyber citizens within a teledemocracy of fast-moving images, representations, and life-style choices" (29).

Surveying the range of recent treatments of class in writing pedagogy, one finds a critical absence of discussion of how the economy and higher education have changed over the past three decades and how those changes are reflected in everyday writing classrooms. All of the dynamic cacophony surrounding and significantly constructing classroom practice is largely silenced in the interest of a narrowed focus that positions postsecondary writing within stable disciplinary and institutional realms—outside of the fast-capitalist logics of socialization and production. An economic and politically mobilizing definition of class is supplanted by descriptions of dialects, habits of communication and consumption, and isolated instances of social embarrassment. In these inert manifestations, class becomes what German sociologists Ulrich Beck and Elisabeth Beck-Gernsheim call a "zombie category": a fossilized term from a past era that no longer has the power to name the material facts on the ground in a way that creates new opportunities for human agency and justice.

For instance, in a recent *College English* devoted to issues of class, Sharon O'Dair relies on very traditional, static notions of institutionality and class in her critique of what she believes are "bad faith" critical writing pedagogies. In "Class Work: Site of Egalitarian Activism or Site of Embourgeoisement?" O'Dair claims higher education as a solidly middle-class endeavor, and describes class as a set of social characteristics and dispositions. It is important to note that though O'Dair is seeking to enter a rhetoric and composition discussion, she self-identifies as "a literary critic interested in the theory and workings of social class, particularly education's role in maintaining and reproducing class distinction" (2003, 594). Her interest in class therefore seems analytical rather than political or moral in the active sense. Moreover, she doesn't exhibit a multiple-literacies perspective that values the languages of diverse peoples—a perspective that arguably now defines the mainstream of rhetoric and composition studies. Disregarding the three decades of work in literacy studies and rhetoric and composition that complicates one-dimensional, instrumentalist notions of Standard English, O'Dair associates recognition of working-class and nonstandard rhetorics with institutional decline:

In this time of great social urgency, perhaps literary critics and composition-ists should not be concerned about standard English, the intricacies of logical argument, or even the writing process; perhaps they should think of them-selves as politicians first, and literary critics or compositionists second, if at all . . . what seems to be at stake here is not just literary criticism or a fine writing style but also the value of intellectual accomplishment and distinction. How far do we go in promoting egalitarianism in the academy? (2003, 597)

O'Dair suggests that working-class students are largely in need of remedi-ation without making the project of remediation historically problematic: "How many students who require remedial instruction in English and mathematics should we admit to undergraduate study—40 percent? 60 percent? More?" (2003, 597). She argues from the general premise that

the vast majority of working-class students are in college because *they* want better occupational opportunities. *They* perceive higher education as a way to achieve such a goal, and that perception is rooted in their understanding that higher education will help them gain access to and perform better in the weird bourgeois or professional worlds they wish to enter. That perception may be somewhat hazy, and *they* may not grasp, for example, that a degree in and of itself is no guarantee of better occupational opportunities or that standard English is the lingua franca of bourgeois and professional life—but when *they* do grasp those facts, they will feel cheated when *they* recall that their composition instructor purposefully decided not to initiate *them* into academic discourse but instead to value the language and knowledge *they* already knew. (2003, 598 [emphasis mine])

There are many things to take issue with here: for instance, the mono-lithic generalizations about "we" and "them"; the belief that she knows enough about *them* and *their* knowledges and languages to make these generalizations about *their* desires and assumptions, but *they* know so little about her institution; the belief that expert knowledge of an aca-demic discourse, like the discourse of literary criticism, makes one any more expert or adept in the discourses of other professions than any other novice. My primary concern, though, is with the presumption that most working-class students aren't really legitimately a part of institu-tions of higher learning—a perspective that I believe wrongly isolates the cultural aspects of class from how it is lived and reproduced in daily life. This is essential because writing and discourse are an integral part of the reproduction of the political economic structures that maintain class inequities. In O'Dair's view, a view that I suspect isn't uncommon, though working-class students attend postsecondary institutions in high numbers, they still don't really constitute those institutions. The socio-material doesn't significantly constitute the real—so *they* are not *we.* They are outsiders to whom the institution/we must continually reach out to its/our detriment. They don't really belong, and it would be better if many of them are therefore, in O'Dair's words, given an "excellent primary and secondary education, as well as excellent secondary and postsecondary vocational training," because this is what is best suited for a working-class consciousness—which, in her construction, remains largely monolithic, implicitly naturalized, and at the very least external to the central concerns of higher education.

What are the assumptions about class, postsecondary literacy, and institutionality that drive the assertion that writing education is the project of a "middle-class professoriate" (2003, 593) and that "colleges and universities have been and continue to be part of middle-class culture" (601)? Evidence abounds that the project of writing instruction at most institutions of higher learning is not carried out by an instructorate which can legitimately be said to be solidly middle class, at least not from a political economic perspective. Higher education is increasingly reliant upon contingent, para-, and nonprofessional teaching labor, and nowhere is this more obviously the case than in postsecondary writing classes. If one defines class narrowly along the lines of educational attainment and privileged cultural knowledge, then an undergraduate degree and an M.A. are the minimum requirements for middle class membership. However, can a teacher really be considered middle class while working part-time or as a contracted laborer at clearly subprofessional wages, and often without benefits? Someone hired to teach courses at a postsecondary institution might be able quote William Blake from memory or talk with intelligence about discourse and cultural studies while she stocks the shelves at night at Barnes and Noble in order to make ends meet, but does that make her "middle class"?

Michael Zweig, in *Working Class Majority* (2000), argues that higher education doesn't necessarily lead to class mobility, but Zweig's argument is that class is more a matter of political economic power than cultural distinction. Recognizing the difference is especially important for an understanding of how class functions in the fast-capitalist economy precisely because outward, "cultural" markers of class from previous eras—clothes, dialects, musical taste—though certainly not gone, are also now not nearly as reliable as markers of class position.

Zweig, an economist who directs the Center for Working Class Life at the University of Michigan, defines class

> in large part based on the power and authority people have at work. The workplace engages people in more than their immediate work, by which they create goods and services. It also engages them in relationships with each other, relationships that are controlled by power. A relative handful of people have great power to organize and direct production, while a much larger number have almost no authority. In a capitalist society such as ours, the first group are the capitalist class, the second group the working class. (2000, 3)

When we, as Zweig suggests, see class in terms of power over production and relationships—in other words, in terms of political economic positioning and processes—rather than in terms of cultural markers of class distinction, we can't assert that higher education across institutions, especially writing education, is solidly middle class. Convincingly wielding the social characteristics of cultural distinction might, in some cases, correlate with power, but it hardly constitutes it.

Zweig argues that culture is more productively and accurately seen as an aspect of the political economic: "Economic and political power are related and reinforce one another. The power to affect our culture comes from control over economic and political resources, but influencing the culture tends to strengthen one's economic and political power as well" (12). When we look at who is actually teaching in higher education and under what conditions, the middle class status of teachers as a whole is quite tenuous. Moreover, the significant majority of all students in postsecondary institutions (73 percent) are classified by the National Center for Educational Statistics (NCES) as "nontraditional," and many of the criteria used by the NCES to define "nontraditional" status—such as works full-time and finances own education—do correlate with "working-class" status.

So what of the relationship between class, writing, and postsecondary institutions? As Jeff Grabill argues, "literacy" has little meaning outside of particular institutional spheres, and "literacy education" does not exist as a transcendent, definable entity—it is always a deployment, a range of actions undertaken with situated (often even explicitly articulated) ideas of what literacy and education are and how they should be pursued. As Grabill puts it: "Institutions give literacies existence, meaning and value" (2001, 7). Institutions are systems of meaning-making and valuation—they are mechanisms of political economic production. When those institutions involve literacy, they create (with varying degrees of specificity) what literacy is and why it is important. They construct what is desirable and undesirable, and they often carry explicit means of shaping how people see literacy and how it is to be evaluated. When institutions deploy their own versions of literacy, they do so according to broader, contentious assumptions about what constitutes the primary identities, roles, and purposes of human beings. For instance, English-only edicts in governmental policy and education are specific, contentious assertions of "American" identity, and when institutions caste literacy in terms of employment, job training, economic competitiveness, political consciousness, and cultural sophistication they emphasize and value different aspects of what it means to be human and what are the most important functions of language. That said, however, it is also important not to see institutions as overly determining, static, or detached from the everyday actions and choices of people: "Institutions are people; they are systems by which people act collectively" (Grabill 2001, 7). Institutions aren't just policies and figments of the imaginary, they are political economic entities: material, historical, continually recreated by the real people who labor within them.

O'Dair characterizes as "nonsense" the arguments of those concerned with class in writing pedagogy, like John Alberti and Joseph Heathcott, who have called for institutions to become more explicitly working class in their orientation (2003, 596). But what Alberti, Heathcott, and Amy Robillard (who examines narrative as an element of working-class cultures) are calling for is not, as O'Dair would characterize it, a degradation of higher education and literacy in the interests of inclusion, but a fuller and more strategic response to what postsecondary educational institutions *actually already are now*. A statistical handful of elite institutions do serve high numbers of privileged students—but as Alberti points out, most are not elite, and most students are not privileged. I would add that most writing teachers aren't either. Higher education as a whole can be seen as solidly middle class only when we ignore that class is an aspect of political economic positioning and power in specific times and places. Rhetoric and composition is likewise bound to be a process of "embourgeoisement" only when we envision it as isolated enculturation or analysis, rather than as ongoing material *praxis* carried out by real people in real locales under real material terms.

Even other more nuanced and politically committed work also tends to favor a definition that is generated more by cultural representation and identification than political economic relations and production—for instance, Tim Libretti's "Sexual Outlaws and Class Struggle: Rethinking History and Class Consciousness from a Queer Perspective" (2004). Libretti's generally provocative and well-structured argument is framed in terms of a binary between two factions. On one side are what he calls "angry white men on the left," a term he borrows from Jesse Lemisch. On the other are people who focus on identity politics in relation to class. In Libretti's binary, people in the "angry white men" faction believe that too much focus on identity politics has splintered the left. The angry white male faction believes that a turning away from class politics and toward diversity issues has left progressive politics without a focus or a means to foster widespread support. Libretti associates this faction with homophobia, racism, and a general ignorance of the relationship between social institutions and economic structures. In contrast, he wants to emphasize the connection between class politics and cultural institutions. Drawing on Lemisch, Mary Bernstein, and Robin D. G. Kelley, he says that "they either don't understand or refuse to acknowledge that class is lived through race and gender" (Kelley, cited in Libretti 2004, 155). Libretti thus builds his position against the image of the antiquated, homophobic, angry white male leftist—a leftist that, he asserts, is too willing to ignore the degree to which capitalism is dependent upon the maintenance of specific social and sexual norms. He locates heterosexual monogamy at the center of the capitalist social system and argues for the importance of "queering" that social institution through a dialectical materialist approach: "Simply put, the full and genuine development of an anticapitalist class consciousness . . . demands a gay perspective and entails, if efficaciously articulated, a politics of gay liberation, of total sexual liberation" (2004, 62). Libretti advocates careful study of the writings of James Baldwin and John Rechy, both of whom articulated a queer identity in relation to class identity, finding that gender and class cannot be teased apart:

> What these authors have provided for the radical imagination seeking to invent new political subjects or write new narratives of class struggle and liberation is the crucial wisdom that this imagination must include a queer dimension if it is going to produce a genuine blueprint for revolution. (2004, 170)

I am convinced of the value of integrating questions of gender and sexuality into discussions of class and identity. I am less convinced, however, that queer identities and lifestyles that are not attached to an explicitly radical economic (rather than culturally centered) politics are threatening to the fundamental social structures of fast-capitalism. This is not the same political culture within which James Baldwin did his primary work. There is much reason to believe that industries in the new economy are becoming very accommodating of nonheterosexual identities and lifestyles. The Human Rights Campaign foundation (HRC)—which rates companies according to their policies concerning lesbian, gay, transgendered, and bisexual employees—found that 265 of Fortune 500 companies offer domestic partner health benefits. Anything less than 100 percent is not enough, but this is enough to indicate a large and growing willingness to accept nonheterosexuals into the normative center of capitalist culture and power as long as its fundamental economic architectures go unchallenged. Moreover, many of the corporations that form the very core of the fast-capitalist economy—from financial sector companies like American Express, Bank of America, and Capital One; to technology companies like Apple, Microsoft, Google, and Intel; to pharmaceutical giants like Eli Lilly and Company and Pfizer—all received the highest ("100") score from the HRC for their policies concerning gay, lesbian, transgendered, and bisexual employees. I wonder whether a "queering" of heterosexual "normalcy" still carries the revolutionary power that Libretti imagines. Among the many oft-cited attributes of fast-capitalism is its cultural agility—its ability to adapt with sophistication to cultural shifts while keeping its foundational political economic structures solidly intact.

In another *College English* article, Jennifer Beech self-identifies as "both scholar and redneck." Beech very usefully describes the historical, cultural complexity of the term "redneck" and points to the fact that most postsecondary university students attend "'second-tier' or 'working class' colleges." She finds that even in these colleges, working-class, "redneck" students are left out of considerations of diversity in pedagogy, which means that we are ignoring or alienating a considerable portion of the current postsecondary population (2004, 176). Beech addresses recent assertions—made by O'Dair, Russel Durst, and Joseph Harris among others—that critical pedagogy ignores the "instrumentalist" motivations that working-class students often carry into higher education. These scholars argue that students want to pursue conventional notions of success—better jobs and middle class cultural "normalcy." Beech counters, very persuasively in my view, that critical pedagogy can critique privilege even as students become more adept at understanding and, if need be, adapting themselves to multiple discourses:

> Critical examinations of language's role in maintaining oppressive race and class structures can productively engage students oppressed by or comfortable with "normative" whiteness, facilitating their ability to critique and resist (deconstruct) oppressive mainstream stereotypes and even allowing for students to imagine and employ (reconstruct) more ethical discursive practices. (2004, 176)

Beech discusses Jeff Foxworthy's jokes, "redneck" music, and a book called *The Redneck Manifesto*.

Beech's article is important; however, as with Libretti, the focus is on social identity largely in isolation from political economic concerns.[4] If, as Beech desires, students do "imagine and employ (reconstruct) more ethical discursive practices," will it bring about awareness of the root causes of economic injustice and systemic exploitation that are built into global economic policies? My concern is that working-class markers like "hillbilly" can take a place among other social identifiers not to be discriminated against on the job or referenced derogatively at socially mixed gatherings. Working-class, rural culture is now already a clearly identified marketing niche—the target of the marketing campaigns of NASCAR and Wal-Mart, music and automobiles. Is a kinder ethics toward culturally disparaged peoples a goal of class identification and study? What about a deeper, more revolutionary and equitable distribution of power, access, and resources? Class is not genetically produced; it isn't something we celebrate with festivals and parades or give its own official month. Class can describe how people live and identify, but we can't lose site of the fact that it is ultimately about unequal relations of power. I recognize the importance of understanding gender, race, and sexuality as aspects of labor and class struggles in the United States,

---

4.   In the same issue of *College English*, Julie Lindquist (2004) advocates developing empathetic responses to class issues. As with Libretti and Beech, I believe that this is valuable work that helped my understanding of my own pedagogy, but I again think we also need class analysis that is explicitly connected to the project of understanding and addressing the structural causes of *economic* injustice. I bring David Seitz's (2004) article, from the same issue of *College English*, into chapter 4. His approach to work memoirs starts from an examination of work that does shift focus to relations of production: the cultural is examined in terms of the economic.

and I also recognize the importance of fostering awareness of the social markers of class distinction (dialect, dress, consumption habits, etc.). However, when the social and cultural (rather than the political economic) aspects of class are the points of emphasis, class is too apt to being appropriated. Corporations can do tolerance workshops and extend benefits to same-sex couples. Classrooms can be forums in which people share experiences and revelations about their own socioeconomic status and resolve to be more sensitive and aware of difference. Meanwhile the irreconcilable contradictions and systematic injustices of the economic system that creates class disparities remain largely unexamined. Class-focused education can even serve an ameliorative political function in higher education in fast-capitalism, as justified anger is directed toward coping and understanding.

In the next chapter, I will offer a pedagogical model that can help highlight structural contradictions and doesn't seek to foster closures, reconciliations, or even "tolerance" of class-based inequalities. In the remainder of this chapter I focus on the broad changes that have occurred in the economy over the last four decades. I believe that critical pedagogical approaches might be more centered on the realization that a significant transformation has occurred in the global economy and that rhetorics of social identification and identifications of points of struggle need to be modified to account for the new terrain. The fast-capitalist economy has outpaced many things, including the ability of those who find reason to take issue with its fundamental logics to sustain a discourse of critique and transformation.

FAST-CAPITALIST LOGICS—FROM THE STEEL MILL TO WAL-MART

> All the profits that you see in American business today come from not paying employee benefits. All the money on Wall Street that they're pushing back and forth comes from people like me paying our own dental bills. [Laughs] Because temping at large corporations is a big deal these days. And you know large corporations don't do anything that doesn't save them money, so they have their work broken up into distinct units that can be done mindlessly. And they bring in temps whenever they need us, and they don't pay us benefits, and they let us go whenever they don't need us anymore. (58)

The above quote was uttered by "Chris Real," a temp worker interviewed for the book *Gig: Americans Talk About Their Jobs* (2000). *Gig* is a fast-capitalist update on Studs Terkel's *Working: People Talk About What They*

Do All Day and How They Feel About What They Do (1972). Terkel's *Working* is deservedly a classic and still a commonplace on reading lists in classes that examine work and class. *Working* was certainly among the many books that helped me, as an undergraduate student, begin to take more ownership over my own working-class upbringing. But reading the book now, over three decades after its first publication, one immediately recognizes that *Working* comes out of a distinctively industrial-economy context. It is still deeply engaging and certainly well worth reading, but its interviews with, among others, mine workers, cab drivers, spot-welders, an "airline stewardess," and a "super market box boy" invite the reader into a world of work that is clearly in the past.

An intense, troubled period of economic, social, and governmental reorganization was underway in the early 1970s and that reorganization has had profound effects on work, education, and discourse. During this transformative period, the power of labor steadily diminished, altering not only the fundamental relationship between employers and labor, but the essence of what it means to be a "worker" and a "citizen." Many of the interviews in Terkel's *Working* can even be read as a portrait of the breaking down of the particular balance mediated by government between workers and industry that had been established by the New Deal. The Keynesian relationship that characterized the political economy of the 1950s and 1960s had been driven by a view that government had a vital role in preventing the abuse and exploitation of workers in a free market economy. This view had not come about naturally, of course. It was an inventive and effective means of containing and eventually disarming the widespread and increasingly politicized anger fueled by the capitalist economic collapse of the 1930s. By the 1960s, however, the American left had largely abandoned an oppositional economic project. This was due to a number of factors. Wealth was being spread more evenly than before across the (white) strata of society, which created a middle class of unprecedented size. Labor unions had been weakened by cold war purges of economic radicals; top-heavy union bureaucracies developed complicitous relationships with management; and the academic/intellectual left turned toward cultural issues and eventually its own conversations, and away from workers' rights and what was happening with relations of production. The celebrations of the social advances of late 1960s and early 1970s counterculture masked fundamental rightward shifts in the American economic structure that disempowered workers and widened gaps in wealth and power. As Louis Uchitell describes it,

The "about face" that came about in the 1970s shifted agency to "entrepreneurial, hard driving managers"—theorizing that a globally competitive economy required giving management maximum flexibility. Job security as a right and an essential component of general well-being—the right to have secure employment—fell away from the political economic discourse. (2006, 6)

A theory of government as a protector of the well-being of all citizens was replaced by a theory of government that facilitated the agency of management for global economic competitiveness. This new theory moved the political focus away from maintaining systemic checks and balances and placed the responsibility for secure employment more exclusively on the workers themselves. Workers began to find themselves in the untenable position of seeking individual solutions to systemic problems. The economic system's failure to create good, secure jobs was made to seem like failures of skill and will in individuals:

Unfettered enterprises, the argument now went, would expand more rapidly and, over the long run, share their rising profits with their workers, doing so voluntarily through job creation and raises. If that did not happen—and it did not happen for tens of millions of people who lost their jobs—well, that was the fault of the job losers themselves. They had failed to acquire the necessary skills and education to qualify for the increasingly sophisticated jobs that were available. (2006, 7)

So changes in the structure of the economy and government shaped the way that workers tended to view themselves, their work, and their rights.

In 1933, U.S. Secretary of Labor Frances Perkins led a march of striking steelworkers in Homestead, Pennsylvania. Prevented from addressing the workers by local town authorities, she marched to the post office to speak to them from federally owned space, signaling that the federal government would stand behind workers in some labor disputes. It is nearly impossible to imagine a high-ranking government official now standing with workers in a labor dispute. In the 1970s, job security as a fundamental right of citizens and an essential component of general well-being fell away from the political discourse and out of legislative policy decisions. In its place came the era of managerial flexibility and worker insecurity—an era in which government hesitated or increasingly refused to intervene in employer/worker disputes; and when it did act, it often acted on behalf of employers. In place of the industrial ideal of the loyal company man came the fast-capitalist ideal of the self-interested entrepreneur. A host of governmental policies—including international trade agreements that included no protections for workers and the so-called "right to work" legislation that weakened unions in states across the country (twenty-two states now have such laws)—have fundamentally changed the terms of work in the United States. In 1981, nearly fifty years after Frances Perkins stood with striking workers on federal land in Homestead, Ronald Reagan invoked executive authority to fire and replace striking air traffic controllers. This is the exclamation point signaling the arrival of a new period of philosophical and economic transformation, the symbol that organized labor no longer had real political clout and that the balance had now shifted largely toward the interests of management and shareholders to the exclusion of those of labor.

Political economic developments have not just changed work, they have changed how people generally self-identify as workers, how they view education and civic life, and how they view themselves in relation to the broader economy. In America, the shift away from a manufacturing to more of a service- and technology-based economy has actually also been a shift toward less-secure white-collar employment. In their most recent comprehensive report (2002/2003), the Economic Policy Institute (EPI) summarizes:

> Job security fell in the 1980s and 1990s as workers began spending less time with one employer. The long-term trend in job stability is disconcerting for a number of reasons. First, workers who are displaced from their jobs often find new ones that pay less and are less likely to offer benefits. Further, many employee benefits, such as health insurance and pensions, are tied to employers. Workers who switch jobs not only tend to start at the firm's minimal number of vacation weeks, but they may have to go through waiting periods for employer-provided health insurance. (Mishel, Bernstein, and Boushey 2003, 9)

According to the report, "low-wage industries [primarily retail, health, and temporary services] accounted for 72.9% of all new jobs in 1989–2000" (see also Galbraith 1998; Osterman 2001). The EPI report tracks a thirty-year trend toward diminished job security and benefits—for all workers, not only less formally educated workers in the manufacturing sector. Since the digital technologies boom of the 1990s, the general assumption has been that high-paying, high-tech jobs are available in large numbers if only more Americans were qualified to take them.

While this assumption diverts attention away from those companies that outsource high-tech jobs in order to keep labor costs low and maximize shareholder profits, it isn't supported by the available statistics. Indeed, the growth in reliance on part-time work and the increasing number of workers who are also in school are among the factors that have tended to make the unemployment rate a weak indicator of job availability and security.

In *Working*, people's expectations and frustrations generally stem from an industrial-era belief that the economy can and should offer workers a degree of permanence and loyalty. This is not to romanticize industrial-era work. Many of the workers' lives are certainly hard, and the jobs fall short of what workers' feel they have a right to expect. Nevertheless, the workers generally see themselves in definable, sustainable occupations rather than in "positions," and there is often clearly a collective identification with a class—sometimes explicitly stated, other times implied or manifested in an identifiable rhetoric. Terry Mason, the "airline stewardess," was only twenty-six at the time that she was interviewed for *Working*, but she had already been on the job for six years and clearly saw herself in a steady, long-term career. Moreover, though the terms of her employment were shockingly sexist (for instance, her airline had an "appearance counselor" who had the power to take women off of shifts if their appearance didn't meet the standard), at that time being an "airline stewardess" brought considerable prestige, a mark of sophistication, and elevated class status. Her family, most of whom had never been on an airplane, boasted to friends of her position and her travel (Turkel 1972, 48–49). Steve Dubui, a steelworker near retirement interviewed for *Working*, had been working since his teens at the same unionized mill for forty years. He had endured a long, hard working life, but he looked forward to retirement and regularly spent time talking with his fellow workers about what they were going to do when they retired. Unfortunately, however, the forces of the new global economy that would have such a devastating impact on workers in the U.S. steel industry in the coming decade were already well underway. He described the changes:

> And they're forcing more work on ya. It's knockin off men, makin' cutbacks here and there to save money. They've knocked off an awful lot of jobs. With the foreign imports of steel they're losin' money. That's what they say. I suppose in order to make a profit they have to cut somewhere. But I told

'em 'After forty years of work, why do you take a man away from me? You're gonna force me into retirement.' All of us were real angry. (1972, 552)

Turnover is so integral to the terms of work in the new economy that having the same job for one's entire adult life is almost unheard of.

The portrait of the working world found in *Gig* (Bowe, Bowe, and Streeter 2001) is in many important ways wholly distinct from that of *Working*. The economy of *Gig* is far more casualized, and the total portrait of work that emerges from its interviews is more about contingency and risk than expectations of permanence and security, cynicism and "free agency" than hopeful expectations and class identification and solidarity. Workers interviewed for *Gig* work in an economy that is driven by digital technologies, thousands of specialized "niche" jobs that are only temporary, and low-level service jobs—such as those in retail and the food industry—that are created by mammoth international corporations like Wal-Mart and McDonald's. Perhaps more importantly, in *Gig* many workers talk of making regular changes in both jobs and careers. As labor historians Paul Le Blanc and John Hinshaw write,

> Since the mid-1970s, the real wages of those fortunate enough to have full-time employment have declined by 20 percent. Even many unionized workers whose wages and benefits have kept pace with inflation share the common view that the labor movement is dominated by entrenched, self-serving bureaucracies having little positive relevance for the lives of working people. And the condition of labor markets will surely deteriorate as corporations and public employers accelerate the process of eliminating full-time employees in favor of temporary workers or so-called self-employed contractors. (2000, 13)

Consistent with the general milieu described by Le Blanc and Hinshaw, the workers of *Gig* seem to expect little loyalty or continuity from their employers, and they often articulate their relationships with their employers as a kind of mutually exploitive gamesmanship. In the new era of managerial techniques that are designed to quickly foster loyalty in ever-evolving workforces—an era in which employees are usually referred to as "associates" and hierarchies are said to be more "flattened"—there is actually much cynicism on both sides of the manager/worker equation. In *Gig*, workers talk about the kind of forced cultures that employers try to create on jobs to increase productivity and a sense of loyalty. For instance, a worker at Kinko's describes training as mostly focusing

on "indoctrinating you into this Kinko's philosophy. . . . I think they
believe that you're less likely to rip them off or be irresponsible if you
feel like you're in a family-type thing. So they get you in all these little
ways. They give you grades. You're treated like a kid" (72). Workers
play along, with low expectations of their employers and carrying the
burden of maintaining employment within an economy that thrives on
short-term, "flexible" labor. A sixty-six-year-old Wal-Mart greeter in *Gig*
who has no intention of ever being without a job makes an interesting
contrast to the nearly retired steelworker in *Working*. Those not in an
economic elite generally don't expect to ever have a retirement phase
in which they don't work at the end of their careers. The media often
presents portraits of seniors at work as positive and voluntary, illustrative
of how the capitalist economy can make even the elderly feel relevant
and productive. The reality is that the economy is seeing the effects of
nearly forty years of the erosion of workers' rights, benefits, and relative
wealth. Many seniors are working because they have to work—and they
get low paying service industry jobs because that is what this economy is
producing in large numbers.

William DeGenario's recent collection *Who Says: Working Class Rhetoric,
Class Consciousness and Community* illustrates the difficulty with fostering
a galvanizing, counter-hegemonic discourse in the current political
economy. DeGenario seeks to identify a distinct, historically continuous
working-class rhetoric. He contrasts this working-class rhetoric to the
work that has formed the canon of traditional rhetorical study, which he
links to elitism and idle privilege. Indeed, he points out that much of the
rhetorical theory that forms our disciplinary canon is "often characterized by a disdain for physical labor and the people who partake in such
work" (2007, 1). He locates the origins of this elitism in Aristotle, and
follows it through Quintilian's figure of "the good man speaking well"
into contemporary conceptualizations of rhetoric. The "good man" [*sic*]
is an educated man who is socially empowered to speak and be heard. In
other words, the good man speaking well is enabled by existing power
structures. In contrast, DeGenario describes working-class rhetorics in
terms of their largely antagonistic dialectic with the very elitist political and social institutions that have largely sustained rhetorical study.
Working-class rhetoricians have not had "the conch" as a birthright,
they have been forced to seize it—and once they have, their rhetoric has
been about power. He seeks to locate a rhetorical history that is alternative to the official, elitist lineage—one that carries a "transformative

function," an imperative to take action. He therefore, perhaps naturally, gravitates toward labor unions in his explanation: "Inspired by the discursive activity of labor unions . . . working-class rhetorics agitate and antagonize the static words on the pages of rhetorical texts and suggest contemporary scholars invent their own class-conscious readings of such texts." (6) This antagonism with power that helps bring about a working-class rhetoric occurs on a variety of terrains, from admissions policies at universities to popular media and workplaces. An essential point for DeGenario, though, is that "class" is still real and class-consciousness is articulated through working-class rhetorics. Therefore, as scholars we need to do more to help people recognize "that class (and by extension, class division and class conflict) exists" (6).

What follows DeGenario's introductory theorization of working-class rhetoric is an intriguing section called "Toward a Working-Class Rhetorical Tradition"—five very readable chapters that deal in some way with the history and rhetoric of the labor movement. This section as a whole persuasively locates a workers' rhetoric of solidarity and opposition, but it locates it in a bygone era. This is where I begin to struggle with the premise of a historically continuous working-class rhetoric. "Working class" is a part of the actionable vocabulary of historic, violent struggles at Matawan, Lowell, Homestead, and Youngstown—struggles that happened during the first half of the last century. It evokes images—fictional and historic—that are deeply embedded in the American historical consciousness: the Joads; tent cities; gun thugs; ruthless, scowling white male industrialists; Marlon Brando and Eva Marie Saint—young and beautiful and finding identity, moral clarity, and a commitment to justice in grainy black and white. One chapter focuses on the rhetoric of Depression-era miner strikes, and two others focus on aspects of labor-oriented rhetoric from the first two decades of the twentieth century. The remaining two chapters examine memorializations of historically important labor battles in Homestead, Pennsylvania, and Youngstown, Ohio—two cities still trying to recover from economic devastation caused by the loss of steel mills that were the locus of these struggles. This section deals not only with labor struggles that are solidly in the past, but also with industries that are no longer a preeminent part of the American economy.

Other pieces in this collection analyze rhetoric in specific, current professions, but in my view fall short of locating a contemporary "working-class rhetoric" that persuasively articulates a common, American working-class consciousness. Workplace rhetoric in working-class jobs is not the same as working-class rhetoric. The concrete workers, truck drivers, and migrant farm workers described in these chapters are clearly "working class" in terms of their economic circumstances, and some are clearly speaking back to power. However, they don't articulate their struggles and identities as part of a common national or international movement. They don't seem united by a mutual awareness of common interests or even a common political consciousness that is shared across occupational realms. These are the elements of a broad and powerful political movement that can be enabled by a common rhetoric of critique and opposition. This doesn't discount the importance of the collection or the lives and struggles it describes. It does, however, complicate the continuity that DeGenario seeks to locate among working-class rhetorics across time. In what ways are the political economic struggles, identifications, and rhetorics of these contemporary workers different from the rhetorics employed at Matawan and Youngstown? Will the same rhetoric work for the workers of *Working* and *Gig?*

The economy has changed dramatically over the past three decades, and though some scholars have addressed those changes, rhetoric and composition as a whole has not developed an adequately rigorous discussion of what they have meant to our work. Given that being working class now doesn't exclude many from higher education, how do the contexts of literacy education shape the rhetorics that are enacted there—how might they change rhetorics of opposition? The political economic context that creates the terms of work for American workers doesn't stop at the university gates. A continued reliance on dated conceptions of higher education and identity markers that are more static and cultural than dynamic and economic prevents us from constructively naming and addressing the terms of work and education in fast-capitalism. If we are looking for starting points for an examination of class in America, we need look no further than our own writing classrooms, where we are likely to find a part-time worker teaching a classroom full of part-time workers, and where marketing images on Web sites and brochures create a slick, icy aesthetic that is largely alien to the daily material lives of most students. Class might not only be the sometime subject *about which* we think and write, it might also be the condition *from which* we think and write. In the following chapter I offer a model for a writing pedagogy that seeks to highlight the character and contradictions of work and education in the current economy. The model emphasizes relations of production at work and in education, as it seeks a galvanizing political rhetoric that is adapted to current economics. An important aspect of this pedagogy is that it is not founded on the need for resolution and there is no prohibition on anger: it actively resists easy closures as it explores the deeply systemic contradictions that are inherent in the worlds of work and education.

4
STUDENTS WORKING

*I get through my days knowing that I am earning my college degree and
keep in mind that these managers who have the power to tell me what to
do today will potentially be working for me after I graduate and obtain
a job they could never have with their level of education and lack of
integrity. . . .*

"Karen," retail worker/student

In *Bait and Switch*, Barbara Ehrenreich investigates life as an unemployed white-collar worker by going "undercover," adopting the identity of a professional writer and public relations specialist looking for work. To do the research for the book, Ehrenreich created a new identity, "Barbara Alexander," drew on the skills and experience she had built in her own "real" career, and marketed herself as a public relations person and event planner. *Bait and Switch* manages to convey some sense of the quietly desperate lives of the tens of millions of people who have white-collar occupations but find themselves in a relatively continuous job search. They are either employed and looking for work because they fear losing their jobs, partially employed as contract workers or in part-time positions with little security and no benefits, employed as temp workers or in retail simply to make ends meet, or fully unemployed.

Because this state of semiemployment is a common predicament in the current American economy, a historically low unemployment rate paints a very distorted picture. Data compiled to calculate the unemployment rate counts only those who are willing to work but have not found any job at all as "unemployed." Much of the real story of employment in this economy is therefore left out. The unemployment rate does not track those who are working part-time or in any job they can find, nor does it track those who have stopped looking for work altogether. In addition to an unemployment rate, the Economic Policy Institute offers an "underemployment rate" as a more accurate indicator of what is happening in this layoff-dependent, more fully casualized economy. The underemployment rate accounts for those who are working part time but want full-time work, those who have stopped looking for work because they are discouraged by lack of success, and those who are not working or looking for work but indicate that they nevertheless want work and have sought it within the past year.

In 2002, while the unemployment rate was 5.8% (relatively low by historical standards, but up nearly two points since 2000), the under-employment rate was 9.5% (Mishel, Bernstein, and Boushey 2003, 223). The unemployment rate is woefully inadequate as an indicator of economic security and job availability in the fast-capitalist economy, which has replaced long-term jobs that offer the opportunity for steady advancement with lower-paying service jobs and part-time, temporary, and contract positions—and which has made layoffs a part of business as usual, even in companies that remain extremely profitable.

Bait and Switch chronicles people's existences in the shadowy, often lonely and depressing world of the white-collar underemployed. After months of dead ends, Ehrenreich finally gets what looks like a promising interview with the insurance company AFLAC. She drives several hours toward what she expects will be a busy corporate office that in some way reflects the public, established image of a company whose brand is now as well known as AFLAC's. What she finds instead is a small, isolated office in rural Virginia that seems to be staffed by only one person, who wears a tie with ducks on it. While she had marketed herself as a public relations person, she quickly comes to understand that the "interview" is for a sales position that pays only on commission. Moreover, the meeting actually isn't as much an interview as it is an informational session for people who might be willing to do insurance sales. The sales positions are contract positions offering no benefits and no operating budget. Coming near the end of the book, the description of this experience solidifies the "bait and switch" metaphor that permeates each chapter. The promise of working in one's field of expertise for a nationally known company that seems well-established turns out to be yet another contract sales job that actually requires upfront money and effort to acquire an insurance broker's license. She would be far removed from the corpora-tion itself, her only connection to it being this one person who works out of an isolated office and shows little actual interest in her skills or goals. There is clearly no possibility of moving into a legitimate, permanent position in the company. So this "interview" might be better described as a sales opportunity with the interviewee as the mark. Drawing on the same rhetoric of individualism and entrepreneurship that permeates the thriving self-help industry that Ehrenreich has been targeted by over the previous months, the AFLAC representative emphasizes "the need to 'hit the ground running' and 'make a total commitment.'" When she asks about health insurance for this job that would involve selling health insurance, he ironically answers, "We're independent contractors; we get our own." She is then told that she won't even get office space or materials: "Our associates use their home offices" (2005, 181).

Throughout *Bait and Switch*, Ehrenreich exposes many of the lows of life in the realm of the white-collar underemployed. A large and growing industry niche that includes job coaches, appearance consultants, get-rich-quick schemes, and quasi-religious (or overtly religious) positive thinking books and seminars has arisen to prey upon this demographic. Typically expensive and offering much promise that it often doesn't deliver upon, this industry responds to the desperation and embarrassment of college-educated, skilled people who have been led to expect that if they "work hard and play by the rules" they will lead economically successful, secure lives. Rather than seeking to help the underemployed understand and address the broad political economic causes of their predicament, this industry sells a mixture of blame and hope driven by highly individualistic philosophies. In this world of winners and losers, people are invited to compare themselves unfavorably to the financially successful and fundamentally change themselves accordingly. In the seminars and consulting sessions Ehrenreich attends, the focus is therefore on redressing her perceived inadequacies (in attitude, dress, and rhetorical packaging of her skills and experiences) and projecting confidence and boundless optimism. Reflecting on her experiences, Ehrenreich writes:

> It goes without saying that a smiling, confident person will do better in an interview than a surly one, but the instruction goes beyond self-presentation in particular interactions: you are to actually feel "positive" and winnerlike. By the same token, you are to let go of any "negative" thoughts, meaning, among other things, resentments lingering from prior job losses. As one web site I quoted warned, "If you are angry with your former employer, or have a negative attitude, it will show." The prohibition on anger seems unlikely to foster true acceptance or "healing," and it certainly silences any conversation about systemic problems. The aching question—why was I let go when I gave the company so much?—is cut off before it can be asked. (2005, 220)

Ehrenreich is addressing the lack of discussion among the underemployed that could lead to recognition and action directed at the root political economic sources of their very pressing and all too common problems. What career coaches, best-selling books like *The Ultimate Secret to Getting Absolutely Everything You Want*, and faith-based networking organizations have in common is a propensity to radically privatize economic issues, making broadly systemic problems that are the result of specific policies and politics seem like individual, biographical problems. So the development of a potentially powerful, collective political awareness and identification is arrested, and this alienated group of underemployed that reveals serious problems with the structure of our current economy becomes just another politically inert marketing demographic:

> When the unemployed and anxiously employed reach out for human help and solidarity, the hands that reach back to them all too often clutch and grab. There are the coaches who want $200 an hour for painstakingly prolonged resume upgrades and pop-psych exhortations. There are the executive-oriented firms that sell office space and contacts doled out one name at a time. And there are, in churches around America, groups that advertise concrete help but have little to offer beyond the consolations of their particular religious sect. In every one of these settings, any potentially subversive conversation about the economy and its corporate governance is suppressed. (2005, 219)

Struggling in quiet isolation, fearing the dire consequences of a health problem, people are compelled to look inward for what is "wrong" with them to make themselves worthy of a job. Many of them end up back in higher education as students or even as adjunct faculty. Indeed, we might justifiably add higher education to the list of entities that "clutch and grab" at the underemployed. Might the formula of *hard work + education = success* be considered another form of *Bait and Switch* for many who buy into it? Certainly distance education and niche programs are largely aimed at an older population of people who are either dissatisfied with their careers or feel that they need further credentialing in order to be more competitive. Moreover, part-time adjunct work offers a veneer of dignity and professionalism to older workers with professional experience who can't find good jobs but don't want to work in, for instance, retail—where the pay is comparable, but the work is repetitive and more transparently low-status.

I have used *Bait and Switch* in a senior–graduate level writing class I teach that uses work as a theme for inquiry and writing. Reflecting on the portrait of economics and work the book depicts, "Paige," an office

worker and student, writes: "We keep working and chasing this unattainable ideal that we have in our minds that work can bring us. . . . I
understand that work will be stressful and make you unhappy, yet I don't
believe that this can happen to me. I am chasing this ideal whether I
think I am or not." Paige had worked since her teens and financed most
of her own university education. She indicates in her journal that she
had never really thought extensively about the relationship between her
work and her education. As she reflected upon those journal entries as
they unfolded over time, however, she came to understand that the two
continually inform one another. She noted a realization growing in her
journal entries that her desire for education is formed, in part, by her
desire to escape the working world that she already inhabits. In these
entries, a dialectic emerges over time about work and education that is
informed by the vocabulary that emerged in the class.

In the initial weeks of the class, we had examined "the American work
ethic" through reading, discussions, and writing about our perceptions
of our own working lives and those that tend to be promoted in the
popular media. During one discussion, I mapped the different perceptions of how we (the class) feel about our challenges and how we tend
to respond to the challenges faced by our communities and society more
generally. At the beginning of the next class, I gave them the following
writing prompt for a journal entry:

> Scan these columns and reflect on whether your own responses to situ-
> ations tends to be more "Individualist" or "Systemic." Think through this
> on paper. Does your perspective surprise you? You will read this aloud
> to a partner.

Individualist	Systemic
One is born into the world and "makes her own way." Economic and educational success are primarily matters of innate ability and one's character.	Socialization, policies and relationships are very important. History, identity and one's given socio-economic status (working-class, middle-class, etc.) are directly relevant to their educational and economic paths and successes.
Wealth and poverty are primarily the result of moral behaviors and "character."	Wealth and poverty are primarily the result of systemic policies and social conditioning.

Individuals can make their own way if they try hard enough.	Material and social environments are very important determinants of one's success.
The ideal for government is a meritocracy in which individuals can help themselves with a minimum of interference. A minimum of governmental interference leaves "an even playing field."	The ideal for government is social justice, which must be ensured by ongoing recognition of how systemic injustice is historically produced and "wired into" social relations and governmental policies.
Stories of success that show people rising from humble circumstances to become successful are inspirational and important.	Collective recognition of systemic problems followed by collective efforts to address those problems is important.
Worthy individuals can transcend their environments mostly through ambition and hard work. The individual can accomplish whatever she wants if she sets her mind to it.	Environments constrain possibilities and shape ambitions and habits. The "individual" and her possibilities are, in part, shaped by her ecology.
Solutions to problems should concentrate on reforming individuals: teaching responsibility and character.	Solutions should concentrate on addressing systemic inequities through the political process.
There is always room at the top, and good policies enable one to get there if one really wants it bad enough.	The top requires a wide bottom for its existence, and policies and social norms go a long way toward ensuring that poverty is perpetuated.

At the end of the semester, as Paige reflected on this conversation and period of the class, she writes that her journal

> continues with the idea about work ideals with [a] discussion of the American work ethic. It seems as if this essay is right on target with the ideas that I had at first about work and what it can give you. This essay, however, explores that idea a little deeper by talking about education, affording clothes for an interview, and character. In this journal I delve deeper by addressing that ideals truly are unattainable if you do not have the means necessary to achieve them. This is an important factor that comes into play again in the journal reflection about being a believer in a systemic system (9/20). In this [journal entry] I acknowledge that it would be ideal to live in an individualistic world where every man can work up the ladder toward the American dream. Keeping with my original thoughts from my first journal,

I default to the idea that people cannot escape the vicious circle they are stuck in. . . . Here I discuss education and how that determines what job market you are prepared to enter. I also discuss luck, and how those who do break the chain of labor they are born into are truly an oddity in the labor market. My ideas remain consistent with my initial reflections, but as I learn more and read more I begin to associate other elements to the idea about the unattainable ideal.

Paige brings her perceptions of her working life and experiences into a critical dialectic with her perceptions of, and work in, education. She finds contradictions there that are both consequential in her own life and not easily resolved.

As a working student who is trying to better her economic circumstances at an urban university, Paige is hardly alone in today's education scene. If Horatio Alger's "Ragged Dick" were written today, young Dick would almost certainly continue to display a strong work ethic, moxie, and boundless optimism on his path to success. However, the fast-capitalist Ragged Dick likely wouldn't follow a trajectory in which he learns a trade and then works his way up in a particular business. Now a requisite step on his path would likely be a degree at a two-year college or a regional university. Moreover, if Dick is a non-native speaker of English, this path might include a detour at some point to gain adequate fluency. Despite many broad changes in the character and perception of higher education over the last thirty years, it continues to hold a place in the public imaginary as an accessible economic and social equalizer. It is seen as a place that is somewhat removed from day-to-day economic survival, where deserving people might "catch up." It is both deeply rooted in the American ethos and a part of the myths of opportunity that drive immigration. Film dramas about high school students from underprivileged families, like *Real Women Have Curves*, typically end with the deserving going off to a happily-ever-after at a university. In the popular television show *America's Extreme Home Makeover*, scholarships for children often take their place among the goodies from Sears and Pottery Barn that are given to families that have fallen on hard times. Like the wedding in a Shakespearian comedy, entry into the university *is* the happy ending. The economic challenges that still plague many students through their educational trajectories and beyond—along with the deeply emotional, powerfully socializing experience of class—are magically shed as students pass through the ivied gates. This image of the university as a path to economic success carries its own powerful metanarrative. It exerts a strong influence on the discursive space of our classrooms; it is an integral part of the marketing of contemporary higher education, and it is linked to the literate development of our students. The ways that students feel comfortable constructing themselves in classes, what they talk and write about, the languages they use when they talk about it, and the value systems they feel compelled to adopt in their writing—all are shaped by where they think they are and what they think they should be doing there.

Not only do most postsecondary students work, according to a recent National Center for Education Statistics (NCES) study—for many, school is even on the margins of lives that center primarily around families and work. Among those whom the study characterized as "highly nontraditional," the majority (67 percent) considered themselves "primarily workers" rather than students.[1] In contrast, only three percent of traditional students self-identified as primarily workers. All nontraditional students are more likely than traditional students to primarily self-identify as workers (National Center for Educational Statistics 2006, 29). Like the majority of the highly nontraditional students in the NCES study, my own students' school-related work is juxtaposed daily with significant hours at jobs.[2] Most students are also already workers, have developed deeply entrenched, complicated identities as workers, and

---

1.   The NCES categorizes a "traditional" student as one "who earns a high school diploma, enrolls full time immediately after finishing high school, depends on parents for financial support, and either does not work during the school year or works part time" (2006). Nontraditional students have the following characteristics:

- delays enrollment (does not enter postsecondary education in the same calendar year that he or she finished high school);
- attends part time for at least part of the academic year;
- works full time (thirty-five hours or more per week) while enrolled;
- is considered financially independent for purposes of determining eligibility for financial aid;
- has dependents other than a spouse (usually children, but sometimes others);
- is a single parent (either not married or married but separated and has dependents); or
- does not have a high school diploma (completed high school with a GED or other high school completion certificate or did not finish high school).

Students are considered to be "minimally nontraditional" if they have only one nontraditional characteristic, "moderately nontraditional" if they have two or three, and "highly nontraditional" if they have four or more.

2.   NCES findings on the overall picture of work among postsecondary students are summarized in chapter 1.

see higher education as a way out of current circumstances. Getting this far in their educations has meant overcoming many challenges beyond those presented by coursework. Jenny, a twenty-two-year-old senior classmate of Paige's, works as a server in a restaurant. She has had seven jobs thus far—in retail, childcare, and as housekeeping staff in a hotel. She writes: "I wouldn't change anything about my work history, because the crummy jobs inspired me to work somewhere better and made me appreciate my subsequent jobs more. My current job makes me happy for now, but it is not something I want to do forever and that inspires me to do well in school and get an even better job." At one point, she quit school and worked two jobs for a year. Nontraditional and first generation college students leave college without getting degrees at significantly higher rates than traditional students and those whose parents were college graduates (National Center for Educational Statistics 2005, 14–15). They thrive within, endure, or just eventually give up on institutions that often do not actively recognize their lives and experiences.

Literacy is interwoven with immediate economic and educational imperatives, and work inside and outside of the university is a part of a broader political economy that confers potentially contentious meanings, values, and identities. If writing is social, productive work that is solicited, enacted, and valued at particular locations, its positioning within its immediate socioeconomic networks and material surroundings is essential to both pedagogy and research. In this chapter I will argue that examination of the terms and significations of fast-capitalism and casualized labor—for instance, what it means to be an "associate" at a retail store, a "contract worker" at a cable company, or an "adjunct writing instructor" in an English department—can lead to more nuanced understanding of how the work of the people who labor under these labels is positioned within the broader economy. These terms can reveal much about how discourse is tied to the everyday material; how it signifies who does what under what circumstances; and how labor, literacy, and materiality are bound up in a dialectical process of identification among writers. I begin with a theoretical framework drawing on Pierre Bourdieu, Lev Vygotsky, and Mikhail Bakhtin that enables an understanding of how identities are formed dialectically in relation to cultural artifacts.

LOCATION AND IDENTITIES IN "FIGURED WORLDS"

As I argued in the introduction, "process" has largely become appropriated by the bureaucratic architectures of FYC and the constraining administrative goals and apparatus that sustain it. Among the most salient features of what might broadly be called the "post-process" movement in rhetoric and composition are its focus on power, location, and institutionalism—on the material spaces of articulation. It "foregrounds the writer's situatedness in history and in his or her writing practice; and it makes visible the 'apparatus of the production of authority' that all writers tend to submerge in their discourse" (Olson 1999, 12). Foucauldian, it is not a naive rejection of authority, but a recognition of how authority derives in particular writing contexts, including within educational settings. Where the writer writes and for whom—i.e., "location"—is therefore profoundly important, as are the immediate circumstances of textual production. Bruce Horner envisions writing classes where students and teachers might examine the historical, social, and institutional foundations of rhetorical conventions and what he calls the "social material conditions of process" (2000, 35). Other recent work brings globalization into the frame of analysis, further complicating the conceptions of literacy that inform writing courses at institutions that primarily serve nontraditional students. Opening up to the broad social realities of writing in fast-capitalism means accounting for and accepting the inevitability of constant evolution and hybridity. For instance, LuMing Mao examines the complicated "border zones" that form the intersection between Chinese and European American rhetoric. Mao's own experiences within this borderland inform the ways he approaches literacy in the writing classroom. Mao explores with his students Western and non-Western ways of reading and writing—fostering understanding of, and sophistication with, multiple literacies. Using language as a starting point, this conception of writing pedagogy consciously situates itself in relation to globalization and the discourses of diverse workplaces, and therefore resists being centered in any genrecized discourse (like "academic writing").

Min-Zhan Lu similarly points to examples that illustrate that English is being used around the globe and is constantly hybridizing, relentlessly changing in particular contexts that bring multiple languages and cultures into play. Lu characterizes this hybridization in economic terms, arguing that the needs and values of global capitalism significantly define the terms of language use and writing pedagogy (2004, 43). Even pedagogies that are informed by multiculturalism and an awareness of multiple literacies can be subsumed by marketplace prerogatives in often unrecognized ways. Lu therefore advocates an interventionist pedagogy for composition that fosters awareness of "relations of injustice":

To intervene with the order of Fast Capitalism, it is the responsibility of Composition to work with the belief that English is enlivened—enlightened—by the work of users intent on using it to limn the actual, imagined, and possible lives of all its speakers, readers, and writers, the work of users intent on using English to describe and, thus, control those circumstances of their life designed by all systems and relations of injustice to submerge them. (44)

She argues that we should see writing education as a way of helping students to "compose against the grain" of the dominating and totalizing discourses of fast-capitalism (46).

Mao and Lu point toward a more radically social pedagogy that situates itself within the global economy of fast-capitalism. Other work that I would also call more radically social emphasizes personal transformation, and like Lu, these scholars are not afraid to assert social justice as a primary concern of writing education. This work ruminates on the purposes of writing pedagogy in ways that show a disaffection with what had became the normal science of the field during the social turn. Specifically, it redresses the field's inability to sustain a discussion of how to do politically engaged pedagogy when it rejected expressivism and embraced a more postmodern view of discourse and subjectivity. Essentially, the practices that shape identity formation fell out of the concerns of many writing pedagogies as adaptation became a primary goal. Much of this work takes a second look at Paulo Freire—understandable, given the historical centrality of Freire to the more overtly political articulations of pedagogy that emerged in the field in the 1980s, but then became the object of scathing critiques in the 1990s. In a recent *College English*, for instance, Robert Yagelski describes a general drift away from political engagement in the field that seems to have paralleled its rejection of expressivism. Addressing the dismissals of Paulo Freire and the disdain for critical pedagogy that became common over the past decade, he counters, "I cannot see how we can justifiably teach writing in ways that reinforce an unjust and unsustainable status quo, nor can I imagine how Freire's message of literacy as a transformative act can be considered irrelevant in the face of deeply troubling developments that raise hard questions about the status quo." Yagelski describes a general lack of consensus in rhetoric and composition concerning *the purpose* of writing during a politically charged and troubling time in which the "struggle [for a broader purpose in writing pedagogy] may have more urgency now than at any time in recent memory" (2006, 533).

Also focusing on finding purpose through engaging more directly with politics in writing pedagogy, Jessica Enoch points to the often overlooked political aspects of Kenneth Burke's pedagogical philosophy, arguing that it should be contextualized within the cold war tension and paranoia of the early 1950s. Enoch links Burke to John Dewey and Freire, and shows that he is not advocating an intellectually distanced critique, as has often recently been assumed, but is rather conceptualizing a pedagogy that leads to critically, politically engaged praxis— action with language. Burke offered his approach as a counter to the increasing tendency to see education in overtly capitalistic terms, specifically as a way of conditioning students for a culture of competition. Burke pointed out fifty years ago that American schooling centered on competition: people learn to compete for grades, then for jobs, and then for power—perhaps on a global scale. Burke "warns that this daily competition can easily translate into rivalry on the national level, where 'national differences' may become 'national conflicts'" (Enoch 2004, 280). Enoch argues that Burke's pedagogical theory can be used as a means of critically examining with students the root societal causes of war—with an eye toward political transformation.

Shari Stenberg similarly describes her desire for a greater sense of purpose and political relevance in the field's approach to pedagogy. Lamenting the lack of "ethical and moral focus" in an intellectual environment that often dismisses the idea of positive historical transformation as a relic of modernity, Stenberg argues that the now well-worn critiques of Freire's humanist-driven pedagogical models have provided little by way of a replacement that is capable of persuasively accounting for and appealing to the emotional lives and moral and spiritual sensibilities of students (2006, 277). Thus, ironically, the desire not to force a particular politics onto students has actually led to a loss of connection with students along personal, moral grounds—we conceive of writing as a form of social action, but we avoid (political) questions of where and why to act. As a means of connecting with students and finding a deeper sense of purpose with them in writing pedagogy, Stenberg advocates liberation theology, which has roots in both Catholicism and leftist political movements in Latin America.

Also drawing on liberation theology, Carl Herndl and Danny A. Bauer advocate what they call a "model of confrontational performance and articulation." They describe a rhetoric that doesn't cater to the assumptions on which exploitive and unjust social structures are founded. It is unabashedly confrontational, as it "seeks to expose the working of hegemony by disrupting common-sense consensus and asserting powerful alternatives to the dominant social formation. It makes apparent what 'normal' discourse obscures: the political, ideological, and metaphysical work of discourse" (2003, 570). Herndl and Bauer's rhetorical model discerns the degree to which subjects "come into being" through writing (581). It recognizes that social dynamics are inextricably bound with the processes of naming—process that are enacted against the backdrop of, and perhaps in conscious opposition to, the cultural dominant:

> When those who had been excluded from the traditional norms of the universal usurp that position and speak as enfranchised subjects, the performative contradiction exposes the exclusionary nature of the conventional norm of universality and broadens the definition, creating a new space and subject position for the previously excluded. (577)

They therefore call upon teachers and students to create a new discursive space and subject position—to "come into being" in politically creative and dynamic ways.

These scholars are, in various ways, locating literacy education. Much of the discussion of "location" in rhetoric and composition has focused on creating relationships between postsecondary institutions and the communities within which they are situated. Service-learning approaches, for instance, are usually centered on reaching out from the institution to the community in some way. Recent discussions of narrative, however, are also concerned with positioning students socially. Ann Robillard, for instance, examines narrative tendencies in working-class students, relating them to a sense of time and trajectory through education. She positions her argument against conceptions of academic discourse that seek to isolate students and their writing in academic settings—in a sense making higher education the limit of the discursive universe, denying the embodied histories of our students. Renee Moreno argues that in the present political climate we must see the literate education of people of color in relation to politically reactionary institutions that are hostile to diverse literacies (see also Sullivan 2003). This work demands that we turn the focus back on our institutions themselves, examining their relationships with (and positions within) a local political economy that shapes literacy and learning. How is any particular educational institution a part of the broader political economic process practices in its locale?

Pierre Bourdieu (1977) and Dorothy Holland, William Lachicotte, Debra Skinner, and Carole Cain (1998) have articulated very useful theories of how identifications form, continually and dialectically, through practice. Bourdieu has become particularly popular in educational and rhetoric-and-composition research of late because his work offers a means of accounting for how social structures shape identity without making those structures homeostatic or overly deterministic. Bourdieu transcends a general tendency to create a false dichotomy between "mechanism and finalism," pointing out that we don't really respond to situations mechanistically, according to explicitly stated instructions or rules—such as they might appear in organizational policies, religious dogmas, or codes of conduct (mechanism). Nor do we, in our everyday lives, pursue clearly identified objectives strictly according to objective plans or explicitly prescribed roles (finalism). Rather,

> the structures constitutive of a particular type of environment (e.g. the material conditions of existence characteristic of a class condition) produce *habitus*, systems of durable, *transposable dispositions*, structured structures predisposed to function as structuring structures, that is, as principles of the generation and structuring of practices and representations which can be objectively "regulated" and "regular" without in any way being the product of obedience to rules, objectively adapted to their goals without presupposing a conscious aiming at ends or an express mastery of the operations necessary to attain them and, being all of this, collectively orchestrated without being the product of the orchestrating action of a conductor. (Bourdieu 1977, 72)

"Transposable dispositions" are formed through practices within social environments and are also perpetuated though social practice. They compel particular agents to respond to situations according to how they have self-identified. The identification also evolves through the response. So the identification is socially formed, but the full range of particular events one encounters in real life can never be anticipated— the responsive actions themselves are interpretive and adaptive. Identity is neither determined nor fixed: it is a general disposition, always evolving and being shaped through practice.

Two aspects of Bourdieu's approach are important to emphasize here and will reemerge later in this chapter. The first is that he is careful not to mark a clear distinction between the internal/personal and the external/social—a proper understanding of identification and sociality for Bourdieu transcends the distinction between the two. We internalize the assumptions that prevail within our social environments, but we also externalize and alter—we are both product and variously creative producers of the social. Second, Bourdieu distinguishes most responses or "moves" from what he calls "genuine strategic intention" (73). The term "strategy" suggests a broad perspective that recognizes a correspondingly broad range of possibilities, and conscious choices made among them. "Moves," in contrast, are made according to perspectives that have been substantially overdetermined by those socializing "structuring structures." An example might be a violent crime in which someone is injured: a person who self-identifies as a "policeman" will respond with a different range of "moves" or habituated responses than a person who self-identifies as a "medical doctor." A less obvious example might be how two people from different socioeconomic classes respond to a waiter approaching a table at a posh restaurant. "Genuine strategic intention," in contrast, suggests a more metaconscious and thorough analysis of a particular situation, and responses calculated to produce more explicitly identified goals. Genuine strategic intention therefore means that an agent is not only negotiating her identity in dialectic with her surroundings, she is to a certain degree aware that she is doing so and making choices and acting accordingly. It therefore connotes a degree of control and agency. So Bourdieu's conception of the social recognizes people's agency, but it also shows how possibilities—for understanding, knowing, and action—are continually shaped by deeply ingrained habits of socialization. It is "moves" that get us through typical days: we don't often act with genuine strategic intention.

Moving from Bourdieu to discussions of specific processes of identification, Dorothy Holland et al. also offer a useful way of thinking through how students encounter "figured worlds." The term "figured worlds" references the recursive relationship between identities and institutionality, and Holland and her colleagues illustrate how this happens in day-to-day practice. Their studies show various agents negotiating identities: through narrative in Alcoholics Anonymous, through an unofficial but deeply engrained lexicon in romance, through an official lexicon in psychological diagnosis, and through caste position in Nepal. They parallel these figured worlds to educational institutions, arguing that the common signifiers and euphemisms of educational bureaucracy are an important part of how identification occurs among students, and they therefore significantly shape both actions and perceptions of possibilities. As with Bourdieu, the relationship between societal structures and consciousness isn't cast as overly deterministic or static. Nor are people constructed as free agents acting according to will or biological disposition without significant social conditioning. They locate a flexible middle ground between a "culturalist" perspective (that views culture as the clothes that are placed on humans that remain the same in all contexts) and a "constructivist" perspective (that sees humans as highly culturally malleable, like liquids that can be poured into bottles):

> We can discern at least three interrelated components of a theoretical refiguring of the relationship between culture and self. First, culturally and socially constructed discourses and practices of the self are recognized as neither the "clothes" of a universally identical self nor the (static) elements of cultural molds into which the self is cast. Rather, differentiated by relations of power and the associated institutional infrastructure, they are conceived as living tools of the self—as artifacts or media that figure the self constitutively, in open-ended ways. Second, and correlatively, the self is treated as always embedded in (social) practice, and as itself a kind of practice. Third, "sites of the self," the loci of self-production or self-processes, are recognized as plural. (Holland et al 1998, 28)

Holland and her colleagues' reference Bakhtin and Vygotsky as they articulate a dialogic, practice-centered theory of identification. Bakhtin's dialogism is connected to Vygotsky's social model of learning and identification, as language is understood as deeply entwined with the formation of consciousness.

Articulation to others and to ourselves is how selves are formed. The formation of self plays out in "figured worlds," frameworks within which perceptions are dialectically formed in day-to-day practice, a process they call "self-authoring." Figured worlds are therefore spaces of authoring that both enable and constrain the possibilities of understanding and articulation. Neither overdetermined by external factors nor formed by independently acting agents, figured worlds are "coproduced" through the "activities, discourses, performances and artifacts" that one experiences, encounters, and enacts in everyday life (Holland et al 1998, 51). Identities are an ongoing outcome of people's efforts to identify within figured worlds.

In Holland and her colleagues' Alcoholics Anonymous case study, new members are initiated through a combination of factors: common readings that help to form a common conceptual vocabulary (Bill Wilson's *Big Book*); close relationships with fellow group members, including a sponsor who assumes a mentoring role; and, perhaps most importantly, the sharing of stylized narratives that conform to a generic pattern and form the basis of the self-identification of "alcoholic" (Holland et al 1998, 66–97). The identity "alcoholic" is *co-produced by* this complex of artifacts. Through hearing the "stories" of others, and then eventually constructing their own stories within the narrative genre that has been established within the organization for sharing, new initiates learn to adopt the self-identification of "alcoholic." One's history and behaviors are made sense of through the lens of this "figuring world," and current and future behaviors and responses are shaped by that ongoing, dialectical identification within the framework of the group. Another case study illuminates how the identities and behaviors of college-age women are shaped, in part, through romantic relationships and perceptions of attractiveness. Women in the study classified men according to a commonly held vocabulary—"brains," "jerks," "jocks," and so on. They also classified each other according to such terms as "Susie sororities" or "dumb broads" (102–3). Though seemingly superficial, these terms were nuanced and prescriptive of behaviors—a part of a broader process of socialization that powerfully shaped identification and decision making. Women's self-identifications, identifications of other women, and behaviors with men were negotiated in relation to these terms. Holland and her colleagues take a Vygotskian approach to understanding this process, one in which

> thoughts and feelings and motivation are formed as the individual develops. The individual comes, in the recurrent contexts of social interaction, to personalize cultural resources, such as figured worlds, languages, and symbols, as means to organize and modify thoughts and emotions. These personalized cultural devices enable and become part of the person's "higher mental functions," to use Vygotsky's terms. (100)

This is how their mode of analysis joins Bakhtin with Vygotsky in a very persuasive and generative model of analysis. They articulate Bakhtin's unceasingly dialectical "space of authoring" as an aspect of Vygotsky's "zone of proximal development." Bakhtin's discursive, dialectical conception of identification relies on a conception of identity as a fluid "position" rather than a fixed and knowable point. They thus describe the self as a part of an active dialectic,

> a position from which meaning is made, a position that is "addressed" by and "answers" others and the "world" (the physical and cultural environment). In answering (which is the stuff of existence), the self "authors" the

world—including itself and others. . . . The authoring self is invisible to itself. The phenomenology of the self is, in Bakhtin's terms, characterized by "openendedness." Because the self is the nexus of a continuing flow of activity and is participating in this activity, it cannot be finalized. It cannot step outside of activity as "itself"; the self as it reflects upon its activity is different from the self that acts. In Bakhtin's view, the self-process must be dialogic. (173)

Vygotsky had shown that learning does not proceed along singular, individualized trajectories, as Piaget might have us believe. Rather, it takes place in radically material, radically social environments. Learning is varied, responsive, and mediated socially by "cultural artifacts," a term that is used quite broadly to reference particular objects, the configuration of environments, and even language. Learning is fostered by activity in "figured worlds." New elements from our daily lives enter into our consciousnesses and eventually become a part of our deep consciousness—our basic frameworks of understanding, identification, and behavioral response. This is what Vygotsky terms "fossilization": we perceive and do without being conscious of why we perceive and do in that particular way (117). Bakhtin adds to Vygotsky through exploring the particular ways that discourse and dialectic contribute to this process. Importantly, figured worlds aren't just created by immediate social and material artifacts, they resonate with their own histories. Doing their own social archaeology of the deeply habituated assumptions concerning gender and relationships that manifested in their study of the figured world of college romance, Holland and her colleagues arrive at the tradition of courtly love. Courtly love has complicated roots in politics and culture that stretch back a thousand years and involve European as well as Eastern elements. The study shows how women's status within relationships with men, as well as their perceptions of love and gender roles, are significantly shaped by the courtly tradition. They also discuss the political functions of courtly love, uncovering how the tradition has been used in historical struggles for power.

To summarize, a few general characteristics of figured worlds are important to how I am articulating writing and writing education here:

- A theme that plays out through the studies is that identities are plural *within* particular people. While people may struggle to define themselves singularly, they actually maintain different identities simultaneously as they move through the various

spheres that constitute their lives. Identity thus has a perpetual
"openendedness," and it is not only evolving, it is multiple and
contingent. It is also innately dialogic, continually involved
in the process of being addressed and responding. Discursive
modes that are still commonplace in standardized writing pedagogies—like traditional, form-driven approaches to argumentation—discipline this tendency through encouraging singular-
ized voices that carry out safely limited purposes.

- Identification and learning are tied to historical, cultural, and
  material artifacts. We build ourselves and our worlds out of the
  materials that are available to us. Holland and her colleagues
  use Levi-Strauss's concept of *bricoleur* in their explanation of
  language as an ideologically loaded material of social construction. The self-author "builds with preexisting materials.
  In authoring the world, in putting words to the world that
  addresses her, the 'I' draws upon the languages, the dialects,
  the words of others to which she has been exposed" (Holland
  et al 1998, 170). Creativity is thus at once enabled and constrained by the available "stuff" of daily life. The languages and
  discourses we use encourage certain situated self-conceptions
  and discourage others.

- Identification and articulation are thus innately tied to history
  and politics. We act within historically figured worlds, and we
  reproduce them and change them with our own actions.

- Bourdieu's "genuine strategic intention" comes out of some
  degree of awareness of the elements that are shaping our identities and behaviors at any given time. This awareness and the
  measured agency that can come out of it can be gained through
  consciously engaged historical and ideological dialectic. The
  ways that figured worlds are figured can only be illuminated
  when we understand their historical contingency and juxtapose
  them against alternatives.

THE FUTURE PERFECT: MARKETING NARRATIVES OF SUCCESS

Students are compelled by the cultural tropes, marketing aesthetics, and
disciplinary norms of higher education to adopt identities that seem to
derive from its figured worlds. To what extent do these figured worlds
mesh with the working, already actively economic lives of students where

other "figuring worlds" might prevail? To what extent are these identities consciously brought into dialectic in educational settings in a way
that fosters "genuine strategic intentions"? In my experiences, students
in English classes might discuss "race" and "gender," Richard Wright
and Virginia Woolf—but they are less likely to write from and about
their own daily, somatic, routinizing experiences of race and gender
working at Neiman Marcus, McDonald's, Wal-Mart, or Hooters. These
worlds also constitute the "stuff" of literate development and identification. They are certainly figured and figuring too—by carefully crafted
public images, by corporate cultures calculated to rationalize behaviors
through training and everyday work procedures, and by specific social
interactions at particular job sites. Likewise, identification in school settings, if examined at all, is probably more commonly relegated to the
realm of representation: the embodied, historical position from which
one identifies and examines remains largely obscure.

Karen, quoted at the beginning of this chapter, sees education as a
chance to move on, and she finds a measure of comfort in feeling superior to her managers and in the belief that she will, at some point, be
in a more powerful position than them. It is notable that she juxtaposes
her identity as a student with her identity as a worker. She is casting
herself as at once the subordinate of her manager (within her work
framework) and his superior (due to the educational trajectory she feels
that she is on). She seeks the strength to endure in one world from the
promise she thinks her efforts in another are creating. She works at a
nationally known retail store she chose to call "Format." As part of an
assignment, she wrote a thick description of a day of work at Format and
then reflected critically on that day. She is required to learn the names
of all of her fellow employees, but she found that "nearly impossible
because it seems as though new people are hired every two weeks." She
complains of indifferent, revolving-door managers as well as sexism.
When examining the language of her employee handbook concerning
equity and sexual harassment, she finds that there are material practices
that are disturbing but fall outside of what is explicitly described as
"sexual harassment":

> Another policy that I am faced with on a daily basis at work is not in the com-
> pany handbook. It may not even be at any other Format store besides ours.
> However, this informal, unwritten rule is quite noticeable within the specific
> store in which I work. My store manager, who I will refer to as "Kevin," has

his own personal method of evaluating potential employees. Although he does evaluate potential employees according to their abilities and work references, he also looks at how physically attractive he perceives them to be. Kevin will not, and never will, even consider hiring a person who in his eyes is unattractive. When he does come across a potential employee who he sees as unattractive, he simply says that they are not Format material.

Karen finds it ironic that while the policies concerning financial issues in the employee handbook are quite specific (for instance, the policies concerning employee discounts), the sexual harassment and equity policies are very general and brief. Notably, she herself never explicitly labels Kevin's behavior as "sexist," and her description of his hiring practices never reaches the level of condemnation. The description constructs the practice as more of an annoyance than a violation of rights.

Among female students' descriptions of their workplaces, behaviors and policies that could easily be labeled sexism on the job are quite common. However, this sexism is rarely personalized or overtly politicized in students' descriptions. Rather, it is accepted as a normal and inevitable part of the common terms of employment on their jobs. This is a primary theme that emerges in analysis of students' work autobiographies—in contrast with their research work, which I address below. While specific instances of sexual harassment are labeled as such, more systemic sexist behaviors and policies are not personalized in the autobiographies, nor are they explicitly challenged as the natural prerogative of employers. Natalie, who makes eight dollars an hour working in the women's shoe department at an upscale retail store, also mentions the pressure on her and her female coworkers to dress well:

> The dress attire at work is business professional with a trendy spin. Our managers expect us to wear trendy clothes and that is due to the fact that I work in the [shoe department] which is more aimed toward teen-agers and the young adult clientele. Often times we are asked to keep up with what is in Fashion Magazines and put outfits together based on that. "Trendsetters" is a key word in my department. Since I work in shoes I use it as the perfect accessory. For me, I will not put a limit on how much I will pay for a pair of shoes, but I try and find clothes that are less expensive.

A concern with appearance incorporates the bodies and identities of these low-paid women into the overall branding/image-making schemes of many of their employers. Their wages and positions make them working class, but they are expected to dress as though they can afford expensive clothes. What is being conveyed to customers within this figured world? That these women make far more than they do? That their primary financial support is coming from someone else—perhaps a man? This body-branding is also a part of how retailers consciously attempt to shape the behaviors and thinking of their employees. A surprising number of female students who work in retail indicate that they are pressured by their employers to buy the clothes at their stores. Sharon says that she is required to dress as a "hip surfer girl" when she goes to work at a mall clothing store for young people. In the figure of the consumer-worker-model, identity, labor, and consumerism are bound together. Katrina, who works at another clothing store, relates a de facto dress requirement to her own self-esteem, competence, and worth as a worker:

> The dress code is not strict, although the guidelines for dress are quite clear. We may wear any color we wish, including other brands of clothing, providing the label of the other brand does not show or is not prominent. In theory, employees could get away with never wearing our company's clothes as long as the labels on our clothes do not show. In reality however, that is a different story. I recall one specific day in which my manager I will call "Charlotte," hassled me about not wearing any clothes from our store. I had only been working there a few days so I did not have adequate time to purchase many articles from the store. Additionally, since our clothing is rather expensive, I did not have an abundant supply of their clothing to choose from in my ward-robe. That day I had chosen a tasteful outfit to wear to work that looked as if it could have at one time come from the store. As I walked through the glass doors, I was ready to work and felt good about the way I looked. I approached Charlotte, my manager, to find out what tasks needed to be completed that day. The very first words out of her mouth as she looked me up and down were, "Don't you own any _____ clothes?" in a condescending tone. I was taken aback by this comment. Questions began to run through my mind in an attempt to decipher the message she was trying to convey to me. Hadn't I dressed fashionably? Didn't my clothes look as though they came from _____? Weren't none of my clothing labels showing? Hadn't I followed the dress code guidelines? I eventually came to the realization that although the dress code did not specifically state that employees must wear _____ cloth-ing, the managers made it a priority to convey their preferences of employees that did wear the company's clothes.

Workplace policies and cultures obviously have a significant influence on these young women's lived experiences as women. By the time they enter a postsecondary classroom, gender has already powerfully shaped the types of employment they seek and find, how they are perceived and treated on jobs, and how they dress and conduct themselves in professional settings. Moreover, their working lives are already deeply intertwined with the figured world of market-niches and branding. Karen has learned that one's conventional attractiveness can make the difference in whether one gets a job. Sharon, Katrina, and Natalie have been oddly positioned as both workers and consumers by their employers, who pressure them to buy clothes that strain or break their bank accounts. Meanwhile, through their writing, "student-selves" work in ongoing dialectic with "worker-selves."

How is writing education in postsecondary institutions positioned in relation to these working lives—how does it function in the overall process of identification of oneself and how one's labor is situated in the economy? How does the trend toward positioning students as consumers shape the identification of students and their perceptions of the character and possibilities of education? Just as with the young women working in retail, we might see the media/marketing/curricular creation of the "college student" as a transposable disposition, a figured way of seeing and responding that is shaped by the cultural artifacts of higher education. In spite of dramatic changes in the landscape of higher education over the past three decades, a particular ideal or aesthetic is still a deeply entrenched part of the popular imaginary—and it continues to shape the public faces of our institutions. My own university's Web site, for instance, portrays students living and learning within a calm, cloistered environment. Aerial photographs depict the campus as an enclosed space dominated and buffered by green. While the internal space of the photographs is new buildings, the surrounding area is forest and athletic fields—visually suggesting a high-tech, intellectual oasis. Students of different races appear in a montage of pictures in various studious and social tableaus. They sit on grass, at benches, in front of computers, or in classes; they walk with friends and play intramural sports; they work in labs and go to basketball games—"student life." The site doesn't completely obscure the fact that the university is in an urban setting. Pictures of the city's skyline and its professional football stadium are included in the campus tour photos. Nevertheless, the general impression created by the Web site, as well as in much of the university's recruiting materials and fund-raising publications, is of students living and learning in a pastoral, at least somewhat protected, space. This is space designed to enable bright people to think and work creatively, engaged with the problems of "the real world" but still not quite "of" them in a day-to-day sense.

I do not believe that the university's depiction is dishonest. It is an attractive campus, and this depiction of campus life doubtlessly helps enrollment and fund-raising. People expect an institution to put its best foot forward in public presentations. Parents, students, and donors are more likely to feel comfortable with a university that plays on the common conception of what a college campus "should" look like: a calming, familiar blend of contemporary and Gothic (or perhaps colonial) architecture and students who are relaxed but engaged. A modern, urban skyline on the distant horizon in some of the photographs only suggests vibrancy, relevance, cutting-edge technology, and the promise of prosperity—the best of both worlds. Our campus is less than fifty years old, and much of it has been constructed in the last twenty-five years. General public conceptions of what a university should look like merge with the university's need to create a campus that is both functional and appeals to that public expectation. This "place" is created by a complicated mixture of cultural expectations, functional needs, and marketing strategies. It is not only structured by deeply embedded cultural perceptions of what a university should be, consistent with the market-driven logics of fast-capitalism, it is consciously constructed with branding and marketing in mind. Building facades, walkways, natural areas, and student activity centers anticipate the expectations of students and parents of college life.

More typical than not, however, my university is not a protected world separate from "the real world" of work and adulthood. Here, students and faculty are very much of our city and our region, and all of our daily lives are shaped by economic relations of production and consumption and the ideologically loaded discourses that sustain them. Ours is a public, urban university enrolling over 21,000 students situated in a sprawling, diverse metropolitan area of over 1.2 million people. Two very busy highways frame the campus and the intersection of two major interstates is less than five minutes away. The majority of our students are commuters, and large, concrete parking decks (along with expansive asphalt parking lots) dominate much of the perimeter of campus. In spite of its thinning green borders, the university is very much a part of the metropolitan region in which it is situated. Parking lots are ubiquitous because ease of access is important. Hurried students typically travel here by car or bus from jobs, or leave here for jobs when they are finished with their classes.

John Alberti has lamented that

> too often our discussions of the future of literary studies and pedagogy in higher education are limited by models of college life rooted in enduring but increasingly misleading images that take the experiences and practices of elite research universities and liberal arts colleges—more accurately, discursive representations of these experiences and practices that are themselves almost stereotypes—as the norm for higher education. (2001, 563)

Alberti points out that the overwhelming majority of students now attend what he calls "working-class" or "second-tier" schools.

While our "second-tier" campus is, to a certain extent, constructed to conform to popular expectations of what a college campus *should* look like, most of our students likewise don't fit the image of the college student from the popular media. Neither privileged nor particularly profligate, most don't party their free time away on fraternity row, few enjoy much leisure time or do a semester of study abroad, few have the space in their lives for activist politics, and few take raucous spring break vacations in exotic locations. Primarily first-generation college students from middle-, lower-middle, or working-class families, the majority of our students pay part or all of their own way through school with their own paychecks and loans. In addition to being students, for at least part of every week they are waiters, package handlers, fast-food workers, telemarketers, front desk clerks, office assistants, landscapers, retail workers, data entry clerks, nannies, baristas, and so on. Older students, many of them in our evening classes, sometimes hold more professional jobs as computer maintenance technicians, teachers, office managers, secretaries, and health care workers. In short, they are not preparing to enter the working world, they *already* help to constitute what the U.S. Department of Labor finds is the largest and fastest-growing job category in the United States, the "service-industry" sector. Most of the jobs created by the "new" or "information-age" economy are service jobs, and most service jobs are low-paying—nearly all of the new jobs created by 2016 will be in the service sector (U.S. Department of Labor 2008).[3]

---

3.   The largest number of new jobs created by 2016 will be in nursing, followed by (in order) retail sales, customer service representatives, and food preparers. A report recently released by the Department of Education focuses on increasing the number of graduates with technology skills, but various economic studies suggest that

As with most other large, public universities, the university employs high numbers of adjunct faculty, who also fit their schoolwork into lives that may include other jobs and classes at other schools. The school's advertising doesn't foreground the fact that we employ large numbers of part-time teachers who make two thousand dollars per class, don't get health benefits, can't afford regular dental care, and are one serious illness away from financial catastrophe. Photographs that accurately depict the daily lives of our students and the majority of our writing faculty might also depict them on gridlocked streets and interstates, searching for spaces in parking lots, or working in cubicles at offices or behind counters at coffee shops—living lives that are anxious, pinched, scattered, and already very "real." The hard-edged realities of casualized teaching labor and commuting student service-workers clashes with the traditional, dreamy aesthetic of higher education as protected, separate, gentrified space. Writing from and about the material conditions of their lives requires students to make a conscious effort to confront, or at least negotiate, the figured worlds of university and student life that are pervasive in media and encouraged by the marketed aesthetic of the university.

However, I don't think that the material conditions of students' lives are a common starting point for inquiry and writing at the university. I think that most of their intellectual work moves smoothly downstream from a traditional conception of education and student life. Certainly, textbooks genericize the student writer, and most do little or nothing that recognizes that students have both jobs and financial concerns that include, but also move beyond, paying tuition. The overwhelming majority of undergraduates will never publish anything academic, but they nevertheless are compelled to write reams of "academic discourse" for the same reason that mall visitors are funneled down spacious hallways with polished faux marble floors. The untidiness of one's lived experiences in the outside world is kept safely at bay. Unfortunately, the term "nontraditional student" often still seems to carry at least a measure of implicit disparagement wherever it is used in academia. It is not a gelled identity in the popular or the professional imaginary. Indeed, in my experience, when colleagues use the term it is a precursor to the identification of some limitation or inconvenience—even reflective of a measure of disappointment with their own careers. The

professional-level, high-tech jobs are already scarce. The category "computers and software engineers" is fifteenth on the Department of Labor list.

implicit assumption is that "nontraditional" is inferior to "traditional." New faculty from graduate programs at more exclusive universities are warned by some new colleagues that they will have to get accustomed to "the students here" in the same tone that white colonial settlers might once have been warned that they will have to adjust to life in the bush. When students' lives enter the picture in often inconvenient ways—for instance, with a child care issue, a transportation issue, or a conflict between a work schedule and an out-of-class activity—it is an intrusion on what is imagined as the proper work and aesthetic of higher education. Meanwhile, teaching jobs at elite universities are scarce and "traditional" college students are now far from average. According to the NCES, in 1999–2000, only 27 percent of undergraduates could be correctly classified as "traditional." Indeed over the past thirty-five years, the entire profile of students has changed considerably. Since 1970, undergraduates have gotten older (39 percent are now older than twenty-five) and more female (56 percent versus 42 percent in 1970). More students are now also part time (39 percent versus 28 percent in 1970).

First-year writing programs continue to be sustained through genericized conceptions of students, academia, and academic discourse. Susan Miller has critiqued the "presexual, preeconomic, prepolitical" juvenilized subject of composition (1991, 87). She argues that this generic writing subject—though far from the reality—has provided a kind of stability for composition's theoretical discourse. The generic student-writer has been a common subject around which curriculum could be built. Writing education remains innocuous and detached, and "composition" maintains a staid and therefore solid, if also paradoxically marginal and subordinate, place in curriculums. The figured world of student life remains largely unproblematized for some very practical reasons. It is difficult to standardize pedagogical approaches that conceive of students as already consequential, already working in a real economy, and already facing the day-to-day challenges of economic survival. Poverty and economic justice may sometimes be the objects of study, but they are less often studied as critical ongoing factors in the present lives of students—a vital part of their experiences and literate development. Meanwhile, students will pursue their lives in the future within the same fundamental political economic framework that creates the conditions within which so many already currently struggle. Pursuing the aesthetic, widely marketed ideal of postsecondary education therefore requires a stubborn tunnel vision that denies, or at least brackets off, many of the harsh realities of work and education in the fast-capitalist economy. We might see the subject positions that students are invited to occupy by particular writing assignments and genres—as well as by programmatic goals, like "learning to write academic prose"—as yet more kinds of transposable dispositions, more means of ameliorative social formation and political control.

"ASSOCIATES," "STUDENTS," "CONSUMERS," ETC.

Many of the important, persistent questions for writing teachers center around the authorial position that our students feel invited to occupy and the subjects that they are encouraged to investigate and write about. Understanding this positionality requires that students gain awareness of, and their own perspectives on, the political economic discourses that shape their everyday lives, at work and at school. Among the characteristics of fast-capitalism is that it has further blurred the lines between education and work. Education and the marketplace exhibit more synergy. Higher education is increasingly explicitly marketed as a form of job training, and it is now more generally constructed in consumerist terms. Likewise, management theories promoted in business schools and best-selling books reflect a sophisticated understanding of the relationship between language, identification, and increased loyalty and productivity. In other words, they resonate with an understanding of language, culture, and the formation of consciousness that has formally been more exclusive to humanities departments.

This phenomenon has been examined in much research over the past decade. For instance, in the influential *The New Work Order: Behind the Language of New Capitalism*, James Paul Gee, Glynda Hull, and Colin Lankshear describe a broad tendency toward discourse-driven social engineering in fast-capitalist business practices. Drawing on research from a training program at a technology firm, they argue that policies and procedures in the contemporary workplace aren't just geared toward managing the behaviors of workers that are directly associated with productivity: they are consciously, unapologetically designed to "indoctrinate"—to change thinking and social habits, even identities. These changes are brought about, in part, through the conscious manipulation of language as a habituated aspect of day-to-day social interaction and as a means of understanding ourselves and the world:

What we are really talking about here is a textual creation of a new discourse
. . . with new social identities: new bosses (now "coaches" and "leaders"),
new middle managers (now "team leaders"), new workers (now "associates",
"partners", "knowledge workers"), and new customers (now also "partners"
and "insiders", who are said to drive the whole process). (1996, 26)

Gee, Hull, and Lankshear go on to characterize this discourse as not
only "imperialistic" but colonizing, poised "to take over practices and
social identities that are (or were) the terrain of other Discourses connected to churches, communities, universities and governments" (26).
The spreading of the discourses and practices of neoliberal economics
into higher education has been the subject of much discussion of late.
David Noble, for instance, notes the increasingly active presence of corporate brands—Burger King, Coca-Cola, Pizza Hut, and so on—on university campuses. Others point to the direct impact of legislative funding
changes designed to harness more of the work of higher education for
private industry (for instance, Martin 1998; Miyoshi 1998; Slaughter and
Leslie 1997). Still others, like Michael Apple, Jill Blackmore, Derek Bok,
and David Geoffrey Smith, note the pervasiveness of market discourses
within discussions of goals and administrative processes in higher education. This work generally describes how "students" are increasingly
construed as "consumers" and education as product within discussions
of administration and curricular goals.[4]

In practice, the boundaries between the "real world" of adulthood
and work and the otherworldly state that still characterizes popular
conceptions of the university is muddied to say the least. The conflation of "student" and "consumer" in education is similar to the
conflation of "associate" and "consumer" in retail. As the discourse
of the fast-capitalist marketplace subsumes the discourses of higher
education, production and consumption are brought into one, more
tightly bound, framework. The creation of a critical space from which
one might examine the broader circumstances of production and
foster a more empowering understanding of consciousness, identity,
and alternity—i.e., strategic intention—is made less likely. Important

---

4.   It should be noted that this shift in higher education is not recognized just by those
      who advocate resistance or point to its shortcomings. A considerable number of
      books, like Frank Newman, Lara Couturier, and Jamie Scurry's *The Future of Higher
      Education: Rhetoric, Reality, and the Risks of the Market* (2004), construct this shift as
      inevitable and either advocate its acceleration, or (in the case of this book) argue
      for its inevitability and advance strategies for managing it.

choices with profound pedagogical ramifications are made not through open, informed deliberative processes among informed scholars, but at the largely invisible level of institutional and curricular architectures. Service-economy jobs and higher education function according to the logics of the new political economy. Both rely on marketed images to at least partially conceal day-to-day material realities. Many universities sell a gentrified ideal of college life for the same reasons and according to the same logics that the Gap uses thin, conventionally attractive models to sell its clothes. Students and teachers are compelled to enter the university looking to assume a new life and identity just as they might when they buy a new outfit: for marketing purposes, "hip surfer girl" becomes "hip coed." Likewise, a part-time teacher who may never have attended a departmental meeting and may have no advanced credentials in the subject she is teaching becomes a "professor."

This structuring also works at the level of local economies. The casualized economy of fast-capitalism relies heavily on part-time, "flexible," and temporary labor—and full- and part-time "students" supply a significant portion of that labor. Moreover, the economy increasingly relies on higher education for ongoing professional training. According to Stanley Aronowitz, 13 percent of the American workforce attends some postsecondary institution (2000, 28). While the higher average age of students over the past thirty years is, in part, explained by the expansion of access to higher education, it is also explained by a labor market that pushes anxious adults back into higher education so they can make themselves more competitive for decent professional jobs. Discussing the broad social ramifications of ongoing changes in management structures and capabilities enabled by erosions of workers' rights and rapid advances in communications technologies, Evan Watkins connects emerging managerial philosophies with technology and displacement in fast-capitalism. This displacement is related to the changing role of higher education in the political economy. As Watkins describes it, "What the new flexible production has made possible is that it is no longer necessary to utilize explicit coercion against labor at home or in colonies abroad. Those peoples or places that are not responsive to the needs (or demands) of capital, or are too far gone to respond 'efficiently,' simply find themselves out of its pathways." Using a new term for what Marx famously identified as the "lumpenproletariat," Watkins calls those workers whose technical skills have become outdated or whose labor is too expensive for a casualized economy "throwaways" (1998,

67). In the very influential *Post-Industrial Lives: Roles and Relationships in the 21st Century*, business sociologists Jerald Hage and Charles H. Powers famously distinguished fast-capitalism from industrial-capitalism in terms of the continual and anxious adaptation required by the latter. Hage and Powers equate human labor capacity in fast-capitalism with the machinery of industrial work, warning that "rapid growth in knowledge not only makes products obsolete, but also means that human capital depreciates quickly" (1992, 39). Always "depreciating" workers must continually update their skills in order to be of value to employers. "Retooled" workers are those that have "updated their knowledge" of areas of specialization as well as the new technologies that are common within chosen professions. When living "post-industrial lives" people are constantly at risk of becoming "unskilled," and skills themselves function as a type of commodity. When moving toward being "unskilled," workers must anticipate the new knowledge they will need and adapt accordingly—or risk quickly becoming victims:

> The technological elimination of unskilled and semiskilled jobs means that a great many people will be caught in a world of despair, lacking marketable skills or hope for the future. That translates into what Marx referred to as the *lumpenproletariat,* an underclass of unemployed or marginally employed individuals living under dire circumstances and surviving by whatever means possible. (1992, 41 [emphasis in original])

Hage and Powers predicted that ongoing fears of falling into an underclass will change not only a variety of social institutions (including education), but also human consciousness itself. "Lifetime education" may, on the surface, seem desirable for those of us who work in higher education—but large numbers of older, "working-age" people going back to school is actually among the outcomes of an economic system that leaves much of the American workforce in a state of perpetual insecurity.

Most student-workers spend part of each week working in low-end jobs that can offer little agency, recognition, pay, or even stability. During the other part of the week students attend classes in institutions that offer the "bait and switch" promise of escaping these "dead-end" jobs even as they reinforce the basic cultural and economic logics that create them. In the context of higher education, the dead-end job of the present doesn't often come into full focus as the subject of legitimate examination and critique. Students' identities and worker identities remain juxtaposed, but aren't often brought into critical dialectic. Work remains on the margins of curricular focus, unvalidated and unexamined, but looming nevertheless as a kind of morality play boogeyman, the impetus for betterment and the cautionary consequence of a lack of ambition and hard work. The implicit goal is to escape it—to adapt to a seemingly immutable environment, rather than to critique it; to become as aware as possible of the forces that shape one's circumstances and consciousness; and to imagine how they might be more just, equitable, and democratic.

WRITING THE POLITICAL ECONOMIC

In the remainder of this chapter I am going to outline a highly dialectical approach to teaching and writing work in composition that seeks to recognize and address some of the deep contradictions that characterize postsecondary writing. A dialectic approach that focuses on political economic structures can highlight opportunities for more strategic intention as it foregrounds the question: how do students' lives as workers and how we do our work in writing education "figure" writing and writers? I have developed a writing class that focuses on work as an ongoing aspect of students' lives as well as the many issues associated with work in the contemporary political economy—from economically driven immigration to welfare-to-work policies. I have built the course from a variety of very helpful models. Ira Shor discussed the importance of examining labor throughout his work, but provided a particularly strong rationale in *Critical Teaching in Everyday Life* (125–54). James Zebroski (1994) describes a very useful model for a writing class centered on the theme of work with considerable depth in *Thinking Through Theory*. I have also participated in conversations concerning work as a theme with fellow members of the Working Class Studies Special Interest Group in listserv exchanges and at a CCCC workshop.

In these classes, my students write about their own lives as workers, they interview others about aspects of the work they do, they examine the discourses of work on the job and at school, and they research broad topics that shape the terms of work in and out of education. The assignments I have used vary and evolve, but generally I start with a thick description of a day in students' working lives or with a "work autobiography." Then students move to essays based on interviews that they do with workers. Group-centered research projects follow, which center on topics that students have generated out of the personal explorations and interviews. Students have explored a variety of topics, including globalization, women in the workplace, the history of the labor movement, labor practices at Wal-Mart, and economically driven immigration. Along the way, they do daily writing, common reading as well as reading for their research topics, and synchronous online discussions. The general trajectory is designed to encourage students to connect the terms of day-to-day work in and out of school with general policy/political issues. In the terms of the political economic as described in the introduction to this book, it brings the micro into dialectic with the macro. Class emerges as an outcome of political economic processes and power (rather than exclusively as a social identifier) or a means of "understanding oneself" outside of the material and the social. John Alberti, Martha Marinara, Shirley Brice Heath, and Amy Robillard have all addressed how working-class students' working lives and perceptions of work can alienate them from their writing selves in academia. This is certainly intertwined with retention problems among nontraditional students. Heath points out that working students often don't feel full identification as students—many dip into and out of higher education to suit immediate needs. Robillard points to "a strong disconnect between the self that works and the self that attends classes." I am very interested in how that disconnect shapes and perhaps undermines what we are trying to accomplish in the classroom. I am interested in fostering dialectic between the self that works in the service economy and the self that attends the university in search of a secure middle-class life.

To be clear, this is a writing class in which the usual elements of process are taught and supported. We develop ideas for research and writing, we journal, we workshop and revise drafts for varying audiences and purposes, and we reflect on our writing and we develop writing portfolios. However, the class fosters an awareness of how articulation—the ways we "come into being" through language—are often overtly framed by political economic factors (Herndl and Bauer 2003, 581). It actively seeks to recognize the relationship between the writer, that which is written, and the immediate educational context within which this process is enacted. Writing is conceived of as a mode through which the writer reflexively struggles with the meanings and identities assigned within fast-capitalist configurations of production and education. In so doing, the pedagogy is designed to create the conditions for novel understandings and identifications. It is intended to highlight contradictions, not resolve them, and class is approached as a political economic (rather than a more purely social) phenomenon.

The first half of class is spent discussing, researching, and writing about issues raised in various readings that center around work. Assigned texts become platforms for discussions of the material present, what it is, and how we may have gotten here. Readings are intended to help situate "work" in American culture. I have assigned historical work from a variety of sources, including excerpts from Frederick Douglass's *Narrative of the Life of Frederick Douglass* and Max Weber's *The Protestant Ethic and the Spirit of Capitalism*.[5] Students locate more contemporary views of work from a variety of sources, including editorials, political speeches, and (of course) popular media.

We also do more contemporary readings. In different classes I have assigned David Shipler's *The Working Poor: Invisible in America*, Michael Zweig's *The Working Class Majority: America's Best Kept Secret*, and Barbara Ehrenreich's *Nickled and Dimed: On (Not) Getting By in America* or her *Bait and Switch*. Shipler's *The Working Poor* has resonated particularly well with students. Shipler relies on intimate profiles and interviews to depict the complex array of factors that contribute to poverty in America—among them, low wages, welfare policies, the cost of health care, poor financial decision making, domestic violence, drug addiction, language and cultural barriers, unequal education, the cost of housing, adolescent sexual abuse, and race and gender. Shipler's book complicates the myth of upward mobility through hard work that continues to play a powerful role in American political discourse as it chronicles the lives of people who simply are not able to pull themselves out of poverty through work. Interestingly, however, many students see aspects of their own lives in Shipler's stories—the book therefore can't be read with the same detachment as the works on most literary reading lists.

Finally, we read some of the narratives from *Gig: Americans Talk About their Jobs*. My students clearly find the working world depicted in *Gig* very familiar, and contentious, overtly political policy issues—like health care coverage, the right to organize, and the right to full-time employment—emerge out of discussions of the interviews. Research and articulation proceed inductively from the lived experiences of the political economic. On this point, I agree with David Seitz and Russell Durst, who

---

5.   John Alberti's reader, *The Working Life*, published by Pearson Longman in 2004, is a very useful text for this type of class. It offers excerpts from Franklin, Weber, and Adam Smith, as well as work from writers as diverse as Woody Guthrie and Nicholas Negroponte.

argue that critical pedagogies that examine work and the contradictions of "the American work ethic" have a much better chance of succeeding when we start where students are—at everyday embodied experience in the world of work and education. Discussions and research on the terms of work on particular jobs blossom into discussions of the terms of work and education in the fast-capitalist economy—how things are, how they have been, and how they might be.

Students compile their own work histories, write descriptions of jobs they currently hold or have held, and examine perceptions of work—how these perceptions are formed and how we might rethink them in light of our critical examinations. The professions covered in a single class can be very broad—from textile mill worker and oil changer to insurance lawyer, software developer, and real estate agent. These narratives become rich texts for classes. Through them, we analyze the discourses of work and the material terms they identify and often mask—including job titles, job descriptions, specialized jargon of various professions, and the surprisingly common terms that people use to describe the jobs they have held in their working lives—"between jobs," "shit work," "dream job," and so on.

During the second half of the class, we turn toward extended group research projects that center on work. Ideas for these research projects often come directly out of the students' work descriptions and interviews. One student who works as a telemarketer, for instance, complained that he increasingly calls households at which no one speaks English. He was frustrated because this wastes *his* time. A front desk clerk at a medical practice whose first language is Spanish complained about the rude comments that patients have made about her accent. Students had very contentious discussions of these experiences, and the contention is very much a part of the politics of our region, which has seen a rapid influx of primarily Hispanic immigrants over the past fifteen years. While some students discussed difficulties with, and resentments about, working with and among those whose native language is Spanish, others conveyed their shock and dismay when they witnessed incidents in which non-native speakers were discriminated against. Discussions about immigrants and language provided an opportunity to contextualize immigration in broader economic and political terms. While the discussion was fractious and even somewhat disturbing (there was no general, satisfying resolution), it did complicate the often overly simplistic assumptions that characterize most popular media treatments of immigration and work. Students researched particular, concrete questions—such as why immigration has been so concentrated in the Southeast over the past decade, and how educational and civic institutions might respond to non-English speakers. Among the interesting projects that came out of that course was a paper written by a woman about race and economics at a restaurant at which she waited tables. She interviewed a Hispanic busser, a cook, and a waiter, noting similarities and differences in biographies, perceptions of work, and education.

Other issues that students have researched in various sections of the class have included:

- Globalization—treaties, outsourcing, debates on points of view, effects on wages and local economies, policies on immigration, the impact of International Monetary Fund policies on the economies of developing nations, and immigration policy.

- Women in the workplace—salary disparities, choices of occupation, advancement, and balancing work and motherhood.

- The labor movement—history, current state of the movement, labor laws, and recent and ongoing confrontations.

- Wal-Mart—effects on local economies, labor violations, and reliance on public money and welfare.

- Education—"the achievement gap," the casualization of teaching labor in higher education, the role marketplace values and needs play in the shaping of curriculum, trends in federal aid for higher education, and the increasing use of contingent teaching labor in higher education.

The factors can also be very specific and personal, and the paths that students take in their writing are often very surprising. One student wrote about her own experience as a fast-food worker and related it to the documentary *Supersize Me,* incorporating some very interesting research on the fast-food industry. Her Web-based, multimodal project made connections between fast food and fast-capitalism, articulating a relationship between poor nutrition, quick calories, and life at the bottom of the economic ladder. Students that examined class and voting patterns created an interactive Web project that presented statistics showing the rate at which voter participation in elections declines with income levels.

Another student investigated voting patterns in an effort to try to understand why working-class people often didn't seem to vote in their own economic interests. She was surprised by the underrepresentation of African Americans among voters; this led to a larger project that linked incarceration rates among African American males with recent legislation in a number of states that made it illegal for convicts to vote. A group of students who were all born outside of the United States developed a Web site focusing on work and immigration. Among that group was a Vietnamese man in his mid-thirties who had started his own small business and a Philippine woman who, as a child, had been sent to the United States to live with relatives to expand her opportunities. Both discussed the difficulties of living, learning, and working in the United States and maintaining the cultural identities of their native countries. The Vietnamese man wrote about the growing gap between Americanized and non-Americanized generations in his family. He explained the difficulties that many new immigrants face as they adjust to life in the United States, and associated a willingness to quickly adapt culturally with the likelihood of relative economic success. The Philippine woman described the growing independence and confidence she had gained as a worker and student. This has caused friction with certain family members, as she is no longer willing to conform to their expectations for her gender. Her work became an examination of the contrasts between a work discourse within which she believes she is more culturally "American," and a discourse of home that she believes limits her in ways she finds increasingly unacceptable. Another student provided an overview of state and federal child support laws, and described her own frustrating struggle to collect the child support that the father of her young son owed. Her project became an examination of the relationship between this legal/bureaucratic discourse and the material realities of both parents' working lives.

HOW DO YOU SOLVE A PROBLEM LIKE SOPHIA?

In his description of the work of rhetoric and composition as material practice, Bruce Horner writes

> if we see the institutional location of the composition course and its inhabitants not as autonomous constraints on actors but as a location reproduced and potentially changed by actors through their practices, then the apparent marginality of that location has potential for both hegemonic and

counterhegemonic work. It is not necessary to somehow escape that location, or attempt to liberate students from it, because it is not separate from the "real world" but both constituted by and constitutive of it. (2000, 57)

While this inquiry-based approach examines work, it doesn't proceed as though the educational context within which we are all working together is neutral or not a part of the total political economic milieu we are seeking to understand and author. It recognizes that we start from an institutional location that, as Horner points out, is continually constituted by us. Therefore we also examine issues like our perceptions of "higher education," the marketing of our institution and its position in our region, the current terms of work in higher education, and the relationship between higher education and the economy.

In the following, I will share work written by a student who enrolled in a section of the course described above. I have chosen to present a problematic case rather than an ideal. I do not offer the work as systematically derived evidence of the success or failure of this approach. I offer it as a means of showing how a dialectical, open-ended approach can illuminate the interrelationship between genre, ideology, situatedness, and literate development in postsecondary writing. The work will show a writer locating herself in the way described by Horner in that she is doing both hegemonic and counter-hegemonic work. However, somewhat complicating what I take to be Horner's assertion, this student does the two simultaneously—asserting self-contradictory voices that ventriloquate the two realms of her everyday life: low-end service work and a student's work in higher education.

The student author is "Sophia," a junior who has worked as a waitress at Shoney's for five years since high school. In the first essay she wrote in the class, a work autobiography called "Maybe This Is My Destiny," Sophia indicates that she enjoys her work in the restaurant. While she makes only $2.15 per hour plus tips and receives no benefits, she nevertheless seems to embrace the role of the happy, if objectified, service worker who is helping her company and herself:

> To be honest with you, in a restaurant good food is not what makes a customer come back, it's how they are treated by their server. It was the determining factor of whether my customer was satisfied or not, and I did all that I could and more to make sure I gave 100% satisfaction. The key to the job was really smiling and being personable. Any customer can get over bad food or bad décor if they have a server that is friendly, jokes around, and acts like they are

interested in him or her. That is why I have never received a bad complaint, the restaurant maybe, but not me.

The rhetoric of this passage could easily be used in a training manual for new servers: her concern is for the satisfaction of the customer and the lack of complaints she has received, and vocabulary like "100% satisfaction," "smiling," "personable," "friendly," and "interested" describes service-work employees as they might be idealized in any training program or manual. Writing as a server in a restaurant, Sophia is speaking largely *from* the figured world of service-work, where she makes the money she needs to survive and pursue her goals, has no recognized identification with others in her economic position, and sees no value in recognition of the political factors that shape her work and relations. She is "a good worker."

In "Maybe This Is My Destiny," Sophia indicates that while all of her fellow waitresses are female, her managers are primarily male. She relates a conversation she had with a manager that, as she put it, "reveals just how sexist the restaurant business [can] be." When she asked one of her managers why all of the waitresses are female, "[he] told me that when most male customers come in they want to have a female server so they can feel like the dominant person. He said that sex sells, and having pretty servers tends to bring customers back." Interestingly, Sophia identified this as sexism, but also indicated that she wasn't particularly troubled by it:

(1) *I knew that this scenario was not politically correct, but once I thought about it I saw just how true it was.* Male customers flirt and compliment my co-workers and I all the time. All we do is smile and flirt right back. *(2) It is sad to say, but that is where most of my good tips come from, and I am not trying to change that as long as everyone is happy, enjoying their food, and not getting too aggressive or offensive.*

I see in Sophia's characterization of the restaurant business as "sexist" and her statement about political correctness mostly a genuflection to her academic context. In this statement she wants to make it clear that she understands how this behavior is to be characterized at the university, and her phrasing could even suggest that the essay serves as a kind of exposé. This is the voice of the working college student with one foot in the classroom, where issues like gender equity are a more serious concern. However, Sophia is only a college student for part of the week. During another substantial part, Sophia is a waitress.

The second statement exhibits a liberal individualist perspective as it is understood in the culture of fast-capitalism, one that sees little value in making connections between politics and one's own working life. As the essay develops, she writes largely from the figured world of low-end service work in the fast-capitalist economy. She accepts the situation as immutable reality, and claims that she is even willing to benefit from sexism that manifests as female subservience if it makes her more money. Sophia doesn't generalize from the situation about the plight of women or gender in the workplace. She was willing to excuse the sexism because of what she saw as its material "truth." An African American first-generation college student, she is earning money to support herself and pay for her education. She recognizes the politics of the situation and suggests that they trouble her, but she simultaneously dismisses this line of critical thought—a line that might lead to more "strategic" rather than purely pragmatic thinking. Adopting a familiar rightist technique of political censure, she suggests that naming her manager's thinking sexist is "political correctness." The implication is that examination of the situation from a political or justice-driven perspective—and perhaps asserting herself as a worker who is deserving of respectful treatment and fair compensation, regardless of gender or attractiveness—is not worthwhile. She claims that she is not offended by the manager's blatant sexism, or what is perhaps a more often latent sexism that permeates her work more generally.

Interestingly, for her research essay, Sophia chose to write about issues that women face at the workplace. While sexism on the job had been a topic that emerged in class discussions, she was not directly prompted to do research on that issue. She joined a group of three other women who chose for their class project to put together a joint Web site that examines women's workplace issues and provides resources for others interested in research or help with particular problems. Her first essay had been entitled "Maybe This Is My Destiny," but the second essay, composed for the Web site, was entitled "The Worth of a Woman." In it, Sophia takes a significantly more condemnatory view of sexism, and moves to a point of view that generalizes from personal experiences, rather than seeing them in wholly individualistic, apolitical terms. "Working women" becomes a generalized category for research and policy, and the perspective seems far more driven by a consciously politicized concern for workers' rights and dignity. She associates economic valuation with gender in both political and cultural terms.

She begins this second essay with a quote from the first:

"Most male customers come into a restaurant wanting to be served by a woman, so they can feel dominant in the situation," according to James Brown, general manager of Shoney's Restaurant. This sexist theory is not only offensive, but in many cases true. *(3) Being a server is typically a women's occupation, and it is an occupation where how much money you make often depends on your physical attributes instead of your personality.* This occupation, along with others, has been laid out as a choice occupation for women, and they are mainly the lowest-paying and least beneficial jobs in the labor force. When either a man or woman mainly dominates an occupation it is considered seg-regation in the work force, and this occurs even though women have more career options than before. Occupational segregation, which includes choice of occupation and wage disparity, is only one of the many discriminations that workingwomen endure in today's society.

Moving from the perspective of worker to academic research writer, Sophia expresses a sense of outrage, but it is qualified. The research that Sophia presents in this essay examines "wage disparity" and "wage depression" (terms she uses) in traditionally female occupations. Here she identifies sexism as a broad political and economic issue—tying it to occupational choices, wages, and systems of valuation. This is very different from the individualist stance of the first essay, where Sophia's identification as a woman only emerges when she relates how her gen-der helps her to make more money because men like to feel superior and flirt. In contrast, in the second essay she speaks largely from the figured world of higher education in a class that is discussing and writing about work and education. In Sophia's research essay, "workingwomen" becomes a category for research and policy, and the perspective is far more driven by a concern for workers' rights and dignity. She starts the essay from her own experience, but moves quickly to research that is statistical and policy-oriented. The overall tone of the second essay con-veys a sense of urgency about the problem of gender-based wage and job discrimination. Mostly gone is the rhetoric of loyal service, customer satisfaction, and adaptive self-entrepreneurialism. In this writing, she employs vocabulary from her reading like "gender segregated workforc-es," "employment conditions," and "government policy processes." She still, however, reinforces some of the viewpoints that she also critiques. In statement three in the passage cited above, for instance, she takes issue with how much money women make being based on appearance, but then says that it should be based on personality—essentially exchanging one beauty pageant attribute for another.

I see very important things happening in these two essays that have to do with genre, discourse, and the figuring worlds of work and school. Clearly the genres of writing invited by the two assignments encourage different points of view. The work autobiography assignment does not explicitly invite students to generalize about their experiences, nor does it ask them to use research. In work autobiographies, student authors very rarely generalize about their positions as workers or the circumstances of workers other than themselves. Likewise, they very rarely use terminology like "equity," "disparity," or "market" that indicates a macro perspective on the political economic or a concern with labor rights. Complaints are very common, but they are highly local and individualized, even when they can easily be generalized in a variety of ways and might be addressed within current labor law. This may be both a product of dominant individualist ideologies in the society at large, as well as the oft-cited tendency of the personal narrative genre (perhaps most famously critiqued by James Berlin [1988]) to reproduce the self-contained, self-interested, rational-choice-making capitalist subject.

The second essay, in contrast, is a "research essay." The assignment asks students to research a topic that comes out of their prior writing, class discussions, or class readings. Here the writing conforms more to students' conceptions of an academic research essay, conceptions that have been shaped over a number of years before they enter an upper-level undergraduate writing class. That conception has also been particularized within this class—by the assignment, by the readings and discussions in class, and by students' "readings" of what I value as their teacher. So it is shaped not only by the genre of the academic research paper—as it exists as a general form in students' imaginaries and how it has been described in this class—but also by a class that fosters the adoption of particular terminologies and critical perspectives. These essays are also shaped, of course, by the research that the students discover and bring into dialectic with their evolving conceptions of themselves and their work. While, as a teacher, I do much to try to ensure that multiple perspectives are represented and valued in the class, the class is certainly slanted toward a labor-rights, social justice point of view. It is therefore unwarranted to identify a radical transformation in Sophia's consciousness based on the contrasts between the two essays because they are written in progressive sequence. The writing in the second essay is just as "figuring" of authorial position, rhetoric, and perspective as that of the first essay. However, that figuring does enable alternative understandings that can generate new insights, especially when students are compelled to compare the two essays. This is an important part of how writing works as a social, dialectical process. As Sophia researches, writes, and engages in dialectic with others and her reading, she is seeing herself as a worker through different lenses—and those lenses are inevitably shaping her self-identification.

Describing how identification occurs from a perspective heavily informed by Vygotsky and Bakhtin, Holland and her colleagues work through the complicated interface between everyday language use and self-identification. Marx writes that "the human essence is no abstraction inherent in each single individual . . . in its reality it is the ensemble of social relations": importantly, Holland emphasizes that Vygotsky and Bakhtin were working from Marxist assumptions about identity and socialization (quoted in Holland et al. 1998, 35). The model of selfhood that informs their research blurs distinctions between the individual and her social context, describing learning and identification as fluid, open-ended, and highly dialectical. Identification is an ongoing, constructive process in which subjects use the available "tools" in their environment to work through who they are and how they should make decisions and act. Moreover, identification changes from environment to environment with social roles and their accompanying discourses. Selfhood is never completed nor contained. When Sophia writes from the position of waitress, though her writing shows evidence of awareness that she is in an academic context she adopts many of the characteristics of her work identity as she writes about her experiences. When she writes a research paper about gender in the workplace, she writes more from a position of scholar-researcher. Neither writing shows a unified "essential self," but both show her undergoing dialectical processes of identification that are tied to situated roles, conceptual vocabularies, and material contexts. She is a working student, and her self-identification is shaped by work at school and Shoney's. When juxtaposed, the worlds of education and service worker bring about many contradictions, but how do we make those contradictions *the object of study*? I opened this section with a question that is also a pun "How Do We Solve a Problem Like Sophia?" For the sake of catchiness, I chose the pun over what might have been a more accurate title, "How Do We Get Sophia to Focus on the Problem"—or the contradictions that shape physical and intellectual labor, power, and opportunity in her everyday life?

For the final essays in the class, I encourage students to adopt a multimodal form (though they have other options). At this point in the semester they have conducted primary and secondary research on a topic. They have written about their own experiences and critically examined the political economics of work and education through various readings and discussions. A multimodal format can enable students to incorporate conflicting or ambivalent perspectives from their work in the class as they work through their own, evolving thinking. The form therefore can foster the creative tension of dialectic as varied viewpoints, voices, and information are juxtaposed. As students blend research writing with narrative accounts of their own experiences, they connect the macro with the micro in interesting and often quite novel ways. The multimodal form gives students the opportunity to move out of the solipsism of narrative and the distanced, linear formalism of more traditional academic research writing. After reading Ehrenreich's *Bait and Switch*, Sophia was very concerned with the issue of job security, and she was asking interesting questions about the role of higher education in her own life and in society more generally. She begins her essay both with an articulation of that concern as the theme of the essay and with an explanation of the form she has chosen to adopt:

> When the parties have ended and you've said goodbye to your college buddies, will you be ready to enter the workforce? Will you have a job waiting on you with open arms? What if you ended up spending months searching for the career that your degree promised you? What if you landed the job of your dreams only to be sent packing with no reasons why? There are many college-educated people that have graduated without immediately landing a job, and even worse, there are many college-educated people that have been pushed out of white-collar employment, and forced to work minimum wage occupations. This could be you. Read on to find out why.
>
> For the final essay I chose to elaborate on the discussion of white-collar recession within the U.S. This is the idea that college-educated, white-collar employees are either being laid-off at high rates, or having difficulty finding employment. I chose the multi-modal format because I wanted to use personal narratives to illustrate the on-going problem that so many people are experiencing. My paper will be an eye-opener for college students that believe having a college degree is all they need to break into corporate America.
>
> Will this be your last resort?
>
> My mother always told me that the only way someone could get a well-paying job was by graduating from a college or university with a good record

and good grades. What if you knew beforehand that going through four or more years of college, and working hard to get your diploma would not guarantee your success in the workforce? Would you go through it? Would you spend the money on tuition and room and board just to find yourself in debt due to student loans, or would you resort to something else? My mother works for the U.S. Post Office, and many of her coworkers are college graduates, some of them even have Masters in a particular field of study, yet they are still working amongst people that never went to college and some that do not even have a high school diploma. Why is that? My mother does not have a college degree, but she makes good money and she is secure in her position, so why should I continue with my college education knowing that I could easily get a job just like hers?

Sophia draws on her mother's work experience to question her own desires and goals for her education. However, this isn't just personal narrative—already she speaks of wages, the present and future of white-collar labor, and the insecurity of the economy. She also explains why she chose this form for the essay, displaying an awareness of the relationship between form and function.

Barbara Ehrenreich's official Web site includes a public board that invites discussion of the experiences she relates and the issues she raises in *Bait and Switch*. Sophia quotes several of the contributors to this discussion board. One quote is from Bruce Swanson, who feels that education is not always the answer:

> I'm a math/chemistry teacher and I've worked as a college instructor, engineer, computer programmer, machine operator, shoe repairman and janitor among many. I also ran a labor union for a while as well at a church. (All true.) Education is the answer only when it is the answer. Right now, it is not. Even when it is, it is a myth that our educational system can deliver. The colleges do not train job ready people; they only produce good candidates for training. The reason for that is that most knowledgeable worker jobs or skilled trade jobs require at least a couple of years on the job full time using the tools of the job to become truly proficient. The educational system simply cannot provide that but the people who run it will never admit it. Education in this country is a great lucrative industry for those staffing it and they exploit the ignorance of the youth eager to work and accumulate. . . .

Among the remarkable aspects of this rhetorical move is that Sophia is finding commonality with other workers as she relates her own positionality with theirs. The form she has chosen invites this multivocality—but the shift is simultaneously conceptual and indicates a move away from the perception that workers' situations are individual toward a perception that economics are relational and collectively created and experienced. Sophia integrates the experiences of others with her own and then examines those experiences in terms of her research. Swanson, the person she quotes here, has not so ironically worked as a contingent college instructor and sees higher education as a piece of a broader economic milieu that is fundamentally insecure and even somewhat predatory in its relationship to the current economy. Sophia is connecting higher education to the "bait and switch" aspects of the current economy. The essay draws on extensive secondary research and connects trends in student loans, white-collar underemployment, and outsourcing—relating all of these factors to her own position as a soon-to-be graduated college student who works, has financed her own education, and has been motivated (in part) by the dream of economic security.

The essay includes elements of analysis, emotionally laden critique, and some alarming statistics about layoffs and the lack of availability of professional-level, high-paying jobs for college graduates. However, in spite of all this, the essay ends with advice for how motivated individuals can break into corporate America:

> In conclusion, studies have shown that having a college degree or higher may not always guarantee you a position within corporate America. While I am not implicating the idea that experiencing college life first hand is not worthwhile, I am issuing a warning for everyone that thinks having a college degree is the gateway to having a successful life. What was once a marketable attribute for any résumé, may not grant you the callbacks that you desire now. I do advise everyone to get involved with internships while in college. Having that experience can make transitioning from college graduate to corporate employee much easier and it can give you the opportunity to have a job after graduation. Most of the time in corporate America, it is not about what you know or how many degrees you have; it is about who you know, and how they can help you. Networking is often the key to success, and if you master that, along with your college education, then gaining a position within a reputable company should be no problem; just make sure that you have a last resort.

Sophia has not become a labor activist in this class. I see this conclusion in a number of ways. She might be said to be adopting a "bootstrap" or "isolated individualist" perspective—a perspective that we had critiqued as a group on many occasions. She warns her readers that a college education isn't "a gateway to a successful life" but she then offers some practical advice for heightening one's chances for success. This advice assumes the hue of self-help—it leaves collective, structural, and political change out of the equation. She speaks of "mastering" networking and gaining experiences through internships. Moreover, she puts faith in the trajectory from higher education to economic success, asserting that with networking skills, experience, and a college education "gaining a position within a reputable company should be no problem." The certitude of this trajectory is aggressively dismantled in *Bait and Switch*, which Sophia professes to admire.

Amy Robillard, in her treatment of the role of narrative in working-class life, notes a need for closure and positive outcomes in working-class narrative. There is a tendency to have faith in a future perfect in which hard work and diligence will be rewarded. The type of open-ended speculation with which academics feel comfortable in their own scholarly work may be uncomfortable for those who have come to higher education looking for security and a sense of control over their own lives. Robillard writes, "I know that my own need for closure could easily lead me to write trite narratives: and *then* and *then* and *then* and *then* a happy ending" (2003, 90). Writing of work memoirs in his own classes, David Seitz has framed this need for closure in the writing of working-class students in terms of the need for control "over their past and future work identities, over tensions between work and family life, over constraints of social class and gender" (2004, 216). Janet Bean similarly claims that "by casting themselves in the role of hero in a narrative of meritocracy, they affirm their ability to control their own lives" (quoted in Seitz 2004, 216). Sophia may very well be making a reflexive move toward security and control after raising such troubling issues in this essay. She still works at Shoney's and is still going into debt to finance her own education—it is understandable that she wants to feel as though she is still on the right track. The marketing of the university, its implicit and explicit promises of economic transcendence and a smoother road ahead, certainly contribute to this disposition.

Overall, Sophia's portfolio showed that she became a better writer in the class—more reflective, more rigorous in her revisions, more assertive, and more focused—in part, because she wrote about things that were relevant to her daily life and work. I could have structured this class and assignment in a way that would have helped Sophia to produce a tighter, more conventional, and seemingly more controlled and politically informed argument in the end that *I* found more satisfying. However, this risks having Sophia do school with me just as she does the happy worker role at Shoney's. Sophia is a writer who has used writing to engage in dialectic with others, complicate her own notions of her work inside and outside of the university, and situate herself with respect to the political economic realities of her position at school and on the job.

I admit that I nevertheless find where she ends up unsatisfying. The problem with this essay is that she wraps things up in a way that isn't true to the problems that it has raised. In the end, she couldn't, perhaps wouldn't, sustain focus on the deep systemic problems and contradictions she describes. Through critical thinking and a thoughtful assimilation of resources, Sophia creates a wonderful tension but doesn't rigorously follow through on it, opting instead for triteness and neat closure. I certainly don't have a problem with optimism in general, but I do when it is clearly denial. She began the class with an essay that sounded at times as though it was written by the ideal employee envisioned in a training manual. In between she asked very good questions, and did research that led her to some troubling revelations. But then she ended her last essay with a paragraph that reinforces the myth of success through hard work and education. I believe my task as a teacher is to keep the endings open, to keep the focus on the complications and contradictions. As Robillard puts it:

> As a writing teacher, I've learned to distrust the neat and tidy endings, the conclusions that look to a bright and happy future despite the contradictions and complications woven through the body of a piece. As a writing teacher, I've learned to distrust the very way of writing that is most comfortable for working-class students. (2003, 90)

The challenge is to continually find ways to help students write in dialectic with the discourses and social practices that shape our lives—to be true to their own discoveries and even their own anger and frustrations. Fostering dialectic means resisting quick, easy closures—those initiated by us and in various ways by our sponsoring institutions. As with many students, I do wish that I could have gone on with Sophia, having her respond to questions about this essay. Though I understand her desire for certainty, I don't think that a pedagogy of hope can ever rest easily with the kind of forced conciliation that Sophia seeks at the end of her essay. She still feels a need to seek biographical solutions to deep systemic problems. In the process she denies both important aspects of her own life, and the conclusions to which her own work and thinking in the class have led her. In my view, a more hopeful future lies elsewhere. Discovering alternatives requires a willingness to confront the economic logics and inherent contradictions of the very educational terrain in which we are all working.

Some of Sophia's classmates investigated labor justice movements inside and outside of the United States and found reason for hope without feeling compelled to write themselves back into a Horatio Alger narrative. One wrote of a movement in Argentina in which workers are taking over factories and managing them as collectives, not only successfully recovering the businesses, but sharing some of the profits with local communities (Lavaca Collective 2007). This is a movement of factory workers, but they are acting strategically in response to world bank policies that are decimating their communities and robbing them of opportunities. Another wrote of the general philosophy and activities of the Jobs with Justice coalition. Another investigated labor unrest at a company owned by Daimler-Benz and located near her own hometown in rural North Carolina—a company that she has considered working for after school. This project was a crash course in labor rights for a moderately conservative engineering student in a state in which less than 3 percent of workers are unionized. Five workers at that plant who were instrumental in its unionization were later fired for leading a strike, and the struggle of "the Freightliner Five" has become a popular cause among U.S. labor activists.

It is important to point out that I was able to structure a class around work, encourage critique of commonplace assumptions about the economy and labor, and create an atmosphere of rigorous debate in this class because I am a tenured faculty member whose credentials and expertise are recognized by his institution. I can afford to be critical of my institution, and if called upon to do so, I can make an informed defense of what I am doing in the classroom and why. My own risk level is very, very small. Many writing teachers don't have the latitude or institutional backing to feel comfortable doing what I do. Like many of the scholars cited in this chapter, I connect myself with a legacy that includes Vygotsky, Bakhtin, Burke, Freire, and hooks and risks seeing pedagogy in terms of a desire for social justice, or as Mark Wood puts it, "a better world." Is there still a place in rhetoric and composition at which we are willing to risk articulating our own contradictions, deep dissatisfactions, and even our angers? Do we then have the courage to risk and act upon our own utopian impulses?

5
WRITING DANGEROUSLY

Last semester Lindsay Hutton "taught" 1,940 students. She met only 70 of them in person. Those were the ones enrolled in the two weekly sections of English composition that she taught in an actual classroom. The hundreds and hundreds of others she knew only as anonymous numbered documents she read on her computer screen and then, with a click of a button, sent back out into the ether. . . . As one of 60 graduate students hired to teach freshman composition at Texas Tech University, Ms. Hutton had a weekly quota of grading.

"Sometimes," Ms. Hutton says, "it feels like a factory."

—Paula Wasley

The above quote describes a graduate student teaching in a university writing program at Texas Tech University called ICON (Interactive Composition Online). The quote is from an article in *The Chronicle of Higher Education* that describes the system (Wasley 2006). The ICON program relies on an interactive, computer-automated system that facilitates the distribution of a writing curriculum, the management of a composition staff, and the assessment of students' writing. According to the article, the system assigns two roles to the staff: "composition instructors" ("CIs") who meet once a week with a section of FYC students, and "document instructors" ("DIs") who grade students' papers from across all sections using an automated, blind system. According to the system's flowchart, CIs meet with students to

> discuss assignments and present general principles of grammar, style, and argumentation, and to discuss their weekly assignments, which are standardized across all 70-odd sections of the two required first-year composition courses. Each assignment cycle includes three drafts of an essay, reflective "writing reviews" commenting on students' own work, and two peer reviews of other students' work, all of which are submitted and stored online (A6).

The system thus brings uniformity to the curriculum and reliability and efficiency to the program's system of assessment and data compilation features. When students complete assignments they submit their papers electronically to the ICON system where each is graded by two DIs. The final grade is an average of the two. If the grades are more than eight points apart, the paper goes to a third DI, and ICON averages the two closest grades. The remaining role for people in this program is that of "faculty managers," who monitor CIs and DIs. Faculty managers use the system to track how much time DIs are spending on each paper, whether the grades are higher or lower than the average, and what types of comments they are giving each paper. If a DI is "falling behind" her quota, the system automatically generates an e-mail notification.

ICON is a number of things: a means of ensuring that a pedagogy is being consistently applied in all classes according to a predetermined set of standards and assumptions; a system of large-scale assessment and accountability; a technologized method of administrative surveillance, resource management, and data collection; and even a commodity, apparently under development for sale to other programs. Not unlike textbooks, ICON is a response to the challenge of teaching writing to large numbers of students using cheap and largely inexperienced academic laborers who don't have professional status. ICON, however, is more in line with fast-capitalist logics of authority, organization, and production for a number of reasons: it uses digital technology to organize and manage the labor of teachers and students who work at disparate times and in isolated locations; it maximizes managerial control through surveillance mechanisms and performance measurements, as well as through ensuring uniformity of important aspects of work (in this case assignments and assessments); and it seeks to address the problem of high turnover and low experience among a casualized labor pool through systematizing the work to such an extent that workers require little background or experience.

The system seems designed primarily to appeal to the interests of administrators who are not credentialed professionals in rhetoric and composition, but who are concerned with cost-efficiency and outcomes measures. ICON brings the work of students and instructors into one very standardized and predictable system that generates mounds of immediate data on student and instructor outputs. According to Fred Kemp, a designer of the system, writes Wasley, it "'produces 201 discrete searchable/sortable chunks of information' on students and teachers." Those who are in a position to do so can know "whether 8 a.m. classes turn in more late papers than 3 p.m. classes . . . whether a class is generating a higher than average number of comma splices or semi-colon errors than other classes . . . whether women comment differently than men. . . . " According to the article, Kemp dismisses critics of the system as "either Luddites with a visceral reaction to anything computerized or don't fully understand the system's operating principles" (A6). It is important to note here that Kemp is arguing on administrative grounds rather than on scholarly grounds. He puts the focus on what he believes are the positive attributes of the operations of the system, rather than on the assumptions about literacy and learning that are hardwired into it. Wasley goes on:

> "Simply to call it an assembly line and say, ipso facto, it's wrong, sounds like a 19th-century point of view," [Kemp] says. "Henry Ford built an awful lot of automobiles, and he made them cheap so that an awful lot of people could buy cars that couldn't have bought cars without the assembly line. So the idea that efficiencies within a system are inherently bad and dehumanizing, I think, is wrong." (A6)

ICON is not just a means of organizing labor and delivering a product, though: it is simultaneously a technocratic deployment of a particular philosophy of writing and learning. This is a part of what makes the Ford analogy inadequate. The "product" here, writing education, is dramatically different from an automobile—when one thinks of the varieties of students in one class of twenty, all of the varieties of legitimate pedagogies that might be employed in the class, all of the various paths of inquiry that might be pursued, the challenges and possibilities that might arise, and the varieties of texts that might be produced, the analogy breaks down very quickly. With ICON, the philosophy must necessarily synchronize well with a mechanized system, and substantive intellectual differences would counter the system's goals. There is no place for an unwieldy social constructivist viewpoint here. Among Kemp's frustrations with the prior system was that instructors "could not agree on either the content or character of good writing." Now those instructors who work in classrooms are expected to focus on "general principles of grammar, style and argumentation," and error counts figure prominently in the data collection. There is a general philosophy of language and learning in the design of ICON, however, and this is important. The philosophy is in the architecture. The description and the deployment of the system sidesteps explicit articulation and meaningful, consequential debate of that philosophy through emphasis on its managerial virtues. Indeed, efficiency is achieved by the system through its very thorough elimination of variance and considerations of its own philosophical contingency. In this directive system, theory is encountered always already deployed, hardwired into its structure: practices that are driven by assumptions that are certainly debatable, and may even be clearly out of step with contemporary composition research, are made settled fact by the technology and the directive operation it facilitates. The opinions and orientations of those who "instruct" and evaluate seem largely inconsequential. Moreover, in terms of this system, student writing also seems consequential to the extent that it yields data for the institution and grades for the students. Students' writing work is appropriated by ICON as a means of assessment and as data. It therefore ceases to be rhetorical in the sense that it is intended to make meaning for an audience (it ceases to be consequentially social), and makes writing an alienating exercise in assessment and data collection. What are student-teachers and student-writers learning about literacy and education from this system? In what ways and toward whose ends is writing enacted? Should these questions be answered in terms of pedagogical philosophy, administrative structure, ideology, or economics?

While I vehemently oppose what ICON does, it does *something* decisive in response to deeply intractable problems that are very common in writing programs across the country (which the designers of ICON did not create). That *something*, however, is to facilitate cheap operational efficiency (rather than confront it) and mask the considerable shortcomings of this response in the language of access, progress, and egalitarianism (a predictable, grammatically correct essay in every driveway!). However, I am not without empathy. WPAs are regularly charged with struggling to lend integrity and substance to large, low-status, low-budget enterprises that experience a high amount of turnover among teachers. I take my place among them. The problems are troubling and no path toward a more positive future is easy or itself unproblematic. ICON certainly has had its critics in rhetoric and composition forums, but in many ways it is only an extreme, technologized version of what already happens in writing programs where teaching and writing are shaped in largely unacknowledged ways according to logics of operational efficiency that operate with indifference to what is happening in scholarship in rhetoric and composition. Philosophies and tactics of program administration can similarly mask contradictions with substantial pedagogical consequences. Upper-level administrators look for ways to make operations at once cheaper, more responsive, and more measurable. WPAs, operating in the position of middle management, are often tasked with maintaining viable writing programs on skeletal budgets with overwhelmingly contingent faculties. Contingent teachers, many whose real status is much closer to retail workers than to vested professionals, are in many cases not entrusted with the agency to make fundamental decisions about the courses in which they assume the position of "teacher." Publishers opportunistically flood the market with textbooks that are designed to appeal to (and reproduce) a generic, philosophically antiquated but ideologically safe middle ground. Spurned on by the marketing of higher education, students at working-class institutions come to us precisely because they want a more economically secure life in an economy that is now characterized by its insecurity. The argument that I have made in this book is that the means of production is not separate from what is being produced. When Ms. Hutton says "it feels like a factory" she seems to be addressing what it is like to work as staff in the ICON system. Certainly, though, writing as a student in that and other highly rationalized programs also assumes a distinct industrial hue.

Much writing program administration discourse might best be called "pragmatist," a term Marc Bousquet uses (I believe rightly) in a controversial article in the *Journal of Advanced Composition* and also in a chapter in *Tenured Bosses and Disposable Teachers: Writing Instruction in the Managed University* (a collection I coedited with Bousquet and Leo Parascondola). Pragmatists generally frame the corporatization of higher education as inevitable and advocate either acquiescence to its inevitability or coping strategies that reflect a wariness of its effects but nevertheless seek to work within "the system" in order to achieve modest goals. Bousquet identifies this figure of the coping, deal-making WPA as the primary subject position of much of the WPA discourse. As the usual disciplinary narrative goes, the WPA describes the particular conditions that she or he is working under and then outlines adjustments and tactics that lead to some modest gains, employing a situated pragmatism that relies heavily on sophistry and canny resourcefulness. As the WPA appeals to the "bottom line" values of those who talk in terms of scalability and cost-cutting, she salvages what she can for quality pedagogy and working conditions.

Bousquet critiques both the model of professionalization around which this pragmatist discourse is centered and the more general strategy of having middle managers act in isolation for the benefit of those who are managed.[1] Among the problems he identifies with the discourse that positions the WPA as pragmatic hero is how it situates rhetoric and the project of writing pedagogy in relation to market logics. This is a very important point that was too often missed in the sometimes vitriolic and reductivist backlash that characterized responses to Bousquet's argument. Parsing through the various positions outlined by (among others) Richard Miller, Bousquet identifies the free market, liberal individualist ideology that is at the core of these pragmatist calls to "face the realities" of writing work in the contemporary university:

> In the pragmatist account, contemporary realities dictate that all nonmarket idealisms will be "dismissed as the plaintive bleating of sheep" but corporate-friendly speech "can be heard as reasoned arguments" (1998, 27). I find this language intrinsically offensive, associating movement idealism and social-project identities and activist collectivity generally with the subhuman, rather than (as I see it) the fundamentally human capacity to think and act cooperatively. (2004, 26)

Critiquing an administrative philosophy that centers on "corporate friendly speech," Bousquet further associates this administrative philosophy with a philosophy of rhetoric:

> More important than the adjectives and analogies [that bolster a corporate point of view], however, is the substructure of assumptions about *what rhetoric is for*. The implicit scene of speech suggested here is of "pleasing the prince," featuring an all-powerful auditor with values beyond challenge and a speaker only able to share power by association with the dominating logic of the scene—a speaker whose very humanity depends upon speaking a complicity with domination. (2004, 26)

Bousquet suggests an important, if still undeveloped, connection between rhetoric-in-action in the hands of WPAs and rhetoric as the subject and practice of writing pedagogy. Both can derive from an ideologically conservative "substructure" in their perceptions of the role of education and rhetoric. To return to Villanueva, "economies are carried rhetorically." Discussions of the economics of work in writing education—discussions that usually only take place in writing program administration forums—are too often discussions of crisis and response,

---

1.   A number of contributors to *Tenured Bosses and Disposable Teachers: Writing Instruction in the Managed University* make similar arguments.

of coping and maneuvering. Antiutopian and conformist at their core, these responses usually assume the form of "moves" rather than "strategies." A disciplinary ethos that promotes pragmatic, acquiescent strategies and rhetorics of administration that are adaptive to the point of self-negation are likely to tend toward pedagogical philosophies and programs that are similarly chastened in their views of the possibilities of education and writing. We are what we do, and at some point the conditions become such that we begin to do more harm than good in writing education.

As a WPA, I understand the lure, and sometimes the necessity, of pragmatism. In order to function as a program administrator in most medium to large institutions it is necessarily to sometimes be complicitous with administrative realities that we abhor: the reliance on part-time teachers is no small part of this. However, I also feel that it is essential to continually name the contradictions and inadeqaucies in our programs, scholarship, and pedagogy—to keep pushing the issues to the forefront and to be willing to make strategic, if controversial, moves to address them. This may very well mean, for instance, cutting back or eliminating first-year writing programs at many sites and concentrating on upper-division courses and majors. Pragmatism leaves the harsh, intellectually debilitating contradictions created by business as usual in postsecondary writing largely unacknowledged. There is therefore no thorough understanding of the ramifications of current practices, and likewise little basis for oppositional consciousness or action among colleagues. Indeed, lack of continual acknowledgement across the spectrum of our professional work—from departmental and university-level discussions of writing to the field's most influential scholarly forums—has the broad effect of naturalizing it. So situations rife with contradictions—for instance, that of a part-time teacher who has no health insurance and works as needed lending her alleged "authority" to students through the "process" pedagogy she gleans from an expensive textbook that is required for all of her students, who, themselves, are mostly part-time workers taking required classes—remain unacknowledged in scholarship and pedagogy.

MAKING WRITING DANGEROUS

The challenge is to find ways to situate ourselves, our work, and writing education within particular locations and under particular conditions that generate new insight and transformative action. This action should

be undertaken with a careful understanding of how administrative decisions shape teaching as a profession and teaching and writing as practices. I ended the previous chapter with a question: Is there still a place
in rhetoric and composition at which we are willing to risk a utopian
impulse? This question can't just be addressed in pedagogies enacted
by tenure-track faculty in the relative bubbles of their own classes, or in
conversations among scholars in specialized realms. It will need to be
addressed with respect to the broad ecologies of writing education—to
labor practices and systems of valuation, policy framing, and material
resources, all of which are aligned according to ideological assumptions.
Rhetoric and composition professionals need to develop a stance and
corresponding vocabulary that both recognizes how administration,
research, and the embodied acts of teaching and writing are integrated,
and that strategically positions that integrated dynamic in relation to the
political economics of higher education.

James Paul Gee, Glynda Hull, and Colin Lankshear argue that literacy
education should evolve to account more fully for relationships between
discourses and social practices within the varied spheres of people's
lives: "Learners should be viewed as lifelong trajectories through these
sites and institutions [work and educational], as stories with multiple
twists and turns. . . . As *their* stories are rapidly and radically changing, we
need to change *our* stories about skills, learning and knowledge" (1996,
6). This is a still largely unheeded call for an inevitably problematic
and even messy professional engagement that critiques and confronts
both academic and fast-capitalist discourses and practices. I am looking
for ways to make administration, teaching, and writing speak back to
the conditions of production, engaging in a critical dialectic with the
locations of their enactment. I am looking for ways to make writing
education consequential, immediate, responsive, and sometimes even
dangerous. What if we turned more of the intellectual energy of our
profession toward understanding and addressing how the economics of
higher education are shaping writing pedagogy? What if the immediate,
material conditions of the classroom became the fully acknowledged
context of the writing and learning that took place there?

I recently taught Gloria Anzaldua's *Borderlands La Frontera: The New
Mestiza* in a graduate rhetoric class. Rereading this remarkable book,
I was again struck by the following quote, which describes Anzaldua's
encounter with a dentist as a young girl:

"We're going to have to do something about your tongue," I hear the anger rising in his voice. My tongue keeps pushing out the wads of cotton, pushing back the drills, the long thin needles. "I've never seen anything as strong or as stubborn," he says. And I think, how do you tame a wild tongue, train it to be quiet, how do you bridle and saddle it? How do you make it lie down? (1999, 75)

Anzaldua worked in the hybrid intersections of language, politics, economics, history, and personhood: she learned to write dangerously. She connected literacy education to the immediate location of its practice, writing from her specific places and times. Her goal wasn't just communication, however, it was transformation—she wanted not only to communicate with her audiences, she wanted to challenge them, and she started by making language and the position from which she speaks primary points of contention. Rhetoric isn't just about adapting to contexts or appealing to the values of audiences. It is also about strategically transforming contexts and about challenging the values of audiences. Finding adequate means of expression in no single discourse or genre, Anzaldua invented her own hybrid discourse: a blending of dialects, languages, and forms. She framed her radically polysemic project in terms of tyranny and rebellion, positioning it against a masculinist culture that is heterosexual and white by default and always threatens to render large parts of her experiences and who she believes herself to be unarticulated. Her "serpent" literate practice is dangerous because it cedes neither history or knowledge as unchallenged givens—it refuses to be convenient or palatable. Rhetorical models are at once examples for partial emulation and opportunities for subversion and novel articulations. She argues that to assume the conventions of a discourse is to risk reproducing its ideological underpinnings, lending tacit support to the historical processes that have led to its ascendancy. Language is inescapably sedimented with the lived political struggles of places and times,

So, if you want to really hurt me, talk badly about my language. Ethnic identity is twin skin to linguisitic identity—I am my language. Until I can take pride in my language, I cannot take pride in myself . . . I will no longer be made to feel ashamed of existing. I will have my voice: Indian, Spanish, white. I will have my serpent's tongue—my woman's voice, my sexual voice, my poet's voice. (1999, 81)

Ngugi wa Thiong'o, an exiled Kenyan novelist, playwright, poet, and activist, similarly writes about the complicated psychologies of postcolonialism. Among the central themes of Ngugi work is the struggle of people to find a mode and language of expression within institutions, including educational systems, which have been forged in conditions of oppression. In his novel *The Wizard of the Crow*, a corrupt government official in a fictional African nation has become obsessed with mirrors and is only capable of repeating the phrases "if" and "if only" as he scratches at his own skin. He seeks help from a shaman, the "Wizard of the Crow," who tells him, "Words are the food, body, mirror, and sound of thought. Do you now see the danger of words that want to come out but are unable to do so? You want to vomit and the mess gets stuck in your throat—you might even choke to death" (2006, 175). When the shaman, who identifies himself as "postcolonial," enables this governmental official to complete his sentences, the patient realizes that the source of the "if only" malady is a deeply historical racial self-hatred, a strong resonance of colonial rule: "If . . . my . . . skin . . . were . . . not . . . black! Oh, if only my skin were white!" (179). Ngugi characters are often seekers of languages of personhood and politics, and the institutions within which they find themselves don't offer adequate answers or satisfactory means of expression. So characters' utterances are multivocal, and often contradictory and incomplete. A single utterance can include a ventriloquation of state power, a strategic movement from English to an indigenous dialect, or (as in this case) tortured omissions and truncated conversations that avoid dangerous realizations about history, power, and identification.

In his fiction and his cultural critique, Ngugi describes literacy education as a powerful means of interpolation. In *Decolonizing the Mind: The Politics of Language in African Literature*, Ngugi argues that

> education, far from giving people the confidence in their ability and capacities to overcome obstacles . . . tends to make them feel their inadequacies, their weaknesses and their incapacities in the face of reality; and their inability to do anything about the [material] conditions governing their lives. They become more and more alienated from themselves and from their natural and social environment. Education as a process of alienation produces a gallery of active stars and an undifferentiated mass of grateful admirers. (1986, 56–57)[2]

I wonder how accurate this description might be of writing education in the "working-class" or "second-tier" institutions that are the majority in higher education in the United States, where service economy rhetorics

---

2.   Also quoted in Moreno (2002, 222).

and logics shape the lives of students on the job and in the classroom. In our roles as teachers, scholars, and administrators, we need to find ways to recognize, account for, and address the political economic factors that shape our work in order not to reproduce "education as a process of alienation." Try as they might, Ngugi characters can never really be "post" colonial in the sense that they can escape their own histories. Likewise teachers and students in postsecondary classrooms cannot escape their own immediate and historical situations; we should turn fully toward them rather than deny them. Language use is always already active, alive with the ideological assertions and omissions carried in any discourse, and straining toward the author's purposes—no matter how expertly or awkwardly. Practices with language likewise don't proceed from privately held "attitudes" or consciousnesses: practices form consciousnesses which, in turn, shape practices. A more fully social view of writing subsumes subjectivity and textuality within a highly fluid, recursive process which embraces possibilities for agency and transformation—both of authors and audiences.

I write this book at a particularly troubled, and I think hopeful, time in American history. The rightist narrative of endless economic growth and democratization through globalization and liberalization of markets seems to have lost much of its pubic credibility with a brutal and costly war in Iraq, revelations of secret prisons and torture, continued growth in wage disparities, record levels of home foreclosures, annual increases in the numbers of people who have no health care coverage, a record national debt, and rising unemployment. This is a time when a socially and environmentally devastating political economic hegemony looks not so hegemonic. It is also a time in which there is a growing global awareness (and accompanying political movement, particularly in Latin America) of the weaknesses, contradictions, and injustices of neoliberalization. This is not a time for pessimism or defeatism concerning the possibilities for education or democracy. We can question old political economic paradigms, understand how they are shaping our educational work, and present hopeful alternatives in the classroom and in our programs. The fullest realization of the power of literacy and learning is far more likely to come about when we conceive of our identities and the identities of our institutions as dynamic, constantly evolving, and subject to being rewritten. The lashing tips of the "serpent's tongues" that might grow in the mouths of teachers and students might be directed toward the circumstances of their own labor and education.

APPENDIX A
Initial Questions

1. What textbook, or textbooks, do you currently use?

2. How long have you used it?

3. Why did you choose this textbook? What were the factors that shaped your decision?

4. Do you often change textbooks?

5. What is your educational background?

6. How many years have you been a college writing teacher?

7. How would you primarily self-identify yourself professionally? Do you see yourself as a part of any particular academic discipline?

8. What are your goals as a writing educator? Can you describe the philosophy or philosophies of language and learning that shape your pedagogy?

9. What research or theory has shaped your thinking about pedagogy? Can you identify yourself with particular theories or pedagogical trends?

10. Can you describe the general assumptions about, or philosophy of, writing and learning that seems to drive the textbook you currently use?

11. Describe the specific role or roles that this textbook (or textbooks) play in your writing pedagogy.

12. Do you think that the textbook lends authority to what you do? If so, how?

APPENDIX B
Code List

IDENTIFICATION

| I: | Professional | IP |
| I: | Imprinting | II |

TEXTBOOK CHOICE

TC:	Cost	TCC
TC:	Support	TCS
TC:	Validation	TCV
TC:	Quality	TCQ
	—Assignments	TCQ—A
	—Sequencing	TCQ—S
	—Readings	TCQ—R
TC:	Accessibility	TCA
TC:	Compactness	TCp
TC:	Textual Features	TCTF
TC:	Instructor's Manual	TCIM

AUTHORITY

A:	External	AE
A:	From Students	AS
A:	Vocabulary	AV

REFERENCES

Alberti, John. 2001. Returning to class: Creating opportunities for multicultural reform at majority second-tier schools. *College English* 63 (5): 561–84.

Anzaldua, Gloria. 1999. *Borderlands la frontera: The new mestiza*. San Francisco: Aunt Lute Books.

Apple, Michael. 2000. Between neoliberalism and neoconservatism: Education and conservatism in a global context. In *Globalization and education: Critical perspectives*, ed. Nicholas Burbules and Carlos Alberto Torres. New York: Routledge. 57–78

Aronowitz, Stanley. 2000. *The knowledge factory: Dismantling the corporate university and creating true higher education*. Boston: Beacon Press.

Atkinson, P. 1990. *The ethnographic imagination: Textual constructions of reality*. New York: Routledge.

Bartholomae, David. 1985. Inventing the university. In *When a writer can't write: Studies in writer's block and other composing problems*, ed. Mike Rose, 134–165. New York: Guilford.

Bauman, Zygmunt. 1997. *Postmodernity and its discontents*. New York: New York University Press.

Bawarshi, Anis. 2003. *Genre and the invention of the writer*. Logan, UT: Utah State University Press.

Bazerman, Charles. 1997. The life of genre, the life of the classroom. In *Genre and writing: Issues, arguments, alternatives*, ed. Wendy Bishop and Hans Ostrom, 19–26. Portsmouth, NH: Boynton/Cook Publishers.

Beck, Ulrich, and Elisabeth Beck-Gernsheim. 2002. *Individualization: Institutionalized individualism and its social and political consequences*. Thousand Oaks, CA: Sage.

Beck, Ulrich, and Elisabeth Beck-Gernsheim. 2002. *Individualization: Institutionalized Individualism and its Social and Political Consequences*. London: SAGE Publications.

Beebee, Thomas O. 1994. *The ideology of genre*. University Park, PA: Pennsylvania State University Press.

Beech, Jennifer. 2004. Redneck and hillbilly discourse in the writing classroom: Classifying critical pedagogies of whiteness. *College English* 67 (2): 172–85.

Berger, Peter L., and Thomas Luckmann. 1967. *The social construction of reality: A treatise in the sociology of knowledge*. New York: Random House.

Berkenkotter, Carol, and Thomas Huckin. 1993. Rethinking genre from a sociocognitive perspective. *Written Communication* 10 (4): 475–509.

Berlin, James A. 1987. *Rhetoric and reality: Writing instruction in American colleges, 1900–1985*. Urbana, IL: NCTE.

Berlin, James A., and Michael J. Vivion, eds. 1992. *Cultural studies in the English classroom*. Portsmouth, NH: Heinemann.

Bizzell, Patricia. 1992. *Academic discourse and critical consciousness*. Pittsburgh, PA: University of Pittsburgh Press.

Blackmore, Jill. 2000. Globalization: A useful concept for feminists. In *Globalization and education: Critical perspectives*, ed. Nicholas Burbules and Carlos Alberto Torres, 133–56. New York: Routledge.

Bleich, David. 1999. In case of fire, throw in what to do with textbooks once you switch to sourcebooks. In *ReVisioning composition textbooks: Conflicts of culture, ideology, and pedagogy*, ed. Xin Liu Gale and Frederic G. Gale, 15–44. Albany, NY: State University of New York Press.

Bok, Derek. 2003. *Universities in the marketplace: The commercialization of higher education.* Princeton, NJ: Princeton University Press.

Bourdieu, Pierre. 1977. *Outline of a theory of practice.* Trans. Richard Nice. Cambridge, MA: Cambridge University Press.

Bousquet, Marc. 2004. Composition as management science. In *Tenured bosses and disposable teachers: Writing instruction in the managed university,* ed. Marc Bousquet, Tony Scott, and Leo Parascondola, 11–35. Carbondale, IL: Southern Illinois University Press.

Bowe, John, Marissa Bowe, and Sabin Streeter. 2000. *Gig: Americans talk about their jobs.* New York: Three Rivers Press.

Brandt, Deborah. 1998. Sponsors of literacy. *College Composition and Communication* 49 (2): 165–85.

Brereton, John C. 1995. *The origins of composition studies in the American college, 1875– 1925: A documentary history.* Pittsburgh, PA: University of Pittsburgh Press.

Crowley, Sharon. 1998. *Composition in the university: Historical and polemical essays.* Pittsburgh, PA: University of Pittsburgh Press.

De Certeau Michel. 1984. *The Practice of Everyday Life.* Berkely, CA: U of California P.

DeGenario, William. 2007. *Who says? Working-class rhetoric, class consciousness, and community.* Pittsburgh, PA: University of Pittsburgh Press.

Devitt, Amy J. 2004. *Writing genres: Rhetoric, philosophy and theory.* Carbondale, IL: Southern Illinois University Press.

Dias, Patrick, Aviva Freedman, Peter Medway, and Anthony Par. 1999. *Worlds apart: Acting and writing in academic and workplace contexts.* New York: Lawrence Erlbaum.

Downing, David B., ed. 1994. *Changing classroom practices: Resources for literary and cultural studies.* Urbana, IL: National Council of Teachers of English.

Du Gay, Paul. 2000. *In praise of bureaucracy: Weber, organization, ethics.* Thousand Oaks, CA: Sage.

Durst, Russell. 1999. *Collision course: Conflict, negotiation, and learning in college composition.* Urbana, IL: National Council of Teachers of English.

Ede, Lisa. 2001. *Work in progress: A guide to academic writing and revising.* Boston, MA: Bedford/St. Martin's.

Ehrenreich, Barbara. 2005. *Bait and switch: The futile pursuit of the American dream.* New York: Henry Holt.

Emerson, Robert, Rachel Fretz, and Linda Shaw. 1995. *Writing ethnographic fieldnotes.* Chicago, IL: University of Chicago Press.

Enoch, Jessica. 2004. Becoming symbol-wise: Kenneth Burke's pedagogy of critical reflection. *College Composition and Communication* 56 (2): 272–96.

Enos, Theresa. 1996. *Gender roles and faculty lives in rhetoric and composition.* Carbondale, IL: Southern Illinois University Press.

Fontaine, Sheryl, and Susan Hunter, eds. 1992. *Writing ourselves into the story: Unheard voices from composition studies.* Carbondale, IL: Southern Illinois University Press.

Foucault, Michel. 1986. What is an Author? *Critical Theory Since 1965.* Hazard Adams and Leroy Searle. Gainesville, FL: University Press of Florida. 138-147.

Fox, Tom. 1990. *The social uses of writing: Politics and pedagogy.* Norwood, NJ: Ablex.

Freedman, Aviva, and Peter Medway. 1994. *Learning and teaching genre.* Portsmouth, NH: Boynton/Cook.

Galbraith, James K. 1998. *Created unequal: The crisis in American pay.* New York: Free Press.

Gale, Xin Liu, and Frederic G. Gale. 1999. Introduction. In *ReVisioning composition textbooks: Conflicts of culture, ideology, and pedagogy,* ed. Xin Liu Gale and Frederic G. Gale, 3–14. Albany, NY: State University of New York Press.

Galeano, Eduardo. 1992. *The book of embraces.* Trans. Cedrick Belfrage with Mark Schafer. New York: W. W. Norton.

Gee, James Paul. 2005. *An introduction to discourse analysis: Theory and method.* New York: Routledge.

Gee, James Paul, Glynda Hull, and Colin Lankshear. 1996. *The new work order: Behind the language of the new capitalism.* Boulder, CO: Westview Press.

Giroux, Henry A., and Susan Searls Giroux. 2004. *Take back higher education: Race, youth, and the crisis of democracy in the post-civil rights era.* New York: Palgrave Macmillan.

Grabill, Jefferey T. 2001. *Community literacy programs and the politics of change.* Albany, NY: State University of New York Press.

Greene, Kristin. 2006. Going hybrid. *Inside Higher Ed.* July 20th, 2006. http://insidehighered.com/views/2006/07/20/strategist (accessed March 24, 2007).

Gunner, Jeanne. 1993. The fate of the Wyoming resolution: A professional seduction. In *Writing ourselves into the story: Unheard voices from composition studies,* ed. Sheryl Fontaine and Susan Hunter, 107–22. Carbondale, IL: Southern Illinois University Press.

Hage, Jerald, and Charles H. Powers. 1992. *Post-industrial lives: Roles and relationships in the 21st century.* Newbury Park, CA: Sage.

Hairston, Maxine. 1990. Comment and response. *College English* 52 (6):694–96.

———. 1992. Diversity, ideology, and teaching writing. *College Composition and Communication* 43 (2): 179–93.

Harrington, Susan, Rita Malenczyk, Irvin Peckham, Keith Rhodes, and Kathleen Blake Yancey. 2001. WPA Outcomes Statement for first-year composition. *College English* 63 (3): 321–25.

Harris, Joseph. 1989. The idea of community in the study of writing. *College Composition and Communication* 40 (1): 11–22.

———. 1997. *A teaching subject: Composition since 1966.* Upper Saddle River, NJ: Prentice.

———. 2000. Meet the new boss, same as the old boss: Class consciousness in composition. *College Composition and Communication* 52 (1): 42–68.

———. 2003. Revision as a critical practice. *College English* 65 (6): 577–92.

Heath, Shirley Brice. 1996. Work, class, and categories: Dilemmas of identity. In *Composition in the twenty-first century,* ed. Lynn Z. Bloom, Donald A. Daiker, and Edward White, 226–42. Carbondale, IL: Southern Illinois University Press.

Heathcott, Joseph. 1999. What kinds of tools? Teaching critical analysis and writing to working class students. In *Teaching working class,* ed. Sherry Lee Linkon, 106–22. Amherst, MA: University of Massachusetts.

Herndl, Carl G., and Danny Bauer. 2003. Speaking matters: Liberation theology, rhetorical performance, and social action. *College Composition and Communication* 54 (4): 558–85.

Holbrook, Sue Ellen. 1991. Women's work: The feminizing of composition. *Rhetoric Review* 9:201–29.

Holland, Dorothy, William Lachicotte, Debra Skinner, and Carole Cain. 1998. *Identity and agency in cultural worlds.* Cambridge, MA: Harvard University Press.

Horner, Bruce. 2000. *Terms of work for composition: A materialist critique.* Albany, NY: State University of New York Press.

Horner, Bruce, and Min-Zhan Lu. 1999. *Representing the "other": Basic writers and the teaching of basic writing.* Urbana, IL: National Council of Teachers of English.

Houghton Mifflin. 2004. Adjuncts.com. http://college.hmco.com/adjuncts (accessed January 3, 2006).

Kitzhaber, Albert R. 1990. *Rhetoric in American colleges, 1850–1900.* Dallas, TX: Southern Methodist University Press.

Latour, Bruno. 1987. *Science in action: How to follow scientists and engineers through society.* Cambridge, MA: Harvard University Press.

Lavaca Collective. 2007. *Sin patrón: Stories from Argentina's worker-run factories.* Chicago, IL: Haymarket Books.

Le Blanc, Paul, and John Hinshaw. 2000. Why the working class still matters. In *U.S. labor in the twentieth century*, ed. John Hinshaw and Paul Le Blanc, 13–23. Amherst, NY: Humanity Books.

Libretti, Tim. 2004. Sexual outlaws and class struggle: Rethinking history and class consciousness from a queer perspective. *College English* 67 (2): 154–71.

Lindquist, Julie. 2004. Class affects, classroom affectations: Working through the paradoxes of strategic empathy. *College English* 67 (2): 187–209.

Lu, Min-Zhan. 2004. An essay on the work of composition: Composing English against the order of fast capitalism. *College Composition and Communication* 56 (1): 16–50.

Mao, LuMing. 2005. Rhetorical borderlands: Chinese American rhetoric in the making. *College Composition and Communication* 56 (5): 426–69.

Marinara, Martha. 1997. When working class students "do" the academy: How we negotiate with alternative literacies. *Journal of Basic Writing* 16 (2): 3–16.

Marshall, Margaret J. 2003. *Response to reform: Composition and the professionalization of teaching*. Carbondale, IL: Southern Illinois University Press.

Martin, Randy. 1998. *Chalk lines: The politics of work in the managed university*. Durham, NC: Duke University Press.

Marx, Karl. 1996. *Capital: A critique of political economy*. Vol. 1. Trans. Ben Fowkes. Intro. by Ernst Mandel. New York: Penguin.

McCloskey, Donald N. 1994. *Knowledge and persuasion in economics*. Cambridge, MA: Cambridge University Press.

Mclaren, Peter. 2000. *Che Guevara, Paulo Freire and the pedagogy of revolution*. New York: Rowman and Littlefield.

Miller, Carolyn. 1984. Genre as social action. *Quarterly Journal of Speech* 70 (2): 151–67.

Miller, Richard. 1999. "Let's do the numbers": Comp droids and the prophets of doom. *Profession*, 99: 96–105.

Miller, Richard E. 1998. The Arts of Complicity: Pragmatism and the Culture of Schooling. *College English* 61 (1): 10-28.

Miller, Susan. 1991. *Textual carnivals: The politics of composition*. Carbondale, IL: Southern Illinois University Press.

Mishel, Lawrence, Jared Bernstein, and Heather Boushey. 2003. *The state of working in America 2002/2003*. Ithaca, NY: ILR Press.

Mishler, Elliot G. 1990. Validation in inquiry-guided research: The role of exemplars in narrative studies. *Harvard Educational Review* 60:415–42.

Miyoshi, Masao. 1998. "Globalization," culture and the university. In *The cultures of globalization*, ed. Frederick Jameson and Masao Miyoshi, 247–272. Durham, NC: Duke University Press.

Moreno, Renee. 2002. "The politics of location": Text as opposition. *College Composition and Communication* 54 (2): 222–42.

Morrow, Raymond. 2006. Forward—Critical theory, globalization, and higher education: Political economy and the cul-de-sac of the postmodernist cultural turn. In *The university, state, and market: The political economy of globalization in the Americas*, ed. Robert A. Rhoades and Carlos Alberto Torres, xvii–xxxiii. Stanford, CA: Stanford University Press.

Murphy, Michael. 2000. New faculty for a new university: Toward a full-time teaching-intensive faculty track in composition. *College Composition and Communication* 52 (1): 14–41.

National Center for Educational Statistics. 2005. The condition of education. http://nces.ed.gov/programs/coe/ (accessed November 26, 2006).

———. 2006. Special analysis: Nontraditional undergraduates. http://nces.ed.gov/pubs2002/2002012.pdf (accessed January 8, 2007).

Newman, Frank, Lara Couturier, and Jamie Scurry. 2004. *The future of higher education: Rhetoric, reality, and the risks of the market*. San Francisco, CA: Josey-Bass.

Newson, Janice, and Howard Buchbinder. 1988. *University means business: Universities, corporations and academic work.* Toronto: Garamond.

Noble, David F. 2002. *Digital diploma mills: The automation of higher education.* New York: Monthly Review Press.

North, Stephen M. 1987. *The making of knowledge in composition.* Portsmouth, NH: Boynton.

O'Dair, Sharon. 2003. Class work: Site of egalitarian activism or site of embourgeoisment? *College English* 65 (6): 593–606.

Ohmann, Richard. 1976. *English in America: A radical view of the profession.* Hanover, NH: Wesleyan University Press.

Olson, Gary. 1999. Toward a post-process composition: Abandoning the rhetoric of assertion. In *Post-process theory: Beyond the writing-process paradigm,* ed. Thomas Kent, 7–15. Carbondale, IL: Southern Illinois University Press.

Osterman, Paul. 2001. *Working in America: A blueprint for the new labor market.* Cambridge, MA: MIT Press,

Parks, Steve. 2000. *Class politics: The movement for the students' right to their own language.* Urbana, IL: National Council of Teachers of English.

Patton, Michael Q. 1990. *Qualitative research and evaluation methods.* Newbury Park, CA: Sage.

Porter, James E, Patricia Sullivan, Stuart Blythe, Jeffery Grabill, and Libby Miles. 2000. Institutional critique: A rhetorical methodology for change. *College Composition and Communication* 51 (4): 610–42.

Report on the Coalition on the Academic Workforce/CCCC survey of faculty in freestanding writing programs for fall 1999. 2001. *College Composition and Communication* 53 (2): 336–48.

Rhoades, Gary. 1998. *Managed professionals: Unionized faculty and restructuring academic labor.* Albany, NY: State University of New York Press.

———. 2004. Afterward: Educating for literacy, working for dignity. In *Tenured bosses and disposable teachers: Writing instruction in the managed university,* ed., Marc Bousquet, Tony Scott, and Leo Parascondola 256–272. Carbondale, IL: Southern Illinois University Press.

Robillard, Amy. 2003. It's time for class: Toward a more complex pedagogy of narrative. *College English* 66 (1): 74–92.

Rubin, Herbert J., and Irene S. Rubin. 1995. *Qualitative interviewing: The art of hearing data.* Thousand Oaks, CA: Sage.

Russell, David R. 1991. *Writing in the academic disciplines, 1870–1990: A curricular history.* Carbondale, IL: Southern Illinois University Press.

———. 1997. Rethinking genre in school and society: An activity theory analysis. *Written Communication* 14:504–54.

Schell, Eileen E. 1998. *Gypsy academics and mother-teachers: Gender, contingent labor and writing instruction.* Portsmouth, NH: Boynton/Cook Publishers.

Schugurensky, Daniel. 2006. The political economy of higher education in the time of global markets: Whither the social responsibility of the university? In *The university, state and market: The political economy of globalization in the Americas,* ed. Robert A. Rhoads and Carlos Alberto Torres, 301–20. Stanford, CA: Stanford University Press.

Scott, Richard. 2001. *Institutions and organizations.* Thousand Oaks, CA: Sage.

Seitz, David. 2004. Making work visible. *College English* 67 (2): 210–21.

Shor, Ira. 1980. *Critical Teaching and Everyday Life.* Boston: South End.

———. 1996. *When students have power: Negotiating authority in a critical pedagogy.* Chicago, IL: University of Chicago Press.

Slaughter, Sheila, and Larry L. Leslie. 1997. *Academic capitalism: Politics, policies, and the entrepreneurial university.* Baltimore, MA: Johns Hopkins University Press.

————. 2004. *Academic capitalism and the new economy: Markets, state, and higher education.* Baltimore, MA: Johns Hopkins University Press.

Slevin, James F. 1991. Depoliticizing and Politicizing Composition Studies. In *The Politics of Writing Instruction: Postsecondary.* Richard Bullock and John Trimbur. Portsmouth, NH: Heinemann. 1-21.

Smith, David Geoffrey. 1999. Economic fundamentalism, globalization, and the public remains of education. *Interchange* 30 (1): 93–117.

Smith, Jeff. 1998. Problems with confrontational teaching. *College Composition and Communication* 49 (2):267–69.

Sobel, Andrew C. 2005. *Political economy and global affairs.* Washington, DC: CQ Press.

Spellmeyer, Kurt. 1999. The great way: Reading and writing in freedom. In *ReVisioning composition textbooks: Conflicts of culture, ideology, and pedagogy,* ed. Xin Liu Gale and Frederic G. Gale, 45–68. Albany, NY: State University of New York Press.

Stenberg, Shari J. 2006. Liberation theology and liberatory pedagogies: Renewing the dialogue. *College English* 68 (3): 271–90.

Strickland, Donna. 2001. Taking dictation: The emergence of writing programs and the cultural contradictions of composition teaching. *College English* 63 (4):457–79.

Sullivan, Patricia. 2003. Composing culture: A place for the personal. *College English* 66 (1): 41–54.

Syverson, Margaret A. 1999. *The wealth of reality: An ecology of composition.* Carbondale, IL: Southern Illinois University Press.

Terry, Les. 1997. Traveling "The hard road to renewal": A continuing conversation with Stuart Hall. *Arena Journal* 8:47–55.

Thiong'o, Ngugi wa. 1986. *Decolonizing the mind: The politics of language in African literature.* London: James Curry.

————. 2006. *Wizard of the crow.* New York: Anchor Books.

Torres, Carlos Alberto. 1998. *Democracy, education, and multiculturalism: Dilemmas of citizenship in a global world.* Lanham, MD: Rowman and Littlefield.

Trimbur, John. 1994. Taking the social turn: Teaching writing post-process. *College Composition and Communication* 45 (1):108–18.

————. 2000. Composition and the circulation of writing. *College Composition and Communication* 52 (2): 188–219.

Terkel, Studs. 1972. *Working: People talk about what they do all day and how they feel about what they do.* New York: Pantheon Books.

Uchitell, Louis. 2006. *The disposable American: Layoffs and their consequences.* New York: Knopf.

U.S. Department of Labor Bureau of Labor Statistics. *Occupational Outlook Handbook, 2008-2009 Edition.* www.bls.gov/oco/oco2003.htm. Retrieved on August 26, 2008.

Villanueva, Victor. 2005. Toward a political economy of rhetoric or a rhetoric of political economy. In *Radical relevance: Toward a scholarship of the whole left,* ed. Laura Gray-Rosendale and Steven Rosendale, 57–68. Albany, NY: State University of New York Press.

Wasley, Paula. 2006. A new way to grade. *The Chronicle of Higher Education* 52 (27): A6. Retrieved September 2, 2008, from Education Research Complete database.

Watkins, Evan. 1998. *Everyday exchanges: Marketwork and capitalist common sense.* Stanford, CA: Stanford University Press.

Weber, Max. 1964. *The theory of social and economic organization.* Ed. and Trans. Alexander Morell Henderson and Talcott Parsons. New York: Free Press.

Weber, Max. 2001. *The Protestant Ethic and the Spirit of Capitalism.* Chicago, IL: Routledge.

Wills, Katherine V. 2004. The lure of "easy" psychic income. In *Tenured bosses and disposable teachers: Writing instruction in the managed university,* ed. Marc Bousquet, Tony Scott, and Leo Parascondola, 201–6. Carbondale, IL: Southern Illinois University Press.

Wood, Mark. 2005. Another world is possible. In *Radical relevance: Toward a scholarship of the whole left*, ed. Laura Gray-Rosendale and Steven Rosendale, 213–37. Albany, NY: State University of New York Press.

Yagelski, Robert P. 2006. "Review: Radical to many in the educational establishment": The writing process movement after the hurricanes. *College English* 68 (5): 531–44.

Yates, JoAnne. 1989. *Control through communication: The rise of system in American management.* Baltimore, MD: Johns Hopkins University Press.

Zebroski, James. 1994. *Thinking through theory: Vygotskian perspectives on the teaching of writing.* Portsmouth, NH: Boynton/Cook.

———. 1998. Toward a theory of theory in composition studies. In *Under construction: Working at the intersections of composition theory, research, and practice*, ed. Christine Farris and Chris M. Anson 30–50. Logan, UT: Utah State University Press.

Zizek, Slavoj. 1989. *The sublime object of ideology.* London: Verso.

Zweig, Michael. 2000. *The working class majority: America's best kept secret.* Ithaca, NY: Cornell University Press.

INDEX

ABOUT THE AUTHOR

Tony Scott is associate professor of English at the University of North Carolina–Charlotte, where he directs the writing program. He has published research on writing assessment, critical pedagogy, and issues associated with labor in postsecondary writing. He teaches graduate and undergraduate classes in writing, technical writing, and theory in rhetoric and composition. He is also active in the National Writing Project.